WAR AND PEACE IN THE TAIWAN STRAIT

CONTEMPORARY ASIA IN THE WORLD

CONTEMPORARY ASIA IN THE WORLD

David C. Kang and Victor D. Cha, Editors

This series aims to address a gap in the public-policy and scholarly discussion of Asia. It seeks to promote books and studies that are on the cutting edge of their disciplines or promote multidisciplinary or interdisciplinary research but are also accessible to a wider readership. The editors seek to showcase the best scholarly and public-policy arguments on Asia from any field, including politics, history, economics, and cultural studies.

For a complete list of books in the series, see page 253.

WAR AND PEACE IN THE TAIWAN STRAIT

SCOTT L. KASTNER

Colulmbia University Press

New York

Columbia University Press
Publishers Since 1893
New York   Chichester, West Sussex
cup.columbia.edu

Library of Congress Cataloging-in-Publication Data
Names: Kastner, Scott L., author.
Title: War and peace in the Taiwan Strait / Scott L. Kastner.
Description: New York : Columbia University Press, 2022. |
Series: Contemporary asia in the world | Includes
bibliographical references and index.
Identifiers: LCCN 2022006072 (print) | LCCN 2022006073 (ebook) |
ISBN 9780231198646 (hardback) | ISBN 9780231198653 (trade paperback) |
ISBN 9780231552738 (ebook)
Subjects: LCSH: Taiwan—Foreign relations—China. | China—Foreign
relations—Taiwan. | Taiwan Strait—Strategic aspects. | National security—
Taiwan. | National security—China.
Classification: LCC DS799.63.C6 K37 2022 (print) | LCC DS799.63.C6 (ebook) |
DDC 327.51249051—dc23/eng/20220415
LC record available at https://lccn.loc.gov/2022006072
LC ebook record available at https://lccn.loc.gov/2022006073

Cover design: Julia Kushnirsky
Cover image: Shutterstock

FOR DINA

CONTENTS

ACKNOWLEDGMENTS

This book is the culmination of a project that started with some conference presentations about ten years ago, and I am deeply indebted to many scholars who have provided constructive feedback over the past decade on some of the ideas developed here, including Nien-chung Chang-Liao, Ping-Kuei Chen, Monique Chu, John Ciorciari, Michael Glosny, Avery Goldstein, Todd Hall, Andy Kennedy, Chun-yi Lee, Tse-kang Leng, Darren Lim, Shirly Lin, Yeh-Chung Lu, Barry Naughton, Hsin-Hsin Pan, Margaret Pearson, Chad Rector, Will Reed, Phil Roeder, Weiyi Shi, Susan Shirk, Stein Tonnesson, Steve Tsang, Yuan-Kang Wang, Chi-hung Wei, Wen-chin Wu, Yu-Shan Wu, and participants in workshops and talks at Stanford University; the University of Michigan; the University of California, San Diego; the University of Nottingham; Western Michigan University; the University of Oxford; the University of Tokyo; Columbia University; Australian National University; Academia Sinica; National Chengchi University; and the Fourth Annual East Asian Peace Conference. At Columbia, I thank David Kang and Victor Cha for their interest in this project, Caelyn Cobb and Monique Briones for their guidance, and the anonymous reviewers for their helpful comments. I am also indebted to Anita O'Brien for her copyediting work, which made this a stronger manuscript. For research assistance, I thank Christine Liu,

Guan Wang, Joseph Yinusa, and Yue Zhang. Parts of this manuscript draw on ideas originally published in an article in the journal *International Security*. Finally, the bulk of this manuscript was completed while I was holed up at home during the pandemic, working at the dining room table. I thank my wife Dina for putting up with me during this time; it is to her that this book is dedicated.

ABBREVIATIONS

A2/AD	antiaccess/area-denial
ARATS	Association for Relations Across the Taiwan Straits
CCP	Chinese Communist Party
CSSTA	Cross-Strait Service Trade Agreement
DPP	Democratic Progressive Party
ECFA	Economic Cooperation Framework Agreement
IT	information technology
KMT	Kuomintang, Nationalist Party
MAC	Taiwan Mainland Affairs Council
NDAA	National Defense Authorization Act
PLA	People's Liberation Army
PRC	People's Republic of China
ROC	Republic of China
SEF	Straits Exchange Foundation
SIPRI	Stockholm International Peace Research Institute
SQ	status quo
TNSS	Taiwan National Security Survey
TRA	Taiwan Relations Act

WAR AND PEACE IN THE TAIWAN STRAIT

INTRODUCTION

Rumors of War in the Taiwan Strait

Only one decade ago, on May 20, 2012, Taiwan's president Ma Ying-jeou talked at length about peace in the Taiwan Strait as he delivered his second inaugural address. The relationship between China and Taiwan had been quite tense in the years before Ma entered office in 2008. Although the People's Republic of China (PRC) has never governed Taiwan, the PRC government claims Taiwan as rightfully part of China. PRC leaders feared that Ma's predecessor, Chen Shui-bian, was maneuvering the self-governing island of Taiwan toward formal independence from China, or at least undermining the prospects for future unification. Beijing's rhetoric at the time was quite threatening—warning of a willingness to pay any costs to prevent Taiwan's formal independence—and in 2005 the PRC's National People's Congress passed an antisecession law, which warned that China would use "nonpeaceful means" in the event of "major incidents of Taiwan's secession from China."

Ma had campaigned in 2008 on a platform of détente with the PRC, promising to stabilize the cross-strait relationship. Looking back at his first four years in office, he observed in 2012 that his government had "resumed institutionalized cross-strait negotiations, signed 16 bilateral agreements [with China] and made cross-strait rapprochement a reality." Cross-strait relations, Ma proclaimed, were at their "most peaceful state . . . in 60 years."[1] The speech was not an exaggeration. The Taiwan Strait was indeed characterized by unprecedented détente during the eight years Ma served as Taiwan's president. The PRC and Taiwan governments engaged in regular dialogue, the cross–Taiwan Strait economic relationship was normalized, and Taiwan opened its doors to tourists from the PRC. For the first time since the end of the Chinese Civil War, it became convenient to travel back and forth between Taiwan and the mainland. The cross-strait rapprochement culminated in an unprecedented meeting in 2015 between the top leaders of the two sides, when Chinese president Xi Jinping met with Ma in Singapore.

The improved cross-strait atmosphere, however, proved to be fleeting. In 2016 Taiwan elected a new president, Tsai Ing-wen, who was less willing than her predecessor to accommodate the PRC on the core sovereignty issues at stake in the dispute. Beijing, in turn, has steadily increased coercive pressure on the island. The PRC halted all dialogue with Taiwan beginning in 2016, and talks have not resumed. More ominously, PRC military activities near Taiwan have increased dramatically over the past few years.[2] Chinese planes have often circumnavigated the island of Taiwan, have frequently entered Taiwan's air defense identification zone, and—breaking with past practice—have started to cross the midline of the Taiwan Strait more often.

Meanwhile, officials in Washington have been sounding the alarm about an increasing danger of war in the Taiwan Strait. In March 2021 testimony to the United States Senate Armed Services Committee, commander of U.S. Indo-Pacific Command Philip Davidson warned that the PRC was adopting an "aggressive posture" in the region and more generally represented the "greatest long-term strategic threat to security in the 21st century." Davidson suggested in particular that a PRC attack against Taiwan to achieve unification was not a distant threat but rather was a danger that is "manifest during this decade, in fact in the next six years."[3] Two weeks later, Davidson's nominated successor, Admiral John Aquilino, testified that Chinese leaders view unification with Taiwan as their top priority, and that "this problem is much closer to us than most think."[4] The Biden administration reportedly had concluded by March 2021 that China was becoming more "impatient and more prepared to test the limits and flirt with the idea of unification."[5] And some U.S.-based analysts have warned of an increasing risk of a cross-strait military conflict in the years ahead.[6] In short, the possibility of war is getting considerable attention in the United States, and China's regular displays of force in the Taiwan Strait—against a backdrop of a generally hostile cross-strait relationship—suggest that armed conflict is a real possibility.

A war in the Taiwan Strait would have the potential to be a catastrophe of almost unimaginable proportions. Most obvious are the human costs—the lives that could be lost or fundamentally altered as a consequence of war and its aftermath. Taiwan and its people are highly vulnerable to PRC air and missile strikes, and the PRC government's willingness to crush opposition in other areas under its control would not bode well for a Taiwan that suffers defeat and occupation. At a minimum, were the PRC to successfully occupy it, Taiwan would almost certainly lose its democracy. And even if it were to emerge with its autonomy intact, the economic costs to the island would be staggering: Taiwan's economy is deeply integrated with the PRC's, and Taiwan depends heavily on international trade, which would likely become disrupted in a war. War also poses substantial risks to China. PRC soldiers—and possibly civilians if things were to escalate—would lose their lives. The PRC's economy, too, is highly integrated into global markets, and the coastal regions that presumably would be most directly affected by a war also happen to be the heart of China's economic dynamism. A major war in the Taiwan Strait could put this economic dynamism at risk, not only because of the possibility of strikes from Taiwan's own capable military, but also because a war could affect the PRC's trade and lead to international sanctions. A war, especially if it were to go poorly for China, could generate domestic instability and embolden new challengers to President Xi. And, of course, the United States could become involved, which would mean two nuclear powers fighting each other directly and the attendant risks implied in such a scenario. Even if the two sides were able to avoid catastrophic escalation, both would face potentially devastating losses in a war against a rival superpower. Finally, Taiwan's integration into global markets—and especially its important role in the production of microchips—means that a war in the Taiwan Strait could have enormous ripple effects on the world economy.

My purpose in writing this book is to better understand how a war in the Taiwan Strait could possibly occur, with the hope that such an understanding could also make war over Taiwan less likely. To be clear, the book is primarily an analytical undertaking. I do not, for instance, pore over PRC military writings or speeches by PRC leaders to assess whether, and how, China might plan an attack against Taiwan. Nor do I undertake systematic analysis of how such a war might play out, or which side might ultimately prevail. And I do not make recommendations concerning which weapons systems or strategic doctrines might best deter armed conflict. Other excellent studies undertake these sorts of analysis.[7] Rather, my aim in this book is to pose—and seek answers to—a set of more fundamental questions: Given the catastrophic costs a war in the Taiwan Strait would potentially entail, why and how would this outcome ever come about in the first place? How likely is a cross-strait war, and is this likelihood increasing? And, how might armed conflict be avoided? Before elaborating on my approach, I first provide a brief overview of the contentious cross–Taiwan Strait relationship.

A BRIEF OVERVIEW OF A CONTENTIOUS RELATIONSHIP

At its core, the dispute between the Taiwan and People's Republic of China governments centers on Taiwan's status: whether Taiwan is, or should be, part of China. The rivalry between the PRC and Taiwan dates to the end of the Chinese Civil War, when Chiang Kai-shek's Nationalist regime (the Republic of China, or ROC) retreated to Taiwan in 1949 as the victorious Chinese Communist Party (CCP) established the PRC on the mainland. Taiwan had previously been incorporated into the Qing Empire in the seventeenth century and had been ceded to Japan after the latter's victory in the Sino-Japanese War of 1894–1895. Taiwan would remain a Japanese colony for half a century, until the end of World War II. During that war the Allied Powers agreed that Taiwan should be returned to China—by then governed by the Nationalists—after Japan's defeat. Taiwan thus became part of the ROC in 1945.

In its original manifestation after 1949, the rivalry across the Taiwan Strait was to a considerable degree a continuation of the long rivalry between the CCP and the Nationalist Party (the Kuomintang or KMT). Although the PRC lacked the capacity to "liberate" the island after 1949 (in no small part due to U.S. security guarantees), establishing control over the island remained a long-term goal. Chiang Kai-shek, for his part, viewed the retreat to Taiwan as temporary and hoped someday to reestablish ROC control on the mainland. Both governments—the ROC on Taiwan and the PRC on the mainland—claimed to represent the rightful government of China, and both viewed Taiwan as part of China. Against this backdrop, tensions remained high in the Taiwan Strait. In the 1950s, for instance, two serious crises erupted over small ROC-controlled islands just off the Chinese mainland. Meanwhile, the United States had not recognized the PRC after its founding in 1949, continuing instead to recognize the ROC as the government of China. In 1955 the United States entered into a formal alliance agreement with the ROC.

The Nationalist government's claim to be the legitimate government of China remained constant even as any hopes to reestablish ROC authority on the mainland became increasingly and obviously unrealistic by the 1970s. The number of countries recognizing the ROC began to decline sharply during that decade, and in 1971 the PRC replaced the ROC in the United Nations. Relations between Washington and Beijing were also improving rapidly in the early 1970s, culminating in President Richard Nixon's visit to China in 1972. The United States and the PRC finally normalized their relationship in January 1979; in turn, Washington broke diplomatic ties with the ROC and abrogated the bilateral alliance treaty. Yet even as Washington recognized the PRC as the sole legal government of China starting in 1979, it did not recognize Taiwan as part of China, instead maintaining an ambiguous approach of "acknowledging" Beijing's position on the issue.

Beijing's approach to Taiwan became more conciliatory starting in the late 1970s, reflecting growing PRC confidence as the ROC became ever more marginalized internationally. Beijing called for a negotiated "peaceful reunification" with the island and in 1981 proposed a model—one country, two systems—under which Taiwan would be afforded a high level of autonomy within the context of a formally unified China. Although Taipei rebuffed these overtures, the ROC nevertheless relaxed its restrictions on interactions with the PRC as the 1980s progressed. For instance, Taiwan lifted its ban on travel to mainland China in 1987 and later in the decade lifted bans on trade and investment with China (all these interactions, however, were still required to be indirect, flowing first through third locations, such as Hong Kong). Relations across the Taiwan Strait appeared to be stabilizing, at least to some extent, by the early 1990s. The ROC government affirmed its continued commitment to national unification as a goal in the Guidelines for National Unification (1991),[8] and both the PRC and Taiwan established quasi-official organizations (the Straits Exchange Foundation, or SEF, in Taiwan; the Association for Relations Across the Taiwan Straits, or ARATS, in the PRC) to serve as intermediaries for engaging with each other. The chairs of SEF and ARATS met with each other in Singapore in 1993, which represented the highest-level interaction between the two sides since the 1940s.

Still, even as the cross-strait relationship appeared to be improving, the underlying nature of the cross-strait dispute was changing, and signs of renewed tensions lurked beneath the surface. By the 1990s the zero-sum nature of the cross-strait rivalry had left Taiwan relatively isolated on the world stage. Fewer than thirty countries still recognized the ROC government, and key remaining allies, such as South Korea and Singapore, broke ties with Taipei in the early 1990s. At the same time, major political changes were unfolding within Taiwan. In the decades after Taiwan's 1945 retrocession to China, the Nationalists governed the island in a highly authoritarian manner. Martial law was in effect, and political dissent was generally not tolerated. Under this regime, mainlanders had dominated the highest echelons of government, and questioning Taiwan's status as a part of China was strictly off-limits.[9] But beginning in the 1980s, Taiwan underwent a process of democratization; martial law was lifted in 1987, and by 1996 Taiwan was holding its first direct presidential election. In an increasingly democratic Taiwan, the nature of the island's relationship with China became the subject of open debate and a salient political issue. In the new environment, politicians responded to, and sometimes tried to cultivate, alternative views of Taiwan's status that diverged from longstanding Nationalist Party orthodoxy. In turn, tensions with Beijing increasingly reflected not disagreement over which side (ROC or PRC) represented the legitimate government of all China, but rather disagreement over whether Taiwan should be considered Chinese at all.

Meanwhile, ROC president Lee Teng-hui (1988–2000) was, by the early 1990s, seeking to reverse Taiwan's growing international isolation. For instance, in early 1994 Lee took a high-profile trip to Southeast Asia, meeting with officials along the way, in what was called a private vacation. And in 1995 Lee was able to obtain a visa from the United States to attend a reunion at his alma mater, Cornell University. While there, Lee delivered a political speech in which he drew attention to the disconnect between Taiwan's political and economic achievements, on the one hand, and its international isolation, on the other.[10] While seeking more international space for Taiwan, Lee also in the early to mid-1990s increasingly appeared to call into question the idea of a "one China" principle, that there is only one China in the world and that Taiwan is part of that China. In the early 1990s the ROC government had essentially recognized that its area of effective governance did not extend to the mainland. Although Lee continued to frame unification as the long-term goal of the ROC (as formalized in the National Unification Guidelines), he also argued that the current reality was that of a divided nation. And in a 1994 interview he seemed to further call into question whether Taiwan should be thought of as Chinese when he suggested that the Nationalist government on Taiwan amounted to a foreign regime (*wailai zhengquan*).[11]

Lee's statements, and especially his trip to Cornell, left PRC leaders increasingly convinced that his ultimate aim was formal Taiwan independence. The Cornell visit also served as the immediate trigger of a prolonged crisis in the Taiwan Strait. The crisis culminated with PRC missile tests in the vicinity of Taiwan ports shortly before Taiwan's first direct presidential election in 1996 (which Lee won in a landslide), and the U.S. decision to dispatch two aircraft carrier battle groups to the area.[12] Although things stabilized to some degree after 1996, relations again became icy in 1999 after Lee characterized the relationship across the Taiwan Strait as "state-to-state relations, or at least special state-to-state relations." Beijing was sharply critical, and in early 2000 it released a white paper attacking Lee and indicating that indefinite delay on reunification would be a legitimate reason for the PRC to use military force.[13] The PRC also froze dialogue through the SEF-ARATS mechanism, demanding a clear recognition of a one China principle as a precondition for resumption.

In 2000 the Nationalists lost power for the first time in Taiwan as Chen Shui-bian of the officially pro-Taiwan independence Democratic Progressive Party (DPP) was elected president.[14] Chen's initial message to China was conciliatory: in his inauguration he noted, for instance, that he would not declare legal independence or change the ROC's official name. But Chen also refused to accept any version of a one China principle, and Beijing refused to negotiate with Chen absent such a step. Dialogue between SEF and ARATS remained frozen throughout the Chen presidency (2000–2008). More generally, relations across the Taiwan Strait were generally quite hostile during most of Chen's tenure in office. Chen in 2002 began to describe the cross-strait relationship as "one country on each side," and in 2003 he advocated for a new constitution for Taiwan. After narrowly winning reelection in 2004, Chen vowed to push for a new constitution in his second term; he further indicated that he believed Taiwan had already achieved "an internal consensus that insists on Taiwan being an independent, sovereign country."[15] During his second term, Chen took a number of concrete steps, such as renaming state entities, to highlight Taiwan's otherness from China.[16] He also promoted a referendum—held at the same time as the presidential election in 2008—asking Taiwan voters to support Taiwan's application to be readmitted to the United Nations under the name Taiwan. Meanwhile, the PRC's National People's Congress in 2005 passed an antisecession law, which threatened the use of "non-peaceful means and other necessary measures" in the event of Taiwan's "secession from China" or "major incidents entailing" secession, or if avenues for peaceful unification were to become "completely exhausted."[17]

The Nationalists stormed back to power in 2008, when Ma Ying-jeou was elected Taiwan's president in a landslide and the KMT won a large majority in Taiwan's Legislative Yuan (the parliament). Ma campaigned on a pragmatic, explicitly pro–status quo platform, emphasizing that he would pursue neither independence nor unification as president. Ma also suggested that Taiwan's future prosperity depended on stable relations with the PRC. During the Lee Teng-hui and Chen Shui-bian presidencies, even though cross-strait political relations were at times quite hostile, cross-strait economic ties were burgeoning. The PRC economy was growing rapidly and had opened the door to foreign investors, and starting in the 1980s Taiwanese businesses rushed into China in ever greater numbers. By the early 2000s China had emerged as Taiwan's top trading partner, and the majority of Taiwan's outbound foreign direct investment flowed to the PRC. Yet political divergence across the strait acted as a brake on this integration, at least to some extent: most notably, even as the PRC became Taiwan's top economic partner, most exchanges with mainland China occurred indirectly. Individuals, for instance, could not take direct flights across the Taiwan Strait but had to pass through third locations like Hong Kong first. Given the growing importance of China to Taiwan's economy, Ma believed that the coexistence of ever-deeper economic integration along with intensifying political divergence was untenable, and that a peaceful cross-strait relationship was an important foundation for Taiwan's long-term economic health. As candidate and as president, he advocated for détente across the Taiwan Strait.

To pave the way for an improved cross-strait relationship, Ma approached the one China issue in a way that departed from his immediate predecessors. In particular, Ma embraced what had been termed the "1992 consensus," referring to an understanding reached between ARATS and SEF that helped to serve as a basis for dialogue in the early 1990s. In 1992 the two organizations separately outlined their respective positions on the one China principle, with ARATS emphasizing that the two sides both "uphold the One-China principle and strive to seek national unification," but the political meaning of the principle would not be stressed in routine interactions. SEF, meanwhile, emphasized that "each side has its own understanding of the meaning of one-China."[18] In embracing the concept of a 1992 consensus, Ma interpreted one China to mean the ROC: the ROC's sovereignty extended over all of China, even though its current geographical proximity covered only Taiwan (along with the offshore islands Mazu and Jinmen and the Penghu Islands).[19] From Beijing's perspective, Ma's willingness to endorse a one China principle in the form of the 1992 consensus was sufficient to resume dialogue across the Taiwan Strait.

China-Taiwan relations stabilized rapidly in 2008, and, as noted earlier, Ma's two terms in office were characterized by an unprecedented détente in cross-strait relations. The two sides reached numerous economic agreements that, collectively, largely normalized the cross-strait economic relationship. These agreements included the establishment of direct contacts across the Taiwan Strait (such as regular direct flights connecting cities in Taiwan to cities on the mainland); an agreement on financial cooperation; and an economic cooperation framework agreement that lowered tariffs on a wide range of goods. Taiwan opened to PRC tourism, and negotiations increasingly ventured beyond economics, with the two sides agreeing to cooperate on issues like nuclear safety. Meanwhile, a tacit diplomatic truce emerged, where the two sides stopped actively seeking to flip the other's diplomatic allies. And the PRC was tolerant of some limited international space for Taiwan, including as an observer at the World Health Organization's World Health Assembly.

Still, during Ma's second term in office there were also signs that the cross-strait détente was beginning to run its course.[20] As the two sides continued to make progress on various functional issues, it was becoming clear that PRC leaders hoped to see discussions on more thorny political issues. In 2013, for instance, Xi Jinping told a Taiwanese envoy that the political disagreements between the two sides could not be "passed from generation to generation."[21] But political negotiations with the PRC—especially if they were to venture into discussions of possible unification—would be deeply controversial, and likely highly unpopular, in Taiwan. Even Ma was not eager to venture into such territory. Meanwhile, a trade in services agreement that Ma had reached with the PRC was facing stiff resistance in Taiwan, ultimately helping to trigger a large protest movement that included a student-led occupation of the Legislative Yuan in 2014. The agreement was never ratified, and in late 2014 the DPP performed very well in Taiwan's local elections. This momentum carried over to 2016, when the DPP returned to power in its own landslide election. Tsai Ing-wen, who had lost to Ma in the election of 2012, won the presidency with over 56 percent of the vote; the KMT candidate finished second with only 31 percent. The DPP also captured a large majority in the Legislative Yuan, meaning that for the first time the party held unified control of Taiwan's government.

Tsai adopted a pragmatic approach to cross-strait sovereignty issues during the campaign and after becoming president. In a speech given in Washington in June 2015, Tsai said that she would "push for the peaceful and stable development of cross-Strait relations in accordance with the will of the Taiwanese people and the existing ROC constitutional order."[22] Earlier, after securing the DPP nomination, she had also signaled commitment to a status quo of "preserving peace in the Taiwan Strait and continuing the current stable development of cross-Strait relations."[23] Once in office, Tsai's approach to cross-strait relations suggested that she hoped to avoid a repeat of the contentious dynamics of the Chen Shui-bian years. In her inaugural speech, Tsai focused first and foremost on domestic issues, such as economic development and expanding the social safety net. When discussing cross-strait relations, she signaled pragmatism by calling for the preservation of "existing mechanisms for dialogue and communication," and by invoking "over twenty years of interactions and negotiations across the Strait [that] have enabled and accumulated outcomes which both sides must collectively cherish and sustain." She also referenced the "1992 talks between the two institutions representing each side across the Strait (SEF & ARATS)," noting that the talks included "joint acknowledgement of setting aside differences to seek common ground," and she reiterated that "this is a historical fact."[24] In short, Tsai appeared to be seeking a middle ground, where she stopped short of accepting a one

China principle (or endorsing the idea of a 1992 consensus) but recognized past progress in cross-strait relations, signaled commitment to the ROC and its constitution, and sought to preserve a peaceful cross-strait status quo.

The PRC was not receptive to Tsai's middle-ground approach, describing her inaugural address as an "incomplete test answer" since she did not recognize the 1992 consensus, nor did she articulate an alternative version of a one China principle.[25] Cross-strait relations, in turn, have dramatically worsened since 2016. Beijing again froze all cross-strait dialogue and over time increased diplomatic, economic, and military pressure on Taiwan. Taiwan was again blocked from participation in the World Health Assembly, and the tacit diplomatic truce that had characterized the previous eight years came to an abrupt end as eight countries established diplomatic ties with the PRC during Tsai's first term in office. China began to limit tourist visits to Taiwan, and PRC military activities near Taiwan increased sharply.

As 2020 approached, the KMT initially appeared poised for a comeback in Taiwan. The Nationalists performed well in the 2018 local elections, including wins in areas that are normally DPP strongholds, like the city of Kaohsiung. But several developments in 2019 ultimately helped fuel a resurgence by Tsai. First, Xi Jinping delivered a speech on the Taiwan issue in early 2019. Although the speech largely reiterated existing PRC policy on Taiwan, it was widely interpreted abroad and in Taiwan as taking a harder line. Xi, for instance, repeated his earlier insistence that the Taiwan issue not be passed down to future generations, and although emphasizing that "Chinese will not fight Chinese," also pointedly refused to rule out the use of force to prevent Taiwan separatism. He also reiterated the PRC's commitment to the one country, two systems framework even as he called on Taiwan to return to the 1992 consensus.[26] Tsai responded with a speech of her own, noting that her government does not accept the 1992 consensus because the PRC's "definition of the '1992 Consensus' is 'one China' and 'one country, two systems.'" She went on to note that Xi's speech "confirmed our misgivings" and emphasized "that Taiwan absolutely will not accept 'one country, two systems.'"[27] The one country, two systems model has never been popular in Taiwan, so it was likely a savvy political move by Tsai to link the model to the 1992 consensus (which the KMT continued to accept as a basis for cross-strait dialogue). Second, the massive protest movement that emerged in Hong Kong in 2019—a response to a proposed extradition law that protestors feared would undercut the region's autonomy under the one country, two systems model in place for Hong Kong— undoubtedly further eroded confidence in the model among Taiwan's public and consequently likely worked to Tsai's political benefit given her outspoken criticism of one country, two systems.[28] Finally, the KMT's nomination of Han Kuo-yu, a populist who had rapidly risen to promi- nence in 2018 as he won the election for mayor of Kaohsiung, appeared to backfire as Han's popularity declined sharply over the course of 2019. In the end, Tsai was reelected in another landslide in early 2020, and the DPP was able to maintain its majority in the legislature.[29]

Cross-strait relations have remained icy since Tsai's reelection, and indeed the PRC's military activities near Taiwan—as noted earlier—have actually intensified. As Taiwan-China relations have deteriorated, mean- while, the U.S.-Taiwan relationship has been getting closer. The United States has recently announced several major arms sales packages for Tai- wan, including the advanced version of the F-16 fighter. The United States has also been announcing frequent naval transits of the Taiwan Strait, several high-ranking current and former officials have recently visited Taiwan, and U.S. secretary of state Antony Blinken warned in April 2021 that it would be a "serious mistake for anyone to try to change the existing status quo by force."[30]

In sum, the Taiwan Strait remains today a potential flashpoint for mil- itary conflict, one that could involve not only Taiwan and China but also possibly the United States as well. Taiwan's sovereign status has been at the center of the cross-strait rivalry, and the nature of the dispute is both complex and dynamic. It is in part a territorial dispute, a dispute over which regime is the rightful government of Taiwan. But the dispute also centers on Taiwan's political identity—the degree to which Taiwan's people and its leaders consider Taiwan to be Chinese and part of China.[31]

As will become clear over the course of this book, one reason the Tai- wan Strait is dangerous is that both the Taiwan government and the

PRC government have at times pursued a mix of status quo and revisionist goals with respect to Taiwan's sovereignty. In Taiwan, there is wide agreement that Taiwan should not be unified with the current PRC—a status quo goal—and wide agreement that Taiwan should have more international space—a revisionist goal. And, as noted above, some in Taiwan advocate for more revisionist goals, such as formalization of Taiwan's de facto independence. In Beijing, there is clearly a desire to see progress on formal unification—a revisionist goal—even as PRC actions are often framed around preventing formal Taiwan independence—a status quo goal. This mix of status quo and revisionist goals, in turn, can make it hard to interpret actions taken by the other side. In Beijing, for instance, there is a tendency to view closer security ties between the United States and Taiwan with alarm, as something that could facilitate Taiwan's permanent separation from China. And in Taipei and Washington, PRC military maneuvers are often seen not as deterring Taiwan independence, but rather as part of an effort to coerce movement toward unification.[32] In the next section, I outline my approach for analyzing this complex and dynamic relationship.

THINKING ABOUT THE PROSPECTS FOR CONFLICT IN THE TAIWAN STRAIT

Given the contentious nature of cross-strait relations, it should come as no surprise that analysts have often pointed to the Taiwan Strait as one of Asia's most dangerous flashpoints. Writing over two decades ago, June Dreyer argued that "of all the issues now straining relations between Washington and Beijing . . . none has more potential for rapid escalation into armed hostilities than the standoff in the Taiwan Strait."[33] A few years later, Alan Romberg described Taiwan as "the only issue in the world today that could realistically lead to war between two major powers."[34] More recently, Susan Thornton, the former assistant secretary of state for East Asian and Pacific affairs, in 2018 described the Taiwan Strait as the most likely flashpoint for conflict between the United States and China.[35] And Robert Blackwill and Phillip Zelikow argue that the Taiwan Strait "is becoming the most dangerous flashpoint in the world," and that "events in and involving [Taiwan] could spark a war that draws in the United States, China, Japan, and possibly others."[36]

Some of this attention, of course, is simply reflective of recent tensions in cross-strait relations, combined with the recent surge in PRC military activity in the air and waters near Taiwan. But many analysts argue that near-term war in the Taiwan Strait is becoming more likely, for a range of reasons. Oriana Mastro, for instance, suggests that factors such as PRC military modernization and insufficient U.S.-led coalition building in the region mean that "cross-strait deterrence is arguably weaker today than at any point since the Korean War."[37] Minxin Pei contends that hardened PRC policy toward Taiwan in recent years under Xi Jinping is increasing the risks of war.[38] Peter Gries and Tao Wang argue that factors such increasing nationalism in China and wishful thinking in Beijing, Washington, and Taipei are combining to make "conflict in the Taiwan Strait . . . more likely than is commonly recognized."[39] Jacques deLisle points out that Beijing is becoming increasingly confident of U.S. decline even as it loses patience over domestic trends in Taiwan.[40] And Tyler Cowen suggests that some long-term trends are likely to turn negative for China—such as the PRC's share of global economic output. In turn, a sense that China's window of opportunity might be closing could incentivize Beijing to launch a war against Taiwan sooner rather than later.[41]

Other analysts, however, are more sanguine about the prospects for peace in the Taiwan Strait, at least in the near term. For instance, Mark Cozad argues that Beijing continues to view its military has having significant weaknesses and in turn concludes that "Chinese political leaders probably remain cautious about . . . a major campaign to force unification with Taiwan."[42] Dennis Blasko notes along similar lines that PRC leaders still "recognize significant shortcomings in the warfighting and command capabilities of the People's Liberation Army (PLA)" more generally.[43] Richard Bush, Bonnie Glaser, and Ryan Hass caution against "hyping" the danger of conflict in the Taiwan Strait, suggesting that a war over Taiwan would both undermine Beijing's global image while threatening more important domestic priorities (such as economic development).[44] The authors also note that Taiwan public opinion is generally cautious on sovereignty issues and is thus unlikely to support actions—such as pursuing formal independence—that are likely to trigger a PRC military response. And others contend that the potentially high economic costs of a cross-strait war are likely to make Beijing cautious in initiating such a conflict.[45]

Why do analysts come to such divergent conclusions about the prospects for conflict in the Taiwan Strait? Part of the problem is that the relationship across the Taiwan Strait is highly complex: China-Taiwan relations are characterized both by a number of factors that exacerbate the risks of conflict and by other factors that help to mitigate those risks. Often, analysts come to different conclusions simply because they weigh the importance of these factors differently. Moreover, future trend lines are hard to predict. For instance, PRC calculations about the efficacy of a military campaign against Taiwan certainly take into account expectations about U.S. behavior—including whether and how the United States would intervene in such a conflict. But U.S. commitments to Taiwan's security have long been ambiguous and have waxed and waned over time; whether U.S. commitments will strengthen or weaken in the future is unknown. Similarly, even as Taiwanese public opinion has generally rejected unification with today's PRC, it has remained pragmatic by rejecting actions (such as a declaration of independence) that might trigger a military response. Whether such pragmatism will persist in the years ahead is likewise difficult to predict. And even factors that seem to be moving unambiguously in a certain direction—such as improving PRC military capabilities—can have ambiguous implications for the likelihood of conflict. Improving capabilities could make war more likely by increasing Beijing's confidence that it could prevail in a war to unify Taiwan. But an expectation that this trend will continue could also encourage patience in Beijing, secure in the belief that it will be in an even better position in the future to maneuver Taiwan toward unification. Making sense of these seemingly contradictory features of cross-strait relations requires systematic analysis to assess how different factors interact with one another in shaping the prospects for conflict and peace in the Taiwan Strait.[46]

My principal aim in writing this book is to develop a framework through which to think, systematically, about the prospects for conflict between China and Taiwan. The framework that I develop draws from a burgeoning international relations literature on the causes of war and begins with a simple observation: there should, in principle, be many peaceful outcomes that would leave both China and Taiwan better off than if they were to fight an actual war. As I explained at the outset, a war in the Taiwan Strait would almost certainly entail tremendous costs for both China and Taiwan—regardless of the war's ultimate outcome. Yet the same can be said of most wars. As James Fearon succinctly puts it, the "central puzzle about war, and also the main reason we study it, is that wars are costly but nonetheless wars recur."[47] Understanding how war could occur in the Taiwan Strait requires grappling with why China and Taiwan might be unable to obtain bargains that would leave everyone better off than the war outcome.

Consider, for instance, the impact of growing PRC military power (perhaps combined with weakening U.S. and Taiwanese deterrence). On the surface, a shift in the balance of power would seem to make the PRC more tempted to attempt to occupy Taiwan using military force. Yet, if the balance of power is drifting in China's favor, and if the PRC increasingly possesses the ability to compel unification, then it is reasonable to ask: Why wouldn't Taiwan be willing to bargain with Beijing? Given how horrible an invasion would be for Taiwan, wouldn't Taipei prefer instead to accommodate the PRC just enough that Beijing prefers peace over war? In short, to understand why wars occur, analysts must grapple with the reality that wars are an inefficient way for states to resolve disputes; in principle, outcomes should exist that leave disputants better off than the war outcome.

In this book I develop a model of cross-strait conflict that draws heavily from the bargaining model of international conflict, which David Lake describes as the "workhorse model" of war in the international relations literature.[48] The bargaining model of war takes the inefficiency of war as a starting point and asks why states are unable to find bargains that would leave all disputants better off than the war outcome. Scholars working in the bargaining model tradition have highlighted two broad causal mechanisms that could lead to war despite its inefficiency. First, information problems can lead to war under certain conditions: leaders might underestimate, for instance, the resolve of their adversaries, and those adversaries might have a difficult time making threats credible. Second, credible commitment problems can give rise to conflict. Simply put, leaders might not trust their adversaries to uphold bargains that all might in principle prefer to fighting a war. I show that both of these causal mechanisms are highly relevant in the case of cross-strait relations, and I use my model to outline several plausible pathways to conflict in the Taiwan Strait. Teasing out the causal logic of conflict, in turn, allows for a more systematic consideration of how different trends in cross-strait relations are affecting the prospects for war between China and Taiwan.

Several conclusions follow from my analysis: First, a cross-strait war could occur through several discrete logics, and the factors that could help mitigate one type of conflict do not necessarily mitigate other types. Second, some war scenarios—particularly those involving a revisionist Taiwan government seeking to formalize a greater level of sovereign status—are becoming less likely as the potential costs of war effectively overwhelm any upside that Taipei might see in risking conflict with Beijing. But, third, the shifting balance of power in the Taiwan Strait is quite worrisome and introduces risks of conflict that are ultimately rooted in credible commitment problems. I argue that these risks are even more pernicious than commonly understood in the literature, but I also argue that powerful mitigating factors remain in place. A cross-strait war, in short, is a real danger, but it is also a danger that is far from inevitable.

PLAN FOR THE BOOK

The remainder of this book proceeds in two parts. Part I focuses on past and likely future trends in cross-strait relations and is structured around several key factors that help to shape the prospects for conflict and peace in the Taiwan Strait. Chapter 1 begins with a discussion of deepening economic ties between China and Taiwan. China, today, is Taiwan's most important overseas economic partner; the PRC is Taiwan's top trade partner and the top destination of its outbound foreign investment. Taiwanese companies are deeply integrated into supply chains that run through mainland China. I trace the historical evolution of the cross-strait economic relationship and summarize its features (noting that after decades of deepening cross-strait economic integration, economic ties between China and Taiwan have leveled off in recent years). I conclude with a discussion of the security implications for Taiwan of being so heavily reliant on economic ties with China. Here I observe that extensive cross-strait economic integration is a double-edged sword for the island. Economic integration raises the costs of conflict, which could act as a stabilizing force. At the same time, it also potentially gives Beijing alternative avenues through which to exert influence in Taiwan.

In chapter 2 I turn my attention to the shifting balance of military power in the Taiwan Strait. China in recent decades has emerged as an economic powerhouse, which in turn has enabled the PRC to invest heavily in its military capabilities. China today is capable of imposing great costs on Taiwan in a military conflict. And as the PRC's military modernization proceeds, some question whether Taiwan (and the United States) will be able to effectively deter a future PRC effort to achieve unification using military force. In the chapter I consider relative PRC military capabilities in several different arenas and speculate on likely future trajectories.

Clearly, any consideration of a cross-strait conflict needs to consider the role of the United States. The United States has been Taiwan's closest security partner for decades and would likely intervene in some capacity were armed conflict to break out in the Taiwan Strait. Chapter 3 considers the U.S. role at length. I describe the U.S. commitment to Taiwan's security as being informal, ambiguous, and to some degree conditional on Taiwan's actions, and I suggest that these characteristics arise from a set of dilemmas the United States faces in the Taiwan Strait. The chapter uses a range of indicators to show that U.S.-Taiwan security relations have been getting closer in recent years, while also emphasizing that these changes have been incremental, and that the level of U.S.

commitment to Taiwan's security continues to be characterized by considerable ambiguity.

The first part of the book concludes with chapter 4, which provides a basic overview of domestic trends on both sides of the Taiwan Strait, and how these trends might affect cross-strait relations. I focus on a few major trends that are likely to have especially large implications for the future prospects for conflict and peace in the Taiwan Strait: declining support for unification with the PRC in Taiwan; a growing prevalence of Taiwan-centric identity among Taiwan's citizens; possible increasing nationalism in the PRC; and shifting views among China's top leaders.

The second part of the book develops a framework through which to analyze how the different trends and features of China-Taiwan relations identified in part I—trends relating to cross-strait economic integration, the shifting balance of military power, the nature of the U.S. commitment to Taiwan, and domestic and societal trends in both Taiwan and the PRC—collectively shape the prospects for war and peace in the Taiwan Strait. I begin in chapter 5 by constructing a simple model of the cross–Taiwan Strait relationship. This model draws directly from bargaining theories of conflict that international relations scholars commonly use to analyze conflict more generally. The model serves as a baseline that I then use in chapters 6 and 7 to explore how two very different types of conflict might emerge in the Taiwan Strait. In chapter 6 I consider a cross-strait conflict that is rooted in efforts by Taiwan to alter the status quo in a way that conflicts with Beijing's preferences, what I refer to as the problem of Taiwan revisionism. In chapter 7 I consider a conflict that is rooted in efforts by the PRC to impose its preferred sovereignty solution on Taiwan, what I refer to as the problem of PRC revisionism. I argue in these chapters that the risks associated with a conflict rooted in Taiwan revisionism are declining, even as the risks of a conflict rooted in PRC revisionism are growing. I argue in particular in chapter 7 that a series of thorny credible commitment problems makes the shifting balance of military power in the Taiwan Strait quite worrisome. The conclusion summarizes my main arguments and discusses how worst-case scenarios might be avoided.

I

PAST AND FUTURE TRENDS IN CROSS-STRAIT RELATIONS

1

ECONOMIC INTEGRATION ACROSS
THE TAIWAN STRAIT

Even in the 1990s, the relationship across the Taiwan Strait was characterized by what Chu Yun-han called a "rather unique bifurcation" that combined rapidly growing economic ties with a hostile political relationship.[1] In the years after Chu's observation, this duality became more puzzling still as cross-strait political relations deteriorated further during the Chen Shui-bian administration, even as the PRC surpassed the United States to become Taiwan's largest trading partner by far. Cross-strait relations had come to epitomize the pithy saying "cold politics, hot economics," which succinctly describes several relationships in the region. Politics across the Taiwan Strait tended to be colder than elsewhere, and the economic relationship was hotter. Perhaps even more remarkable, the cross-strait economic relationship came to flourish even though Taiwan's government maintained a range of restrictions on economic interactions with China. Indeed, China became Taiwan's largest trading partner at a time when there was virtually no direct travel across the Taiwan Strait. Taiwan businesspeople wishing to travel to the mainland needed to pass through Hong Kong, or other third locations, first.

More recently, during the détente that emerged during the Ma Ying-jeou administration, the PRC and Taiwan signed a number of agreements that largely normalized the bilateral economic relationship.

Direct travel is now allowed, and many of the restrictions on investment have been eased. However, a more normalized economic relationship has not translated into accelerating economic integration. To the contrary, as labor costs increase in China, the period of explosive growth in cross-strait economic ties appears to be over. Nor has a more normal economic relationship transformed the bilateral political relationship; since the election of Tsai Ing-wen in 2016, the cross-strait relationship has returned to the realm of "cold politics, hot economics." Still, even if cross-strait trade and investment flows are not expanding as rapidly as in the past, economic interactions continue to be extensive. The PRC remains Taiwan's primary economic partner, and China continues to derive considerable benefits as well from bilateral economic exchange. Assessing the prospects for conflict and peace in the Taiwan Strait clearly requires grappling with these extensive economic ties, if for no other reason than the massive economic disruptions that a war in the Taiwan Strait would be sure to trigger.

In this chapter, I provide an overview of the evolving cross-strait economic relationship. I begin with a history of the relationship, summarizing the rapid growth in cross-strait economic ties over time. I discuss the factors that have pushed the two economies closer together, as well as the political controversies that economic integration has given rise to in Taiwan. The second part of the chapter then considers some of the security implications of extensive cross-strait economic integration. I observe that economic ties can be a double-edged sword for Taiwan, helping to bring prosperity (and perhaps helping to deter military conflict), but also generating significant security risks for the island.

HISTORY OF THE CROSS-STRAIT ECONOMIC RELATIONSHIP

The rapid growth in cross-strait economic ties largely parallels China's astonishing rise as a global economic superpower. At the dawn of the post-Mao economic reforms, China was a highly autarkic economy;

despite having the world's largest population, roughly three dozen countries traded more than the PRC.[2] Within a few short decades, however, China has emerged as—depending on methodology—either the world's largest or second largest economy, its largest trading state, and one of the primary destinations for foreign direct investment. Today China stands as the primary trading partner for nearly every country in its immediate periphery and indeed is the top trading partner for a growing number of countries across the globe, from Africa to Latin America.

Seen in this light, Taiwan's economic integration with China is not especially unusual. In fact, cross-strait relations might be even more puzzling today if Taiwan were to have managed to divorce itself from these broader trends by fencing itself off from the economic giant just one hundred miles to the west. Still, context is critical. When economic integration across the Taiwan Strait began to surge in the late 1980s, the two sides of the strait had no official interactions with each other. The obstacles facing Taiwanese entrepreneurs wishing to invest in China were substantial, and by the mid-1990s the two sides were locked in an intense, and prolonged, military crisis. Taiwan may not be an outlier in its extensive economic linkages with China, but those ties emerged against a backdrop—an exceptionally antagonistic political relationship—that we might normally expect to quash economic integration. Consider, for instance, the limited commercial integration that we see in other cases of intense political rivalry—on the Korean Peninsula, in South Asia, or in the Middle East.[3] How did this come about?

EARLY BEGINNINGS: CHANGING CROSS-STRAIT ECONOMIC RELATIONS IN THE 1980S

Prior to the 1980s, economic ties across the Taiwan Strait were extremely limited. Since the Nationalist retreat to Taiwan at the close of the Chinese Civil War in 1949, the ROC government had banned all contact, which included economic contact, with the PRC. Of course, even in the absence of these bans, the incentives for extensive economic interactions across the Taiwan Strait were limited. The combination of a centrally planned economy, economic mismanagement under Mao, and a highly autarkic development strategy all served to temper any enthusiasm Taiwanese companies might have had to do business in China. Instead, Taiwan looked east: by the early 1980s, nearly half of all Taiwan exports flowed to the United States. Cross-strait trade was limited to a small amount of indirect trade through Hong Kong in products like traditional Chinese medicines; in 1978 this trade amounted to only US$47 million.[4]

During the 1980s, however, several factors combined to encourage rapid growth in cross-strait economic exchange. Most important, China was changing dramatically. After Deng Xiaoping consolidated power in the late 1970s, China initiated an economic reform program that included increased openness to the world economy. Initial steps in this regard were tentative. Most notably, the PRC in 1979 established four special economic zones—open to international trade and designed to attract foreign investors—in Fujian and Guangdong provinces, and in 1984 it opened an additional fourteen cities to foreign trade and investment. More dramatic opening occurred in the later 1980s as the PRC implemented a broader coastal development strategy, which was designed specifically to lure low-wage manufacturing from more developed regions in East Asia to China's coast. Key elements of the strategy included decentralization of investment regulations (allowing local authorities more freedom to devise policies meant to attract foreign investors), lower barriers to imports of raw materials used in the production of exports, and increased legal protections to foreign companies.[5]

Meanwhile, as noted in the introduction, the PRC's approach to Taiwan changed sharply after the United States established formal diplomatic ties with Beijing—and severed official ties with Taiwan—in 1979. Beijing replaced the old rhetoric of "liberation" with a new rhetoric of "peaceful reunification." Chinese officials promised that Taiwan, if it were to agree to unify, would be able to maintain a high degree of political and economic autonomy, a formula that came to be known as "one country, two systems." As part of this changed policy, the PRC openly welcomed increased economic exchange with Taiwan. This welcoming attitude toward cross-strait economic ties was highlighted in the nine-point plan for national unification proposed in 1981 by Marshal Ye

Jianying (then vice-chair of the National People's Congress Standing Committee). More specifically, the plan called for the opening up of direct travel, postal, and commercial linkages across the Taiwan Strait and advocated increased economic and cultural exchange between the two sides.[6]

Significant changes were also taking place in Taiwan. From the mid-1950s until the early 1980s, the economy averaged 8.7 percent annual growth, making it one of the fastest growing economies in the world. Living standards improved rapidly: real per capita income grew at an annual rate of 7 percent during the 1960s and 1970s, while income inequality declined.[7] Taiwan's per capita income ranked eighty-fifth in the world in the early 1960s but jumped nearly fifty spots in the ranking by the mid-1980s.[8] By the late 1960s Taiwan citizens had enjoyed nine years of free compulsory education, and by the late 1970s the literacy rate approached 90 percent.[9] In this environment, Taiwan's labor costs began to rise sharply, and the island's comparative advantage in low-cost, labor-intensive manufacturing began to erode. Furthermore, after years of growing current account surpluses, the ROC government by the mid-1980s was coming under pressure from the United States to allow its currency, the New Taiwan dollar, to appreciate in value. The second half of the decade saw a sharp increase in the currency's value, further undercutting the competitiveness of Taiwan's labor-intensive industries in foreign markets. Faced with these constraints, the island's low-end manufacturers had growing incentive to move production abroad to places with lower labor costs. Not surprisingly, mainland China's proximity, low labor costs, shared language and culture, and economic reforms and welcoming posture toward cross-strait economic links combined to make investment in the PRC an increasingly attractive option for Taiwan manufacturers.[10]

Against this backdrop, trade flows across the strait and Taiwanese investment in the PRC began to rise during the 1980s. By 1985 cross-strait trade exceeded US$1 billion according to some estimates, and small-scale, labor-intensive industries were beginning to relocate to the mainland.[11] In many cases, these operations simply disassembled key equipment, shipped it through Hong Kong, and then reassembled in mainland China.[12] Although these interactions remained illegal, in practice the Taiwan government began to tolerate limited investments in the mid-1980s (primarily undertaken by small, labor-intensive industries). After martial law was lifted in 1987, the Taiwan government legalized indirect travel to the PRC, which effectively undermined the government's ability to monitor and control small-scale economic flows across the Taiwan Strait.[13] Soon Taiwanese investment in labor-intensive industries—industries that had become increasingly uncompetitive in Taiwan—began to pour into mainland China. By the early 1990s the ROC government was easing restrictions on cross-strait economic ties largely to try to keep up with facts on the ground.[14] As Chu Yun-han puts it, "adaptable small and medium-sized enterprises simply rampaged through the official investment ban" so the "state was forced to modify its policy to accommodate the fait accompli."[15] Taiwan also began to ease restrictions on imports from the PRC, although inward flows remained (and, indeed, remain to this day) much more limited than outbound flows to the mainland.

THE 1990S: DEEPENING INTEGRATION, GROWING CONCERNS IN TAIWAN

The rapid growth in cross-strait economic ties during the late 1980s and early 1990s was largely driven by Taiwan's small and medium-sized firms that produced in labor-intensive industries (such as shoe and garment manufacturers) that had become increasingly uncompetitive in Taiwan. Moreover, as Rigger observes, these businesses often avoided local suppliers in China.[16] Rather, entire supply chains would typically migrate to the mainland together, "reproducing the clustered production process they had used in Taiwan." Thus the movement of a few initial firms to China led to a wave of connected suppliers moving to China as well.[17] As this process unfolded, the mainland quickly emerged as one of Taiwan's most important economic partners. Statistics in the 1980s and early 1990s were notoriously unreliable since much Taiwan investment in and trade with the PRC was still illegal and hence likely unreported.

However, Taiwan's Mainland Affairs Council estimated that Taiwan's exports to mainland China represented more than 16 percent of the island's total exports by 1993. Approved Taiwan investment in the PRC exceeded US$1 billion for the first time that year, and PRC statistics suggested that the actual amount of investment exceeded US$3 billion.[18]

Although the initial wave of economic integration across the Taiwan Strait was driven by Taiwan's smaller, labor-intensive firms, after 1992 Taiwan's larger firms also began to show increasing interest in the PRC market. Much of this interest was driven by changes that were taking place within China. In the immediate aftermath of the 1989 post-Tiananmen Square crackdown, economic growth and the reform program stalled as hard-liners reasserted authority in Beijing.[19] By 1992, however, reformers again seized the upper hand. Deng Xiaoping famously toured southern China early in the year, touting the virtues of economic reform while critiquing conservatives. In the aftermath of that trip, economic reforms—including new reforms that liberalized access to China for foreign investors—picked up steam and economic growth skyrocketed.[20] The new reform momentum, in turn, attracted more of Taiwan's larger enterprises, which hoped to tap into China's rapidly growing domestic market (as opposed to earlier investors who were mostly exporting what they produced in China). Furthermore, some larger upstream firms were also being driven to China by the large number of downstream small manufacturers that had already moved there, since those smaller firms made up a key portion of their customer base.[21] Thus, during the early-to-mid-1990s, the average size of Taiwan investments in China increased sharply, and to an increasing degree Taiwan's larger enterprises began to invest in production facilities in the PRC.

The ROC's political leadership in the 1990s viewed deepening cross-strait economic integration, and in particular the interest in China exhibited by Taiwan's large enterprise groups, with increasing concern. Partly this concern was economic, and in particular a fear that the PRC's burgeoning economy could trigger an exodus of Taiwan firms that would effectively hollow-out the island's economy. But Taiwanese officials also worried about the political implications of overreliance on the PRC market. Beijing clearly and openly viewed economic ties across the Taiwan Strait as advancing its goal of unification, which naturally made officials in Taipei suspicious of growing cross-strait linkages.[22] These suspicions would intensify as cross-strait relations worsened in the aftermath of Lee Teng-hui's visit to Cornell University in 1995.

The Lee government took a number of steps to try to limit Taiwan's economic dependence on China during the 1990s. First, the government encouraged diversification of Taiwan's foreign economic ties. The "Go South" strategy, the most visible effort in this regard, aimed to increase Taiwan's economic linkages with Southeast Asian countries as an alternative to the PRC market.[23] Among the concrete steps taken to encourage firms to invest in Southeast Asia were ROC government loans to businesses investing in the region. Second, the Taiwan government at times offered incentives—such as reduced taxes or relaxed environmental standards—to firms that agreed to invest in Taiwan instead of the PRC.[24] Third, after 1996, the Lee administration also began to tighten restrictions on mainland investment. Lee's "go slow, be patient" policy placed a cap of $US50 million on individual investment projects in China and banned investments in major infrastructure projects.[25] These efforts corresponded to some drop-off in investment flows during the late 1990s: Taiwan government approved investments in mainland China dropped from approximately US$1.6 billion in 1997 to approximately US$1.3 billion in 1999. PRC statistics also suggested a decline in both contracted and realized Taiwan investment in China after 1996.[26]

Ultimately, however, efforts during the Lee administration to limit Taiwan's economic dependence on China proved to a considerable degree ineffectual. The Go South strategy faced limited enthusiasm from the Taiwan business community, which was more attracted to shared culture, language, and kinship ties and the booming market just across the Taiwan Strait. The Asian financial crisis, which hit many Southeast Asian economies hard in the late 1990s, further undercut the policy. Meanwhile, efforts to restrict investments in China faced resistance from Taiwan businesses.[27] While the go slow, be patient policy was successful in stemming the flow of high-profile infrastructure investments in

China, it made only a relatively small dent in long-term trends.[28] By the end of the decade, Taiwanese investment in China was again rising, driven in large part by the growing migration of Taiwan's high-technology production facilities to the PRC.[29] As with earlier waves of investment in the PRC, Taiwan's high-tech sector hoped to take advantage of lower production costs in China to maintain a competitive edge in global markets. Taiwanese companies had already established themselves as global leaders in a range of information technology (IT) products like motherboards, monitors, and, by the late 1990s, laptop computers. By the early 2000s, Taiwanese IT companies were producing as much in mainland China as they were in Taiwan, and even Taiwan's vaunted notebook computer industry was setting up production facilities in China.[30]

THE CHEN SHUI-BIAN ERA AND THE INTENSIFYING DICHOTOMY BETWEEN ECONOMICS AND POLITICS

The election of Chen Shui-bian as Taiwan's president in 2000 thus occurred as the cross-strait economic relationship continued to deepen despite efforts under Lee to stem those trends. Chen, as noted in the introduction, initially took a pragmatic approach to cross-strait relations. In addition to pledging to avoid taking steps—such as declaring independence—that might trigger conflict with China, Chen promised to relax some of Taiwan's restrictions on cross-strait economic ties. During his first year in office, Chen repeatedly expressed interest in lifting the ban on direct exchanges across the Taiwan Strait, and in 2001 he tasked an advisory conference—which included many of the island's most prominent businesspeople—with crafting recommendations concerning economic policy and cross-strait relations. The conference, in turn, recommended ditching the go slow, be patient policy and replacing it with an "active opening, effective management" policy instead. More specifically, the conference recommended loosening restrictions on capital flows across the Taiwan Strait, and a more aggressive effort to establish direct linkages (trade, travel, and communications—known as the "three direct links"—which had not existed since the end of the civil war) across the Taiwan Strait.[31]

Chen Shui-bian endorsed the advisory conference recommendations, and over the next year the Taiwan government relaxed a number of restrictions on investment in China. These liberalizing measures included lifting the $50 million ban on individual investment projects in China that had been put in place during the Lee administration; streamlining the process through which investments in mainland China are approved; allowing direct investment in the PRC (rather than requiring companies to route investments through companies in third locations, such as Hong Kong); allowing listed companies to invest a greater share of their capital in China; and lifting Taiwan's ban on semiconductor investments in the PRC.[32] The Chen government also took some steps to open direct links across the Taiwan Strait. In late 2001 Taiwan initiated the "mini three links" (*xiao san tong*), which permitted direct links between the ROC-governed island of Jinmen and mainland China. In 2003 the Chen government allowed charter flights to travel between Taiwan and China during the Chinese New Year (when many Taiwanese businesspeople travel back to Taiwan), though these flights were required to touch down briefly in Hong Kong; in 2005 charter flights that only needed to pass through Hong Kong's airspace were allowed during the holidays.[33]

Despite these liberalizing steps, however, Taiwan's restrictions on cross-strait economic exchange remained considerable for the remainder of Chen's time in office. Most notably, the ban on direct links across the Taiwan Strait—with the exceptions just noted—remained in place, meaning that trade and travel for the most part continued to be done via third locations like Hong Kong. The key barrier to opening direct links was political: cross-strait dialogue, which had occurred at the quasi-official level during the 1990s, was frozen throughout the Chen presidency (as noted in the introduction). The PRC government, starting in 2002, proposed a way around the impasse by suggesting negotiations via unofficial talks held between private organizations (such as trade associations). Chen rejected this proposal, however, insisting that negotiations on this sensitive topic must also involve government representatives at some level.[34] Meanwhile, on the investment front, the Chen government pursued few new liberalizing reforms after the policy changes of 2001–2002.

Cross-strait economic ties, however, expanded rapidly during the Chen administration despite the persistent ban on direct links and continued restrictions on Taiwan investment in China. According to Taiwan Mainland Affairs Council (MAC) estimates, cross-strait trade exploded from US$31 billion in 2000 to over US$105 billion in 2008; PRC customs statistics show an even more dramatic increase, from US$30 billion in 2000 to over US$129 billion in 2008.[35] According to the MAC estimates, trade with China grew from under 11 percent of Taiwan's foreign trade in 2000 to over 21 percent by 2008.[36] In 2003 mainland China surpassed the United States to become Taiwan's largest trading partner, and by the end of Chen's presidency trade with China nearly doubled trade with the United States.[37] Investment flows across the Taiwan Strait also grew rapidly during the Chen era: investment in the PRC approved by the Taiwan government rose from US$2.6 billion in 2000 to US$10.7 billion in 2008.[38] Investment continued to flow heavily toward high-tech sectors, including electronic components and computers.[39] The official numbers almost certainly understated actual Taiwan investment flows by a large margin. For instance, it was widely estimated, even by the mid-2000s, that accumulated Taiwan investment in China already exceeded US$100 billion.[40] Furthermore, more and more Taiwanese were moving to China, and by the 2000s young Taiwanese were increasingly going to China for education or to launch careers. Estimates often put the number of Taiwanese living in China at one million (a large number considering Taiwan's total population at the time was approximately twenty-three million), although, as Rigger writes, "no one really knows how many Taiwanese are living in mainland China . . . but everyone agrees the numbers are huge and growing."[41]

Perhaps most remarkable, the rapid growth in cross-strait economic ties during the Chen Shui-bian administration occurred during a time of tense, and deteriorating, cross-strait political relations. Intuitively, this deteriorating political environment—where Beijing was overtly threatening war with Taiwan even as it appeared to be harassing some

Taiwan businesses for their political identification back home—
should seemingly have acted as a brake on the cross-strait economic
relationship. Yet a number of factors acted to mitigate the impact of a
toxic bilateral political relationship on economic ties. Most important,
the Chinese economy continued to boom. As China continued to
grow and integrate into global markets (the PRC entered the World
Trade Organization in 2001, further cementing its status as an emerging
trade powerhouse), its economic allure to the Taiwan business community was simply irresistible. As Rigger writes, moving production
facilities to China gave many Taiwan businesses a new lease on life as
production costs continued to rise in Taiwan, and China's deepening
integration into global markets made it an ideal destination.[42] For much
of Taiwan's business community, staying out of China simply wasn't a
realistic option.

A second factor that enabled cross-strait economic ties to thrive
despite political tensions centered on Beijing's approach to Taiwan.
Although the PRC was often harsh in its criticism of Chen Shui-bian,
and at times appeared to sanction pro-Chen businesses operating in
China, for the most part Beijing tried to keep political tensions from
undermining the bilateral economic relationship. Even during the 1995–
1996 Taiwan Strait crisis, when cross-strait tensions were at their recent
peak, Beijing tried to reassure the Taiwan business community that their
investments in China were safe.[43] The efforts to target pro-Chen businesses in the 2000s, meanwhile, tended to focus on a very few high-
profile cases, and officials discounted the degree to which they implied
a broader crackdown.[44] Beijing had strong incentives to keep politics
from destroying the cross-strait economic relations: even though economic ties represented a much larger share of Taiwan's economy than
the PRC's, it was clear that the mainland benefited enormously from
these ties. Douglas Fuller, writing in 2008, argued that Taiwanese companies contributed to China's technological development by, among
other things, training workers (such as engineers in the semiconductor
industry) or through venture capital investments.[45]

Finally, businesses were able to insulate themselves from politics to
a considerable extent. They had already proven adept at avoiding Taiwan restrictions on cross-strait commerce; since the 1990s, Taiwan's

restrictions were often trying to catch up with the facts on the ground. But, more generally, Taiwan businesspeople operating in China have tended to adopt a low profile on political issues, so as to avoid being targeted with harassment on the mainland and becoming entangled in political controversies in Taiwan.[46]

MA YING-JEOU AND DEEPER LIBERALIZATION

The landslide election of Ma Ying-jeou as Taiwan's president in 2008 led to dramatic changes in the cross-strait economic relationship. Endorsing a weak version of a one China principle in the form of the 1992 consensus, the Ma administration was quickly able to restart dialogue with the PRC via the SEF-ARATS channel that Beijing had suspended since the late 1990s. The two sides engaged in numerous rounds of dialogue during Ma's eight years in office, reaching twenty-three separate agreements that—as Richard Bush has put it—collectively helped to normalize, liberalize, and institutionalize the cross-strait economic relationship.[47]

Once cross-strait dialogue resumed, the two sides moved rapidly to open direct links across the Taiwan Strait. Although some progress had been made during the Chen administration on this issue—with the opening of the "mini three links" and the occasional authorization of direct charter flights—for the most part the ban on direct ties remained in place when Ma took office in May 2008. In June the PRC and Taiwan agreed to establish direct charter flights for tourists.[48] More sweeping agreements were reached in November when the two sides agreed to open regular direct flights, as well as direct cargo shipping and mail services, between the two sides; these new direct ties commenced in December 2008.[49] Soon, hundreds of flights per week connected numerous cities in Taiwan and mainland China; travel across the strait had been transformed from a full-day affair involving a stopover in Hong Kong to routine trips that in some cases took little more than an hour.

In 2010 the PRC and Taiwan signed an Economic Cooperation Framework Agreement (ECFA); the agreement was quickly ratified by Taiwan's Legislative Yuan and took effect in that same year. The ECFA laid out an ambitious agenda for further liberalization in cross-strait economic ties, including reduced barriers to trade and investment, increased cooperation on issues such as intellectual property rights and investment protection, and negotiations over a dispute settlement mechanism. The two sides agreed that the ECFA would be followed by subsequent agreements to address these issues; in particular, four follow-on agreements were planned, to address trade in goods, trade in services, investment protection, and a dispute settlement mechanism.[50] The ECFA also included an "early harvest" program where the two sides agreed to reduce tariffs on 539 products that Taiwanese companies exported to China, and on 267 Chinese exports to Taiwan. Several service sectors were also part of the early harvest program. In sum, the ECFA both produced immediate liberalization via its early harvest program and served as a roadmap for further liberalization and institutionalization of the cross-strait economic relationship.[51] Against this backdrop of liberalization, trade between the two sides continued to grow during the first Ma administration after an initial blip caused by the global financial crisis. By 2011 bilateral trade exceeded $129 billion, according to Taiwan customs statistics.[52]

Taiwan also opened its door to PRC tourists during the first Ma administration. Negotiators from the PRC and Taiwan reached an initial agreement in 2008 allowing PRC tour groups to visit Taiwan, and in 2011 the two sides agreed to allow individual tourists from a limited number of Chinese cities.[53] The opening of Taiwan to PRC tourists, in turn, led to a rapid increase in mainland Chinese visitors to Taiwan, from under 300,000 in 2008 to over four million in 2015; by 2015 the vast majority of PRC visitors to Taiwan were tourists.[54]

BACKLASH: THE LATE MA ADMINISTRATION AND THE RISE OF TSAI ING-WEN

Ma Ying-jeou's reelection in 2012 as Taiwan's president appeared to confirm another four years of continued liberalization in cross-strait economic ties. However, Ma's cross-strait economic policies became highly contentious in Taiwan. The backlash against further liberalization helped to trigger the Sunflower Movement in 2014 and to pave the way for a return to power by the DPP in 2016.

Opposition to Ma's liberalizing cross-strait economic policy was already building during the ECFA negotiations. The Democratic Progressive Party was highly critical of the agreement and organized large-scale protests against it in 2010; Tsai Ing-wen, the DPP chair at the time, argued that the agreement was negotiated without transparency and warned that it would primarily benefit large corporations and not average Taiwanese.[55] Although this opposition did not stop ECFA from being signed and ratified, it did augur trouble for further steps toward liberalization: the PRC and Taiwan signed only two of the planned four follow-on agreements to the ECFA—an investment protection agreement in 2012,[56] and the Cross-Strait Service Trade Agreement (CSSTA) in 2013.

The signing of the CSSTA proved to be a turning point in the evolving cross-strait economic relationship. In the agreement, China agreed to open eighty service-sector industries to Taiwan investors, while Taiwan agreed to open sixty-four of its service-sector industries (ranging from beauty parlors to tourism to banking, among others) to PRC investors. The CSSTA quickly became highly contentious, with DPP legislators protesting the Ma administration's plans to enact the agreement without legislative ratification. The major parties later agreed—in the face of growing public outcry—to a legislative review process; however, the process broke down as the DPP accused the KMT of trying to ram the legislation through the Legislative Yuan without sufficient review, while the KMT accused the DPP of obstruction. In March 2014 the KMT moved the CSSTA to the floor of the legislature, triggering a student-led occupation of the Legislative Yuan that lasted for twenty-four days and a broader protest movement that came to be known as the Sunflower Movement. Opponents of the CSSTA organized a huge protest in Taipei in late March, and public opinion polls suggested tepid societal support for the agreement. Ultimately, Ma was forced to withdraw the agreement from the Legislative Yuan, and it was never ratified. The episode also led to the sidelining of a trade in goods bill that was to have been finalized after the CSSTA. The dramatic liberalizing trend in cross-strait economic relations that characterized much of the Ma presidency, in short, had stalled by 2014.[57]

By late 2014 it had become clear that political winds were shifting in Taiwan, as Ma's approval ratings dropped in the aftermath of the Sunflower Movement, and as the DPP performed very strongly in December 2014 local elections. In 2016 Tsai Ing-wen of the DPP was elected president in a landslide, and for the first time the party also secured a majority in the Legislative Yuan. As noted in the introduction, cross-strait relations became more hostile after Tsai's election; Tsai refused to endorse the "92 consensus" or any other version of a "one China" principle, and the PRC in turn cut off all dialogue with the Taiwan government and has since ratcheted up military, diplomatic, and economic pressure on the island. Existing economic agreements remained in place, however, and the two economies remained highly integrated.

Still, it is worth emphasizing that economic trends have to some extent leveled off in recent years, and on some dimensions economic ties have actually weakened. For instance, growth in cross-strait trade slowed considerably in the years after 2012.[58] As the U.S.-China trade war escalated in the late 2010s, meanwhile, some Taiwan firms—which often rely heavily on exports to the United States—were considering moving production facilities back to Taiwan.[59] Furthermore, as I will discuss at greater length in the next section, PRC tourist visits to Taiwan declined; this drop became more precipitous in the run-up to Taiwan's election of 2020 (even before the coronavirus crisis fully shut down such travel). And the Tsai administration launched an ambitious New Southbound policy, which aimed—harkening back to Lee Teng-hui's Go South strategy—to encourage greater linkages with Southeast Asia while easing dependence on the mainland China market.[60]

SUMMARY OF THE CROSS-STRAIT ECONOMIC RELATIONSHIP TIMELINE

In sum, the mainland China and Taiwan economies have become deeply interconnected. Economic integration proceeded rapidly during the 1990s and 2000s, despite what was a tense and at times highly confrontational bilateral political relationship. Economic ties continued to deepen during the détente that emerged after Ma Ying-jeou was elected Taiwan president in 2008, and the Ma administration reached numerous agreements with the PRC that further liberalized and normalized bilateral economic relations. These agreements, however, were contentious within Taiwan, and the CSSTA in particular helped to trigger a large protest movement that signaled an end to the period of aggressive liberalization. Since then, economic interdependence between the two sides remains substantial, but cross-strait economic ties have not continued to grow rapidly as in preceding decades, and on some dimensions economic ties have weakened to some degree.

CROSS-STRAIT ECONOMIC INTEGRATION AS A DOUBLE-EDGED SWORD FOR TAIWAN

Clearly, cross-strait economic integration has long been a contentious political issue in Taiwan. Part of this contentiousness parallels the sorts of controversies that typically arise when countries open their markets to international competition. For instance, even as some businesses benefited tremendously from access to the PRC market, some worried about the possibility of hollowed-out industry and worsening labor market conditions as firms moved production facilities to China. Yet the controversies surrounding cross-strait economic integration also have a strong security-related dimension, where many worry not simply that economic integration might have pernicious economic consequences for particular groups in Taiwan, but more broadly that cross-strait economic ties introduce a range of security vulnerabilities to the island. Indeed, PRC officials have at times been quite frank that they view economic ties as advancing China's political goals vis-à-vis Taiwan.

To the degree that economic ties do pose security risks for Taiwan, they represent a double-edged sword, and Taiwan, by integrating with

China, is in essence taking a gamble that enormous economic benefits outweigh the risks introduced by economic ties. In this section, I briefly elaborate on this trade-off by focusing on one particular concern often raised by those worried about cross-strait economic integration: that deepening economic ties are likely to increase Beijing's influence over Taiwan. After briefly outlining how economic ties could potentially lead to increased PRC influence, I observe that evidence of such an effect is mixed. I conclude this section by noting that because economic ties can also have positive impacts on Taiwan's security, assessing the net security implications is difficult.

HOW MIGHT CROSS-STRAIT ECONOMIC TIES TRANSLATE INTO CHINESE INFLUENCE?

To begin to unpack the sources of Chinese economic leverage over Taiwan, it is first important to consider how cross-strait economic ties might translate into political influence. Economic ties can potentially lead to influence through a range of causal processes, some of which involve conscious policy decisions and some of which arise naturally in the absence of intent to influence. A few examples of these different causal logics are discussed here.

Coercive economic sanctions. Here, China explicitly or implicitly threatens sanctions if the target doesn't comply with some demand, or China imposes sanctions to punish a target for undertaking actions or policies that Beijing dislikes. These threats can be directed against the Taiwan government, or against actors (such as businesses operating in China) that will be harmed directly by the sanctions. Sanctions can be designed to change target behavior, or they could serve as a signal to other actors that particular actions have consequences. For instance, Beijing might punish a few businesspeople who are insufficiently "pro-China" in order to send a message to others doing business in China.[61]

Positive inducements. Rather than threaten sticks, China can also offer carrots in exchange for a target doing something that the PRC wants. Again, the target can be the Taiwan government (where the PRC offers economic benefits in exchange for preferred policies), but the PRC might also target firms, individual politicians, or even voters with positive inducements. Inducements might have an explicit quid pro quo (such as a bribe) but might also seek to shape behavior by "winning hearts and minds."[62]

Creating vested interests in stability. PRC officials have long subscribed to a belief that economic integration has a transformative effect on Taiwan society and politics by generating vested interests in a stable and close cross-strait political relationship—that is, by creating a "China lobby" in Taiwan.[63] The large community of Taiwan businesses operating in China, for instance, might lobby for policies in Taiwan that align with Beijing's objectives and vote for candidates seeking stable relations with Beijing. Taiwan's economic dependence on China might lead individual voters to support candidates who don't want to rock the boat in cross-strait political relations. Note that this effect could occur even in the absence of PRC policies that deliberately try to leverage economic ties for political aims—that is, economic ties should naturally create vested interests.[64]

TO WHAT DEGREE HAVE ECONOMIC TIES ACTUALLY TRANSLATED INTO PRC INFLUENCE IN TAIWAN?

To begin, it is worth noting that China's general economic policy toward Taiwan dating to the late 1970s appears to have been at least partly rooted in a desire to increase influence over political trends on the island. Early policy initiatives, such as the "9 points plan," encouraged enhanced cross-strait economic exchanges, and PRC officials have long argued that Taiwan's deepening economic dependence on China advances cross-strait relations and helps to facilitate political unification.[65] Moving beyond these general observations, it is clear that the PRC has at times sought to leverage economic ties as a tool of influence. Some prominent examples are listed in this section.

The political behavior of Taiwan businesses with interests in China

Beijing has long viewed the large Taiwanese business community operating in China as a potential source of PRC influence in Taiwan. At times, the PRC has encouraged Taishang (Taiwan businesses operating in China) to lobby in Taiwan for certain policies.[66] For example, Beijing encouraged Taishang to oppose Lee Teng-hui's "special state-to-state relations" formulation in 1999.[67] Beijing has encouraged Taishang to go back to Taiwan to vote in elections (for instance, Chinese airlines sometimes offer discounted tickets to travel to Taiwan during elections),[68] and the PRC has at times threatened Taishang that appeared to be supporting the "wrong" causes or candidates in Taiwan. For instance, during the Chen Shui-bian administration, Beijing warned that pro-independence Taishang were not welcome in China and pressured several businesspeople who had supported Chen. Finally, it is worth emphasizing that Taishang have a vested interest in stable cross-strait relations, and so may advocate for a friendly relationship with Beijing even in the absence of PRC overt efforts to use them as a tool of influence.[69]

Some evidence suggests that the Taishang are the source of limited increased PRC influence in Taiwan. PRC pressure on pro-DPP Taishang during the Chen administration, for instance, appeared to have a chilling effect that discouraged Taishang from being outspoken supporters of the DPP.[70] And some Taiwanese businesspeople who are heavily invested in China are vocal in their support for policies conducive to cross-strait stability and are willing to interject themselves into political debates.[71] However, the extent to which the PRC has been able to leverage the Taishang as a source of political influence should not be overstated. Most important, while some wealthy businesspeople with mainland investments have been outspoken in Taiwan politics, most Taishang tend to adopt a low profile on political matters, hoping to avoid being targeted in China or being cast as villains in Taiwan.[72] Taishang as a group are also not highly organized in Taiwan politics.[73] Moreover, a number of studies suggest that Taiwanese living in China tend to retain a separate Taiwanese identity, so it isn't clear the extent to which Taishang represent a clear "pro-China" constituency in any event.[74] Finally, past efforts at coercion have been quite limited in scope. The attack on pro-independence Taishang in the early 2000s, for instance, appeared to be mostly aimed at a few very high-profile businesspeople who had publicly supported Chen Shui-bian.[75]

Agricultural inducements

During the Hu Jintao administration, the PRC launched an effort to "win the hearts and minds of Taiwanese" via an economic inducements policy. For instance, it lifted import barriers to a range of Taiwanese agricultural exports in the mid-2000s, with the hope that Taiwan farmers would become more willing to support the party—the KMT—that favored increased economic ties and closer relations with Beijing. During the Ma Ying-jeou administration, delegations led by officials from China at times engaged in buying sprees in Taiwan, purchasing large amounts of Taiwan produce.[76] And Beijing also experimented with more direct efforts to increase support among Taiwan farmers during this period. In one highly reported-on case, a state-run Chinese corporation promised to purchase milkfish for a set price from fish farmers in the Syuejia municipality in southern Taiwan.[77] The program was put in place after a visit to the town by the Deputy Director of China's Association for Relations across the Taiwan Straits.

Existing scholarship suggests that these efforts have had, at best, limited impact on voting behavior in Taiwan. One recent study finds that China's post-2005 agriculture trade barrier reductions had no significant impact on the 2008 election: areas that benefited from the reductions were no more likely to vote KMT than other areas, once controls were introduced.[78] Another study found that the Syuejia milkfish initiative led to an increase in KMT support relative to expectations in recent elections. The effect was small, however, and was limited to areas that directly benefited from the incentives, leading the authors to conclude that the fish-buying effort was not cost-effective.[79]

Tourism sanctions

After Tsai Ing-wen and the DPP swept Taiwan's elections in 2016, the PRC responded by cutting back tourism to the island; in particular, Beijing pressured tour groups to cut visits there. The (implicit) sanctions were an effort to punish Tsai for refusing to recognize the 1992 consensus and were part of a broader coercive campaign directed against Taiwan since 2016. PRC tourist visits to Taiwan dropped sharply in 2016 and 2017.[80] More recently, in the run-up to Taiwan's presidential election of 2020, the PRC introduced more stringent restrictions on tourism—including a ban on individual tourism—which led to a sharp drop in tourists during the fall of 2019.[81]

Assessing the effectiveness of the tourism sanctions is not straightforward, since the sanctions were implicit and the goal of the sanctions is not entirely clear. If the goal was simply to demonstrate to Taiwan that there are costs associated with refusing to endorse a one China principle, then sanctions—in combination with other actions, such as stepped-up military coercion directed against the island and efforts to squeeze Taiwan's international space—have probably succeeded to some degree. The sanctions have also led to some protests in Taiwan by individuals working in sectors that have been harmed by the decline in PRC tourism. On the other hand, the sanctions did not lead to a change in China policy by the Tsai government, and the Taiwan government countered by stepping up efforts to attract tourists from other locations, such as Southeast Asia. Increased tourism from places other than China, in turn, largely negated the drop-off in Chinese tourism (in terms of number of visitors).[82] And, of course, Tsai was reelected as president in a landslide in January 2020.

Summary of the PRC's use of economic ties to influence Taiwan

The three cases just examined suggest that Beijing's efforts to leverage economic ties with Taiwan for political aims have had at best limited success to date. But each case shows the potential for influence. Taiwanese businesspeople who are invested in China, for instance, can at times wield considerable political clout in Taiwan. The milkfish case suggests that efforts to buy Taiwan hearts and minds is expensive, but one academic study suggests that the effort was at least marginally successful. And the tourism case demonstrates that China possesses ample means to punish Taiwan for pursuing policies at odds with Beijing's interests.

These cases are certainly not the only examples of PRC efforts to leverage economic ties as a tool of influence in Taiwan. In 2018, for instance, the PRC introduced thirty-one new inducements meant to attract increased Taiwan investment and to encourage more Taiwanese to move to and study in China. The inducements were obviously politically motivated, aiming to both increase Taiwan's dependence on China and lure away talent.[83]

It is also worth emphasizing that it can be hard to determine ex ante whether a particular economic undertaking might lead to influence, or even whether there is intent to influence. In one recent example, Taiwan's Ministry of Economic Affairs Investment Commission rejected a bid by a company with links to China to build a skyscraper complex in Taipei, citing national security concerns. The commission's decision appears to be based on an abundance of caution, given the firm's links to China; whether the project would actually lead to PRC influence, or indeed whether there is even intent to influence in this case, is less clear.[84] Regardless of intent, however, the case also highlights an important reality: that Taiwan is not simply powerless in the face of PRC economic influence attempts. Rather, as Christina Lai emphasizes, Taiwan has a range of strategies that it can deploy to counter these efforts, such as some of the diversification efforts described earlier in this chapter.[85]

Finally, although cross-strait economic ties clearly generate some security risks for Taiwan, this does not necessarily mean that those economic ties have a net negative impact on Taiwan's security. Indeed, economic ties with China have been a central part of Taiwan's economic development for the past several decades. The idea that economic ties make Taiwan potentially vulnerable to economic coercion is largely premised on the sense that the island reaps considerable benefits from those ties, and that the costs of cutting those ties would be substantial. If we imagine a counterfactual world in which Taipei sealed itself off from China economically, it is quite likely that Taiwan in such a world would be significantly poorer than it is today. In turn, power asymmetries—the subject of the next chapter—might have shifted even more dramatically in China's favor in the absence of cross-strait economic exchange. It is worth noting here as well that economic ties— because they bring extensive benefits to the PRC—may also act as a constraint on Beijing's willingness to use force against Taiwan, given how economically disruptive military conflict would likely be. At a minimum, extensive cross-strait economic integration raises the costs of military conflict for both sides and so should help to induce some caution in both Taipei and Beijing. In part II of this book, I consider at greater length the implications of increased costs of conflict for the prospects for war and peace in the Taiwan Strait.

In sum, Taiwan faces complex tradeoffs in its economic relationship with China. Economic ties have brought considerable economic benefits to the island, but they have been contentious—both because of their distributive effects in Taiwan and because they potentially introduce security risks to Taiwan. However, assessing whether the security risks outweigh the potential economic gains of integration—or, indeed, whether economic ties on balance do more harm than good for Taiwan's security—is a complex undertaking unlikely to yield clear answers. Given this uncertainty, it is perhaps unsurprising that Taiwan has over the past several decades acquiesced to—and at times openly welcomed— extensive and deepening cross-strait economic ties.

CONCLUSION: ECONOMIC INTERDEPENDENCE ACROSS THE TAIWAN STRAIT

Even though the pace of cross-strait economic integration has slowed in recent years and some ties—such as PRC tourism in Taiwan—have weakened, Taiwan's economy remains deeply intertwined with mainland

China's, and extensive China-Taiwan economic ties remain a defining feature of the relationship. Economic interdependence blossomed even as cross-strait political relations were at times quite hostile, and economic relations have remained resilient even as political relations have become more adversarial since 2016. While it hardly appears that robust economic ties in any way obviate the potential for military conflict in the Taiwan Strait, they certainly raise the stakes of such conflict and thus likely act as a stabilizing factor to some extent. Whether the stabilizing impact of economic ties is enough to counteract other, more destabilizing trends is less obvious, however. The next chapters deal with some of these other trends, beginning with a shifting balance of military power.

2

THE SHIFTING BALANCE OF MILITARY POWER IN THE TAIWAN STRAIT

T he deepening of cross-strait economic integration described in the previous chapter has occurred against a broader backdrop of China's rise as a great power. The economic reforms initiated starting in the late 1970s have unleashed tremendous economic dynamism and growth in the PRC. China's dynamic economy, in turn, has enabled the PRC to pour greater resources into its military, such that today China ranks second only to the United States in money spent on national defense. Even though Taiwan is an advanced economy that maintains a formidable defense capability, these trends mean that the cross-strait military balance is shifting sharply in China's favor. China already undoubtedly possesses the capacity to impose great costs on Taiwan in a military conflict. And looking to the future, some analysts doubt Taiwan's long-term defensibility in the event of a cross-strait conflict, or the capacity of the United States to intervene effectively in a cross-strait war.

Intuitively, the balance of military power in the Taiwan Strait should be a critical variable that helps to shape the prospects for war and peace between China and Taiwan. All else equal, improving PRC capabilities make it more likely that China would prevail in a conflict at acceptable cost and should thus have an important impact on Beijing's willingness to use force to advance its cross-strait goals. In this chapter I present an overview of the shifting balance of military power in the Taiwan Strait. I begin with a summary of big-picture trends in this regard. I then consider Chinese capabilities in four specific arenas: PRC strike capabilities against Taiwan; the ability of the PRC to isolate Taiwan using a blockade; PRC capabilities in the "gray zone"; and the capacity of the PRC to launch an invasion and occupation of Taiwan. I discuss each arena with reference to both Taiwan's capabilities and U.S. capabilities in the region (since the United States would likely become involved in a cross-strait military conflict in some capacity). Finally, I briefly consider possible future trends.

IMPROVING PRC RELATIVE MILITARY CAPABILITIES IN THE TAIWAN STRAIT: THE BIG PICTURE

Two decades ago, analysts of China's military tended to be confident in Taiwan's capacity to defend itself, at least in the near term. For instance, the U.S. Department of Defense highlighted some of the challenges the PRC would face in a Taiwan Strait conflict, noting that in the short term the People's Liberation Army (PLA) would "have only a limited capability to conduct integrated operations against Taiwan."[1] A RAND Corporation study in 2000 likewise concluded that "any near-term PRC attempt to invade Taiwan would likely be a very bloody affair with a significant probability of failure."[2] Since then, however, China's military capabilities have improved dramatically. Indeed, in recent decades a chasm has emerged between the PRC's military budget and Taiwan's military budget. The Stockholm International Peace Research Institute (SIPRI)—widely used as a credible source of military spending worldwide—estimates that in 1995, military spending in China was roughly double spending in Taiwan: the PRC spent US$26 billion compared to approximately US$13 billion in Taiwan (both in constant 2018 dollars). Since the mid-1990s, however, military spending has grown rapidly in China while staying relatively constant in Taiwan. By 2019, military spending in the PRC had surged to approximately $266 billion, more than twenty times Taiwan's estimated spending of $11 billion (still in constant 2018 dollars).[3] In other words, in the past twenty-five years, military spending grew roughly tenfold in China, even as military spending actually *declined* in Taiwan, once inflation is factored in.

Of course, military spending does not translate seamlessly into military capabilities, and Taiwan has numerous important advantages in any potential military clash—particularly in a conflict where the PRC seeks to invade and occupy the island. An invasion of Taiwan would require the PLA to undertake a dangerous crossing of the Taiwan Strait, known for its tricky currents and changing weather. It would require an amphibious assault on an island with limited usable beachheads. Much of the island itself is mountainous and covered with dense forests, increasing the risks of a prolonged insurgency even were the PRC to conquer major urban centers. And it is possible—perhaps even likely—that the United States would intervene in some capacity in the event of a cross-strait conflict. Yet, even accounting for these favorable factors, the reality remains that Taiwan is a small island that lies very close to an emerging colossus: today China's economy is more than twenty times larger than Taiwan's, and its population is roughly fifty times greater. If China continues its rapid ascent, Taiwan's security challenges will likely become ever more daunting.

Moreover, not only has PRC military spending increased rapidly in recent decades, but that increased spending has been motivated to a considerable degree by a desire to prepare for Taiwan conflict contingencies. The U.S. Defense Intelligence Agency, for instance, assesses that "Beijing's longstanding interest to eventually compel Taiwan's reunification with the mainland and deter any attempt by Taiwan to declare independence has served as the primary driver for China's military modernization."[4] Likewise, Michael Glosny writes that "China's military modernization has focused on deterring Taiwan independence and preparing for a military response if deterrence fails."[5] Joel Wuthnow echoes this assessment in observing that a Taiwan contingency has "spur[red] the development of short- and long-range ballistic missiles, amphibious and airborne units, and other capabilities targeted at Taiwan and intervening U.S. forces."[6] Given Taiwan's prominence as a driver in PRC military modernization efforts, it is not surprising that rapid growth in PRC military spending has led to a sharp increase in PRC capabilities relevant to a possible conflict in the Taiwan Strait. This shift in the balance of power has dramatic consequences for how an actual military conflict would play out in the Taiwan Strait, even if the United States were to intervene. A recent RAND Corporation report, for instance, concludes that U.S. advantages in a Taiwan contingency have eroded considerably since the mid-1990s.[7]

In sum, China's dramatic ascent as an economic powerhouse has enabled PRC military spending to dwarf spending in Taiwan in recent years. Moreover, the implications of this growing chasm are especially relevant for military contingencies in the Taiwan Strait, since Taiwan has been a primary motivator of PRC military spending. The next section summarizes in greater detail relative PRC advances in several specific arenas.

IMPROVING PRC RELATIVE CAPABILITIES IN SPECIFIC CONTEXTS

Improving PRC relative military capabilities are manifested in several arenas, including a growing capacity to strike targets in Taiwan (with missile and air forces), increased capacity to isolate Taiwan via blockades, and greater ability to undertake "gray zone" operations. China still appears to lack the capacity to launch a successful invasion and occupation of Taiwan, though its relative capabilities in this regard are also improving. This section briefly summarizes enhanced PRC military capabilities in each of these four areas.

RAPIDLY IMPROVING PRC STRIKE CAPABILITIES

Writing two decades ago, Robert Ross argued that China already was able to effectively deter Taiwan independence because of its ability to impose tremendous costs on the island.[8] Since then, China's ability to undertake a costly strike campaign against Taiwan has continued to improve. As Oriana Mastro and Ian Easton put it, the PRC "has the world's most active land-based ballistic and cruise missile program."[9] William Murray estimates that the number of land-based missiles deployed by China within range of Taiwan grew from approximately 350 in 2002 to more than 1,100 by 2012,[10] and the U.S. government estimates that the PLA by 2019 had hundreds of ground-launched cruise missiles and up to 1,500 land-based ballistic missiles that could be utilized in an attack against Taiwan.[11] These missiles could be used to deter steps by Taiwan toward independence and perhaps as a way of punishing the island if it were to cross PRC red lines. They could also be employed to weaken Taiwan's defenses prior to an attempted amphibious assault on the island. Although Taiwan has invested in ballistic missile defense systems and other capabilities to counter this threat, some analysts are pessimistic about the defensibility of Taiwan's fixed military targets.[12] Murray writes, for instance, that the "competition between Chinese [missiles] and Taiwan's Patriot interceptors is . . . one Taiwan cannot win, and probably cannot afford to continue."[13] A study by the RAND Corporation likewise concludes that China's improving missile capabilities mean that it "soon may be impossible for the United States and Taiwan to protect the island's military and civilian infrastructure from serious damage."[14] Mark Stokes has remarked that China's growing missile arsenal implies that "every citizen of Taiwan lives within seven minutes of destruction, and they know that."[15]

Rapidly improving air capabilities have reinforced the PRC's capacity to strike targets in Taiwan. According to Pentagon estimates, China possessed only 65 modern combat aircraft in 2000. By 2020, however, the Pentagon estimated that China possessed approximately 800 modern fighters, part of a force that included 1,500 fighters and 450 attack bombers overall. Taiwan, on the other hand, possessed only about 400 total fighters and no attack bombers.[16] While PRC fighters are not all deployed near Taiwan, many could be easily redeployed for use in a Taiwan conflict, since China has about forty air bases close enough to Taiwan for unrefueled operations over the island.[17] Meanwhile, although Taiwan (and the United States) have long had a qualitative edge due to factors like better pilot training, this edge may also be eroding with improving PLA training.[18] These trends in missile and air capabilities led a RAND Corporation study in 2009 to conclude that Taiwan could no longer be confident about maintaining air supremacy in the event of a cross-strait conflict, even if the United States were to intervene.[19] Eric Heginbotham et al. assess that PRC and U.S. forces have approximate parity in attaining air superiority in a Taiwan conflict, while PRC forces would be advantaged in attacks on air bases.[20] In short, as Michael Hunzeker et al. succinctly put it, "U.S. analysts largely agree that the PLA already has the ability to carry out a devastating strike campaign against Taiwan."[21]

PRC ABILITY TO ISOLATE TAIWAN

China might also pursue a blockade against Taiwan, either as a prelude to invasion or as a means of coercion in its own right. Though PRC capabilities in this regard have clearly improved, there remains considerable uncertainty concerning whether China currently has the ability to impose an effective blockade on Taiwan. Analysts also disagree on whether China is likely to have this capability in the future.[22]

On the one hand, PRC naval capabilities have improved dramatically in recent decades. China has a large and rapidly modernizing fleet that by the mid-2010s included at least ninety modern submarines and surface ships (up from about sixteen in 2000).[23] Meanwhile, Taiwan has a relatively small navy that is "equipped with mostly aging platforms that . . . are well past their prime."[24] Bernard Cole, writing in 2007, noted that the naval balance was already shifting sharply in China's favor: although China and Taiwan were "roughly equal in surface combatant capability" at the time, the PLA Navy already possessed "much superior" submarine and aviation capabilities.[25] Moreover, China has in recent decades invested in asymmetrical capabilities, sometimes referred to as antiaccess/area-denial (A2/AD) capabilities, that would likely complicate the ability of the U.S. Navy to intervene in a conflict on or near Taiwan. China's rapidly improving ballistic and cruise missile capabilities (including the deployment of anti-ship ballistic missiles), along with its increasingly advanced submarines, surface ships, and fighter jets, significantly increase the risk of U.S. operations near China's coast in wartime.[26] In an analysis of China's improving A2/AD capabilities, Stephen Biddle and Ivan Oelrich conclude that the PRC will have increasing ability over the next two decades to impose a blockade against Taiwan, and that the United States would have difficulty countering this threat even if it were to intervene.[27]

On the other hand, imposing an effective blockade of Taiwan would entail significant challenges for China. First, and perhaps most important, it is far from clear that even a blockade that succeeded in cutting off Taiwan's trade would succeed in coercing Taiwan to yield on sovereignty issues. As Michael Beckley notes, "No blockade in the past 200 years has coerced a country into surrendering its sovereignty."[28] Moreover, even though the PRC certainly has the ability to damage Taiwan ports and increase risks of shipping by laying mines and using submarines and surface ships to threaten blockade runners, it is also the case that the PRC would be assuming great risks in implementing such a course of action. Beckley observes, for instance, that the United States would be able to impose significant costs on China without directly trying to break the blockade, such as by imposing a blockade of its own on oil shipments through the Strait of Malacca or general financial sanctions.[29] And if the United States were to intervene directly, its advanced antisubmarine warfare capabilities would pose a grave threat to PRC submarines that attempt to enforce a blockade.[30] Finally, as James Holmes writes, blockades "are slow-moving affairs."[31] Though perhaps useful as part of an invasion strategy, a blockade in itself would likely appall the international community and perhaps galvanize support for U.S. intervention.[32]

In sum, although PRC capacity to impose a blockade on Taiwan has clearly been improving, analysts disagree concerning how effective such a blockade would likely end up being. The PRC could certainly greatly disrupt shipping to and from Taiwan, and this capacity is likely to increase over time. On the other hand, it is far from obvious that even a blockade that effectively isolates Taiwan would lead to significant policy concessions from Taipei. And China would be taking considerable risks in undertaking a blockade, including risks to its ships and submarines that attempt to enforce it, as well as risking other types of retaliation from the United States.[33]

IMPROVING PRC CAPACITY TO UNDERTAKE GRAY ZONE OPERATIONS NEAR TAIWAN

A recent RAND report defines the *gray zone* as "an operational space between peace and war, involving coercive actions to change the status quo below a threshold that, in most cases, would prompt a conventional military response, often by blurring the line between military and non-military actions and the attribution for events."[34] Obviously, such a definition potentially encompasses a wide range of activities and could include both military and nonmilitary operations. For instance, some have characterized activities such as election meddling (via disinformation campaigns, etc.), diplomatic pressure (such as convincing Taiwan's diplomatic allies to switch recognition to the PRC), or economic coercion (such as sanctions or forced technology transfer) as gray zone operations.[35] Here, I focus my attention on PRC gray zone uses of military capabilities.

It is clear that China in recent years has been more willing to use its military forces to undertake a range of gray zone operations near Taiwan. For instance, since 2019 PLA fighters have frequently crossed the midline of the Taiwan Strait, and over the past few years Chinese strategic bombers have sometimes circumnavigated the island of Taiwan. The U.S.-China Economic and Security Review Commission reports data showing that these flights have occurred frequently since the election of Tsai Ing-wen as Taiwan's president in 2016, and that 2020 in particular saw a sharp increase in activity.[36]

PRC gray zone uses of military forces, such as sending fighters across the midline of the Taiwan Strait or entering Taiwanese airspace, can in theory be used to advance a number of different objectives. Cole, for instance, suggests that the operations may be part of a broader "psychological warfare" campaign directed at Taiwan, an effort to reinforce a sense of vulnerability on the island.[37] Admiral Lee Hsi-ming, the former chief of general staff of Taiwan's military, made this point in especially vivid terms in a recent interview: "You say it's your garden, but it turns out that it is your neighbor who's hanging out in the garden all the time. With that action, they are making a statement that it's their garden."[38] In addition to intimidation, these sorts of PRC gray zone military operations, then, act as a "salami-slicing" tactic that over time helps to change facts on the ground; they signal greater PRC control over the air and seas near Taiwan. The operations could also serve an intelligence-gathering function for the PLA (including improving understanding of how Taiwan or the United States responds to PRC incursions), and the constant need to scramble aircraft to respond to PRC incursions could have the effect of increasing wear-and-tear on already stretched Taiwanese air and naval forces.[39]

Of course, this uptick is largely reflective of policy decisions in Beijing—and not a direct result of shifts in the military balance of power in the Taiwan Strait. However, the shifting balance of power does have implications for how effective these sorts of operations are likely to be, and how effectively Taiwan can respond. In particular, as the PRC's numerical advantages in aircraft and naval vessels continue to grow, it becomes more and more taxing for Taiwan to attempt to counter each individual gray zone incursion. As Hunzeker et al. persuasively argue, if Taiwan tries to keep up in this regard—for instance, by investing in large numbers of advanced fighter aircraft needed to intercept PRC jets— the opportunity costs become untenable: high-end fighter jets and naval vessels are extremely expensive and do not represent the most cost-effective way to deter an actual invasion of Taiwan. Thus, over time, as the balance of power continues to shift and as the PRC numerical advantage in fighter jets and naval assets continues to grow, Taiwan may ultimately need to cede much of the gray zone to the PRC.[40]

PRC CAPACITY TO INVADE AND OCCUPY TAIWAN

Although China's relative military capabilities have clearly been improving, an attempt at invasion and occupation of Taiwan still presents daunting challenges for the PLA. At a minimum, the PRC would be taking a great deal of risk were it to engage in such an operation, including the possibility of escalation to a major war with the United States. Whether the PRC could successfully invade and occupy Taiwan—either now or in the near future—has been the subject of disagreement among analysts. Some argue that PRC officials appear to be growing more confident of the PLA's abilities to successfully execute an invasion of Taiwan and point especially to China's improving A2/AD capabilities, which could limit U.S. intervention options. Others remain skeptical of PRC capacity to launch a successful invasion for the foreseeable future.

As of a few years ago, most analysts of cross-strait military trends doubted the PRC's near-term capacity and willingness to launch an invasion of Taiwan. David Shlapak et al., for instance, undertook a detailed analysis of the cross-strait military balance, which included an entire chapter focused on an invasion scenario. Although the authors argued that the overall balance was shifting in the PRC's favor, they pointed to several factors that would greatly complicate an invasion attempt, including lack of PLA experience, lack of sufficient amphibious lift capacity, and defensive advantages for Taiwan that enable effective defense even in the absence of air superiority. As such, they concluded that an invasion attempt remained "a bold and possibly foolish gamble on Beijing's part."[41] The Pentagon's annual report for 2014 on China's military likewise emphasized that an attempted invasion of Taiwan would involve considerable military and political risk, and that the PLA did "not appear to be building the conventional amphibious lift required to support such a campaign" in any event.[42] Easton noted in 2014 that PLA writings remained relatively pessimistic about the overall military balance in the Taiwan Strait, including the ability to achieve air and sea superiority. He suggested that this pessimism, in turn, could explain limited PRC investments in amphibious lift capacity: "It makes little sense for any navy to spend limited resources on ships that would be rapidly sunk in combat."[43]

Many—perhaps most—U.S.-based analysts argue that a Taiwan invasion will continue to present daunting challenges for the PRC in the years ahead, even as the overall balance of power continues to drift in

China's direction. Denny Roy argues, for example, that PLA forces would face uncertain prospects for success even absent U.S. intervention, emphasizing in particular that invading forces would be highly vulnerable to Taiwan defenses and that the PLA has limited wartime experience and no recent experience with such a complex operation.[44] Meanwhile, Biddle and Oelrich argue that the same trends in A2/AD that will complicate U.S. intervention in a cross-strait contingency (and that make Taiwan vulnerable to blockade) will also—when deployed by Taiwan—make "a Chinese amphibious invasion prohibitively costly."[45] These arguments are echoed by Beckley, who highlights a number of factors likely to complicate a potential amphibious invasion in the years ahead. For instance, Taiwan's geography (rough terrain and cliffs on the eastern side of the island; mud and sand bars extending off the coast to the west) means that the island has relatively few potential landing places for an amphibious assault, so Chinese forces would face highly concentrated resistance. Furthermore, Beckley argues that the United States would have the capacity to impose devastating losses on a PLA invasion force, even given improving PRC A2/AD capabilities. In particular, the use of U.S. attack submarines and long-range stealth bombers would greatly increase the risks faced by PRC amphibious ships crossing the Taiwan Strait and the risks faced by PLA soldiers trying to establish a beachhead on Taiwan.[46] Finally, the Pentagon's annual report for 2020 on China's military continues to highlight the difficulties involved in launching a successful invasion, concluding that it would represent a "significant political and military risk" for China.[47]

Still, although an amphibious invasion of Taiwan will likely remain a highly risky proposition for China in the years ahead, the PRC has nevertheless made advances in this regard. Despite its emphasis on the risks of an invasion, the Pentagon's 2020 report also observes that China "continues to build capabilities that would contribute to a full-scale invasion," including the recent completion of its first helicopter dock amphibious assault ship.[48] Thomas Shugart argues, moreover, that analysts should be careful in making inferences about China's cross-strait sealift capacity based on currently available platforms, since "China may be able to close this gap faster than may be commonly understood."[49]

Furthermore, improving PRC strike capabilities highlighted earlier are salient in an invasion scenario, since they would likely be used to degrade Taiwan's defenses and would also threaten U.S. forces deployed in the region. Indeed, some analysts have emphasized U.S. vulnerabilities in this regard, particularly to a PRC first strike; Shugart warns, for instance, that China could choose to launch a preemptive strike on U.S. forces in the region if Beijing believes a conflict in the Taiwan Strait is inevitable.[50] Mastro further highlights improving PRC capacity to disrupt U.S. command and control and early warning systems, as well as to undertake cyberattacks that could cause major disruptions within the United States itself.[51] These improving capabilities, in turn, potentially open the door to a fait accompli strategy, where the PRC seeks to invade Taiwan before the United States could intervene due to either a PRC preemptive strike or the threat of one.[52] Finally, although PLA writings recognize continued weaknesses in a hypothetical war against the United States, PRC confidence about its ability to undertake an invasion of Taiwan may be increasing.[53]

DISCUSSION OF PRC'S IMPROVING CAPABILITIES

PRC relative capabilities for a range of Taiwan-related contingencies have clearly improved quite dramatically. At a minimum, the PRC is already able to impose extremely high costs on Taiwan through a strike campaign, and Taiwan is finding it increasingly difficult to respond effectively to PRC gray zone operations. The PRC also has improved capacity to impose a blockade on Taiwan, although doing so would entail considerable risk, and analysts disagree about whether the PRC could use a blockade to compel concessions on sovereignty issues. The biggest question marks center on an invasion scenario. Here, analysts generally agree that an invasion would be an enormously risky undertaking for China, and many remain skeptical of PRC prospects for success. Others suggest, however, that PRC confidence is increasing, and that improving PRC A2/AD capabilities could limit U.S. ability to intervene. In short, the overall trend in the cross-strait military balance of power has been shifting in China's favor. This does not mean that use of force is now—or will in the future be—an attractive option for Beijing. Rather, it means that use of military force is probably more attractive—with the very important caveat of holding all else equal—than it was earlier this century.

CONCLUSIONS: LOOKING TOWARD THE FUTURE

Future trends in the cross-strait balance of power will hinge on numerous factors, ranging from domestic political factors in China, to U.S. interests in the region, to Taiwan's defense strategy. Here, for simplicity, I focus on a few big questions, the answers to which will have major implications for future trends in the cross-strait military balance. I organize these questions around future developments in China, in Taiwan, and in the United States.

CHINA

The most important long-term driver of a shifting balance of military power in the Taiwan Strait has been China's rapid ascent as an economic superpower. Yet China today faces serious challenges that call into question continued robust economic growth. For instance, the country faces an aging workforce, rising wages, and a large debt-to-GDP ratio. Economic reforms have slowed under Xi Jinping, and the country faces a relatively hostile international environment, including the trade war with the United States. These factors are likely to undercut the dynamism of China's economy to some degree. On the other hand, Chinese leaders have proven themselves highly adept at avoiding economic crises for the past several decades, and even an economy that is growing more slowly than in the past will remain formidable and capable of supporting continued military modernization.[54] A key question in this regard centers on continued efforts to upgrade technology sectors and to develop indigenous innovation, which could help to foster further modernization of China's weapons systems. Meanwhile, although continued growth and innovation to some degree will help to shape what is possible in terms of PRC military modernization in the future, PRC domestic and foreign policy priorities will also determine the degree to which economic and technological advances will be leveraged to improve PRC relative capabilities in the Taiwan Strait. While Taiwan—for reasons that I will elaborate on in chapter 4—will likely remain a key PRC priority, the PRC's growing global military presence could both divert resources from preparation for a Taiwan contingency and become a source of new vulnerabilities. Indeed, Wuthnow argues that the United States should pursue a strategy of seeking "system overload" in the years ahead: the United States should plan to challenge the PLA in multiple theaters during a Taiwan contingency, which would overwhelm China's ability to fight in numerous theaters at the same time and erode its capacity to wage a successful campaign in the Taiwan Strait. As the PRC's global presence continues to grow, these sorts of concerns could act as a constraint on PLA relative capabilities in the Taiwan Strait.[55]

TAIWAN

How Taiwan adapts to improving PRC military capabilities will also shape the future of the cross-strait balance of power. Perhaps the most important factor here centers on Taiwan's resolve: its willingness to pay costs to deter, and if necessary, defeat a PRC attack. If Taiwan's population and government are strongly committed to maintaining de facto independence, then China's growing capacity to impose high costs on Taiwan (via a strike campaign and/or blockade) will not be enough to compel surrender in the event of a cross-strait conflict. A high level of Taiwan resolve, then, means that China will be able to coerce unification only if it is able to mount a successful invasion and occupation of the island. Moreover, high Taiwanese resolve also implies a willingness to continue to invest in the acquisition and development of weapons systems needed to deter a PRC invasion, meaning that strong resolve also has considerable implications for the future capacity of the PRC to launch a successful invasion.

Public opinion polls can provide some insight into resolve. One 2020 poll, for instance, found that over 70 percent of respondents believe most Taiwanese would resist a PRC attack on the island, and up to a third indicated a willingness to participate directly in a war effort. These numbers suggest that a PRC attack on Taiwan would likely meet considerable resistance. Moreover, both numbers are significantly higher than in previous years, almost certainly reflecting a more hostile cross-strait environment along with the PRC's harsh crackdown in Hong Kong (which presumably further increases skepticism in Taiwan about what a unified China might look like).[56] In chapter 4 I will discuss public opinion trends at greater length. It is worth noting here, however, that the future trajectory of Taiwan's resolve to fight a war is likely endogenous to the degree to which the PRC is seen as threatening on the island.

The future evolution of the cross-strait balance of power will also be determined, in part, by the development of Taiwan's military capabilities and how well the ROC military will be able to leverage limited resources (in terms of both money and manpower) to counter advances made by the PLA. In light of PLA advances, many U.S.-based analysts have called on Taiwan to pursue an asymmetric defense strategy modeled on the experience of other states that have deterred and/or defeated much more powerful militaries; here, limited resources would be focused heavily on an invasion scenario while accepting inability to compete with the PLA in other arenas such as the gray zone.[57] Taiwan has recently embraced some elements of an asymmetric strategy in its Overall Defense Concept, introduced in 2017. As Admiral Lee Hsi-min, the principal architect of the strategy, puts it, the strategy aims to complement a small number of high-quality advanced platforms (such as the F-16V) with large numbers of relatively small, easily maintained, and inexpensive weapons systems. The former help to address vulnerabilities in the gray zone, while the latter can help to deter, and if needed defeat, an invasion attempt. Examples of relatively inexpensive systems that, if deployed in large numbers, could greatly complicate a PRC invasion include drones, mobile coastal defense missiles, and man-portable air defense missiles.[58] To the degree that Taiwan develops robust asymmetric capabilities, it will mean that a PRC invasion would be both more costly to China and ultimately less likely to succeed.[59]

THE UNITED STATES

Finally, future U.S. capabilities in the region and the evolution of the U.S. commitment to Taiwan's security will have a large effect on the cross-strait balance of power. At a minimum, the possibility of U.S. intervention means that Chinese initiation of the use of force would be a tremendously risky decision; the United States is also the only country willing to sell advanced weapons to Taiwan. As China's capabilities continue to grow, Taiwan's ability to deter and ultimately repel an attack will hinge to a considerable degree on U.S. capacity to intervene effectively. Will the United States, for instance, develop effective systems and strategies to address improving PRC A2/AD capabilities? Perhaps even more important, U.S. resolve to intervene will remain a critical factor: to what degree will the United States be committed to Taiwan's security moving forward? That is, to what extent would Washington be willing to pay high costs, in terms of both money and possible lives lost, to defend Taiwan were the island to come under attack? The following chapter considers the U.S. security commitment to Taiwan in greater detail.

3

THE U.S. COMMITMENT TO TAIWAN

The previous chapter emphasized that the role of the United States is central to the balance of military power in the Taiwan Strait. The possibility of U.S. intervention in a cross-strait military conflict, at a minimum, raises Beijing's expected costs of conflict and makes more difficult any effort to invade and occupy Taiwan. In chapter 2 I focused primarily on relative capabilities, and the discussion relating to the United States centered on whether Washington has—and is likely to maintain—the *capacity* to intervene effectively in a cross-strait conflict. In this chapter I focus on what is perhaps an even more fundamental question: whether the United States has the *resolve* to intervene in the event of armed conflict in the Taiwan Strait.

I begin with some brief background on the U.S.-Taiwan security relationship. Here I note that the U.S. commitment to Taiwan has been informal, ambiguous, and to some degree conditional on Taiwan's actions, and I argue in the next section that these features of the U.S. commitment arise from a set of difficult dilemmas the country faces in the Taiwan Strait. The third part of the chapter assesses recent trends in Washington's commitments to Taiwan by analyzing several concrete indicators of the two governments' security relations. I show that security relations have been getting closer in recent years, but I also emphasize that these changes have mostly been incremental, and that the level of U.S. commitment to Taiwan's security remains ambiguous.

BACKGROUND: THE POST-1979 RESIDUAL COMMITMENT TO TAIWAN

Security cooperation between the United States and ROC has a long history. During World War II the two were allies in the effort to defeat Japan. As the Chinese Civil War intensified in the late 1940s, the United States provided significant aid to the KMT—even as the Truman administration grew more fatalistic about the regime's prospects. After the Nationalist retreat to Taiwan, the United States initially signaled that it would not intervene to protect the Nationalist regime but then helped to ensure the survival of the ROC government by commencing naval patrols in the Taiwan Strait after war broke out in Korea. And later, in 1954, the two governments signed a formal alliance agreement. In subsequent years, the United States stationed troops in Taiwan, and the island served as an important base during the Vietnam War. But formal security ties between the United States and the ROC came to an end with the normalization of the U.S.-PRC relationship in 1979: during the normalization process, Washington agreed to sever diplomatic ties with Taipei and to abrogate the bilateral alliance agreement.

Still, the U.S. and Taiwan governments maintained extensive security ties even after 1979. Although Washington recognized the PRC as the sole legal government of China, it took an ambiguous stance concerning Taiwan's status: in the Normalization Communiqué (December 1978), Washington "acknowledges" but notably does not accept or endorse the PRC position that Taiwan is a part of China (echoing the Shanghai Communiqué of 1972, albeit in more straightforward language).[1] And in early 1979 the U.S. Congress passed, and President Carter signed into law, the Taiwan Relations Act (TRA). As Steven Goldstein and Randall Schriver observe, the language in the U.S.-ROC

Mutual Defense Treaty of 1954 was—like most U.S. alliance treaties—somewhat ambiguous concerning U.S. commitments to the island; the TRA, they write, effectively "recasts" this language in a more "lengthy and convoluted form."[2] For instance, it declares that "any effort to determine the future of Taiwan by other than peaceful means" would be "of grave concern to the United States," and that the "President and the Congress shall determine, in accordance with constitutional processes, appropriate action by the United States in response to any such danger." The TRA also stipulates that the United States would continue to sell to Taiwan "such defense articles and defense services in such quantity as may be necessary to maintain a sufficient self-defense capability."[3] And although the United States and China later issued a third joint communiqué in which the United States pledged to reduce arms sales to Taiwan over time, recently declassified materials suggest the Reagan administration did not view the communiqué as a major constraint on U.S. arms sales policies, and the United States has continued to sell weapons to Taiwan to this day.[4] Moreover, at the same time it issued what became known as the "Six Assurances" to Taiwan, promising (among other things) not to engage in prior consultation with Beijing on arms sales to Taiwan, or to pressure Taiwan to enter into negotiations with the PRC.[5] Thus, even though the United States and Taiwan ended formal diplomatic ties in 1979, the United States has maintained some level of commitment to Taiwan's security. This commitment, in turn, has at least three interrelated features that merit further elaboration.

First, the U.S. security commitment to Taiwan is mostly informal. Although there are formal U.S. laws—including most notably the TRA—that outline some level of commitment to Taiwan, at a bilateral level cooperation occurs in the absence of official ties. To be certain, in many ways bilateral U.S.-Taiwan relations take on the appearance of a normal relationship. For instance, the United States does not maintain an embassy in Taiwan, but the American Institute in Taiwan functions largely as an embassy, is staffed by Foreign Service officers, and is housed in a large new building in Taipei. But Washington has also limited how far it goes in giving appearances of an official relationship. The informal nature of bilateral security ties most obviously manifests in the lack of an alliance agreement but also extends to many other facets of the security relationship. To give a few examples: the United States does not station troops in Taiwan or send military vessels to its ports; public high-level meetings between Taiwan and U.S. security officials are rare; and the two sides do not undertake large-scale joint military exercises. As I will show later in this chapter, we still see considerable variation over time in the closeness of bilateral security ties within the confines of an informal security relationship, and broadly speaking these ties have grown closer in recent years.

Second, and relatedly, the U.S. commitment to Taiwan is much more ambiguous than is the U.S. commitment to most formal allies. Of course, the language of most U.S. alliance treaties is ambiguous to some degree. For instance, as noted earlier, the U.S.-ROC Mutual Defense Treaty of 1954 (using language common to many U.S. alliance treaties) somewhat vaguely commits the United States to "act to meet the common danger in accordance with its constitutional processes" in the event of an attack on Taiwan. Yet typically Washington reduces such ambiguity by taking steps and issuing statements that signal stronger commitment. The United States stations troops throughout the world, something that enhances commitment by ensuring that its forces would likely be directly involved in an attack on an ally's territory. But it has generally eschewed stationing troops in Taiwan since severing official ties in 1979. Similarly, when the PRC undertakes threatening actions toward Taiwan, U.S. public statements have typically been more circumspect than other cases where allies face a clear threat. For example, officials have often issued unambiguous statements of commitment to defending South Korea in the event of war (sometimes referring to this commitment as "iron-clad").[6] In contrast, when the PRC sent fighter jets across the median line in the Taiwan Strait in 2019 (in what was generally seen as a sharp escalation in China's military intimidation of Taiwan), the State Department quoted from the TRA in responding ambiguously: "Beijing's efforts to unilaterally alter the status quo are harmful and do not contribute to regional stability. . . . Consistent with the Taiwan Relations Act, the U.S. considers any effort to determine the future of Taiwan by other than peaceful means, including by boycotts or embargoes, of grave concern to the U.S."[7] More generally, as Richard Bush writes, "U.S. officials cite the Taiwan Relations Act, speak in general terms about Washington's 'abiding interest' in peace and stability in the Taiwan Strait, and reiterate opposition to either side's unilaterally changing the status quo—without saying how the United States would respond to such an attempt."[8]

Finally, the degree to which the United States has signaled commitment to Taiwan has varied over time and has been conditional in part on Taiwan's own domestic and foreign policies. More specifically, the United States has in the past signaled reduced support for Taiwan when the island's leaders pursue policies that—from Washington's standpoint—appear to be moving Taiwan in the direction of formal independence. U.S. policy has long been that Washington opposes "unilateral" changes to the status quo in the Taiwan Strait. In 2004 Assistant Secretary of State for East Asian and Pacific Affairs James A. Kelly elaborated on this policy in testimony to Congress: "The U.S. does not support independence for Taiwan or unilateral moves that would change the status quo as we define it. . . . For Beijing, this means no use of force or threat to use force against Taiwan. For Taipei, it means exercising prudence in managing all aspects of cross-Strait relations. For both sides, it means no statements or actions that would unilaterally alter Taiwan's status."[9] During the Chen Shui-bian administration in particular, the United States was frequently critical of Taiwan's policies, such as the decision to hold a referendum—asking the Taiwan public to support applying to UN membership under the name "Taiwan"—at the same time as the presidential election of 2008.[10] Although Washington did not publicly and explicitly warn that support for Taiwan would be less likely were the United States to view a PRC attack as being provoked by actions taken in Taipei, the public criticism of Taipei essentially suggested as much. Thus whether the United States would come to Taiwan's defense in a cross-strait war is likely conditioned in part on the degree to which Washington views Taipei as having taken unnecessarily provocative actions that helped to trigger a PRC military response.

In sum, although the United States broke formal ties with the ROC in 1979, it has maintained extensive security ties with the island. It continues to sell weapons to Taiwan and to signal interest in peaceful resolution of the Taiwan issue (and to oppose PRC military coercion against the island), and it maintains extensive bilateral contacts with military and defense officials in Taiwan. At the same time, however, the U.S. security commitment to Taiwan is informal, more ambiguous than most other U.S. security commitments worldwide, and at least somewhat conditional on Taiwan's behavior. In the next section I elaborate on the dilemmas that give rise to these characteristics of the U.S. commitment.

ROOTS OF AN INFORMAL, AMBIGUOUS, CONDITIONAL U.S. COMMITMENT

As emphasized in the previous section, Washington clearly retained some interest in Taiwan's security even after breaking formal ties with the island in 1979. However, the United States faces two dilemmas that have complicated this general interest in Taiwan's security: First, it faces a moral hazard dilemma in its relationship with Taiwan, where Washington has reason to worry that strong commitments to Taiwan will lead Taiwan to pursue policies that are not in Washington's interest. Second, the U.S. interest in Taiwan's security at times conflicts with a desire to maintain constructive (or at least peaceful) relations with China. In turn, the United States has had to consider how efforts to advance Taiwan's security might affect broader U.S.-China relations, and, indeed, how increased turbulence in U.S.-China relations might affect Taiwan's security. Below I elaborate briefly on each of these dilemmas and show how they contribute to informality, ambiguity, and conditionality in U.S. commitments to Taiwan.[11]

The first dilemma that Washington has faced is a moral hazard problem. Moral hazard, simply put, refers to the tendency of insurance to encourage more risky behavior. Having fire insurance, for instance, might lead to somewhat less diligence in clearing brush around a house. Likewise, a bank that knows it is likely to be bailed out in a recession might undertake more risky loans than it otherwise would. Security commitments can create moral hazard when a defending state (the United States) and a protégé state (Taiwan) have at least partially diverging interests. In the 1950s U.S. officials worried that a strong alliance commitment to Taiwan might encourage Chiang Kai-shek to instigate a renewed war against the CCP in the hopes of dragging the United States into the fight to reestablish Nationalist authority over mainland China. Today, the insurance provided by U.S. security commitments could encourage two types of—from Washington's perspective—risky behavior in Taipei.

First, unambiguous security commitments could disincentivize Taiwan from investing in its own military capabilities, since there will be a stronger expectation of extensive U.S. intervention in any cross-strait conflict scenario. I suspect, however, that this problem is becoming less salient over time, since even a strong U.S. commitment is increasingly unlikely—in itself—to guarantee Taiwan's security given shifts in the cross-strait balance of military power (and the PRC's growing ability to complicate U.S. intervention). Regardless of U.S. willingness to intervene, Taiwan's security increasingly requires robust domestic investments in asymmetric capabilities to deter Beijing.

Second, stronger U.S. security commitments could potentially encourage Taiwan to pursue sovereignty-related policies that diverge from U.S. interests. More specifically, although the United States has signaled that it shares Taiwan's interest in peaceful resolution of disputes with China and opposes PRC coercion against the island, it is less clear (as touched on in the previous section) that the United States has any interest in Taiwan formalizing its de facto independence—or, indeed, in Taiwan taking steps in that direction. The PRC has signaled repeatedly that it views formal Taiwan independence as a cause of war, and that Taiwan is taking on some risk by pursuing policies that appear to be moving the island in the direction of independence.[12] From Washington's standpoint, steps to formalize Taiwan's de facto independence are "needlessly provocative," mostly symbolic actions that have little substantive effect on Taiwan's democracy or security but do trigger strong PRC reactions.[13] Thus the United States sometimes faces a version of an "entrapment" dilemma in the Taiwan Strait, where it seeks to deter PRC coercion against Taiwan but wishes to avoid being dragged into a conflict with the PRC over goals—like Taiwan independence—that it does not prioritize.[14] Washington, in turn, is at times cautious in its support for Taiwan, wishing to avoid the appearance of a clear and unconditional commitment to the island's security that might green light actions by Taiwan that are likely to raise tensions in the Taiwan Strait and increase the risk of conflict with China.

The second dilemma the United States has faced centers on a trade-off between Washington's interest in Taiwan's security and a U.S. interest in maintaining peaceful relations with China. Although U.S.-China relations ebbed and flowed in the decades after the Cold War (and included periods of significant tension), the Bush I, Clinton, Bush II, and Obama administrations all sought stability in relations with Beijing. Even though the United States and China often have competing interests, each of these administrations also viewed some level of U.S.-China cooperation as important in addressing a number of issues on which the two countries have had at least partially convergent interests, such as nuclear nonproliferation, global terrorism, and climate change. In turn, to the degree that the United States values good relations with China, Washington's ability to signal support for Taiwan is constrained.

In general, establishing credibility to defend an ally if that ally comes under attack is inherently difficult. In this case, U.S. intervention in a cross-strait war would mean fighting against a militarily capable and nuclear-armed PRC. To make its defense commitments more credible, in turn, the United States often takes steps such as signing formal alliance agreements or stationing troops on an ally's territory.[15] But if Washington were to try to enhance the credibility of its commitment to Taiwan along these lines, it would risk destabilizing relations with Beijing. When the United States and China normalized their relationship in the 1970s, the United States committed to having only unofficial relations with Taiwan, and the PRC has clearly signaled that any effort to reestablish official political or security ties with Taiwan would create a crisis in U.S.-China relations. Thus although the United States has been willing to explore the boundaries of this normalization bargain, to the degree that it wants to maintain a stable relationship with the PRC, it must stick to the basic contours of the bargain struck in the 1970s. Strong signals of commitment to Taiwan, like entering into a formal alliance agreement with the ROC or stationing U.S. troops in Taiwan, would undoubtedly be viewed in Beijing as unacceptable. In turn, U.S. commitments to Taiwan have been relatively informal and ambiguous.

RECENT TRENDS: MOVING TOWARD ABANDONMENT OR GETTING CLOSER?

Though broadly informal, ambiguous, and conditional, the strength of the U.S. commitment to Taiwan's security has varied over time and is often the source of debate within the United States.[16] For instance, as cross-strait relations stabilized during the Ma Ying-jeou administration, several U.S.-based analysts questioned the desirability of commitments to Taiwan. Some suggested that scaling back support might pave the way toward a better U.S.-China relationship,[17] or that U.S. commitments to Taiwan would become unsustainable in any event as Chinese military power grows.[18] Others pushed back against the idea of "abandoning" Taiwan at the time,[19] and more recently—as cross-strait tensions have increased again—some analysts have called on the United States to strengthen its commitment by making ties with the island more formal and less ambiguous.[20] Indeed, a conventional wisdom is taking hold that U.S.-Taiwan security relations have been improving in recent years.[21]

In this section I examine recent trends in U.S.-Taiwan security relations, focusing on several concrete indicators of the bilateral security relationship, including U.S. arms sales to Taiwan, interactions with Taiwan's civilian and military officials, naval transits of the Taiwan Strait, and legislation relating to Taiwan's security, as well as how Taiwan is treated in U.S. strategic writings and statements. In each case, I assess whether recent trends are indicative of a strengthening relationship on that dimension. I show that the security relationship has indeed gotten closer in recent years, although changes have generally been incremental and the relationship remains largely informal, ambiguous, and conditional.

ARMS SALES TO TAIWAN

U.S. arms sales to Taiwan have been a contentious issue in U.S.-China relations since normalization. Washington refused to terminate arms sales after severing formal ties with Taiwan, and the Taiwan Relations Act of 1979 requires that the United States make defensive weapons available to Taiwan. The PRC strongly protests such sales and at times has threatened stronger retaliation.[22] In turn, arms sales serve as a useful barometer of U.S.-Taiwan security ties because they demonstrate a willingness to risk friction in U.S.-China relations.[23] More specifically, a stronger commitment is suggested to the degree that the United States is willing to risk PRC retaliation by selling large quantities and more advanced weapons to Taiwan.

Figure 3.1 shows the value of approved U.S. arms sales to Taiwan by year, in constant U.S. dollars. Clearly, arms sales are somewhat "lumpy," in that arms sales packages occur at somewhat irregular intervals and the dollar value of sales bounces around considerably from year to year. Thus figure 3.1 also includes the five-year moving average of U.S. arms sales, which is perhaps a better indicator of long-term trends given this lumpiness.

The figure shows that U.S. approved arms sales to Taiwan have remained relatively steady over the past three decades. The five-year moving average increased to over US$4 billion in the early 2010s, reflecting several large weapons sales packages from 2007 to 2011, but then dropped off considerably in the late Obama and early Trump administrations. But in 2019 several large packages were approved, leading to a sharp jump in the moving average, to a level above where it was in the late 1990s through most of the 2000s but still lower than the early 2010s. It is also worth noting that very recent arms sales packages have included items that suggest an upgrade in what the United States is willing to sell

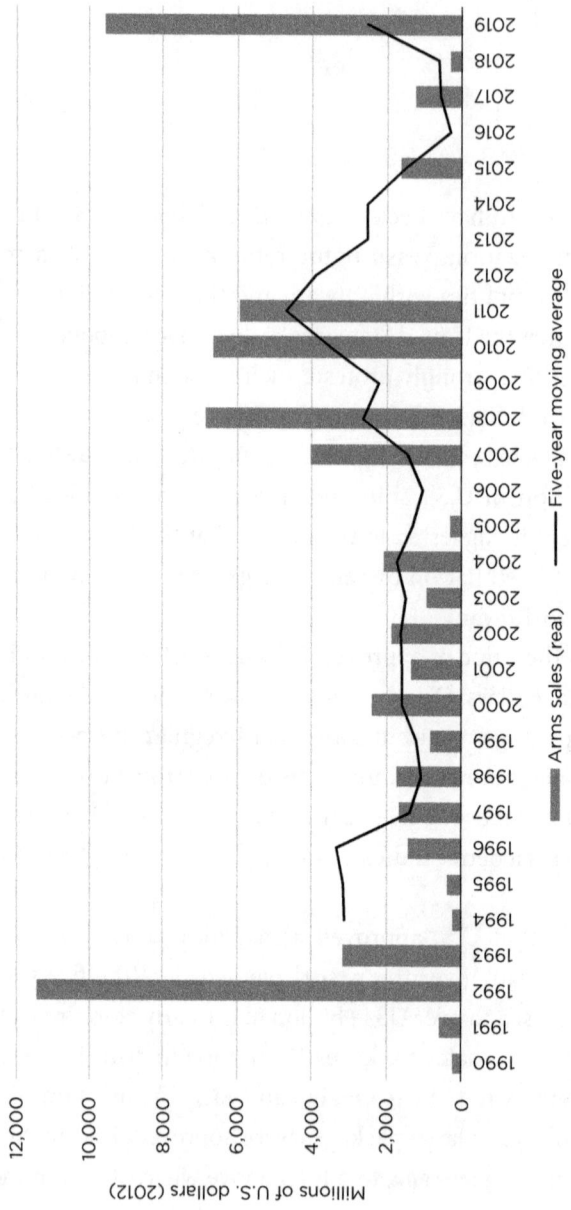

FIGURE 3.1 Approved U.S. arms sales to Taiwan (inflation-adjusted dollars).

Data since 2014 comes from the Defense Security Cooperation Agency, Major Arms Sales, https://www.dsca.mil/major-arms-sales; earlier data are from Shirly A. Kan, "Taiwan: Major U.S. Arms Sales Since 1990," CRS Report, August 29, 2014, https://fas.org/sgp/crs/weapons/RL30957.pdf. Totals are adjusted to constant 2012 dollars based on the U.S. Bureau of Economic Analysis GDP deflator as reported by the St. Louis Federal Reserve, https://fred.stlouisfed.org/series/GDPDEF#0.

Taiwan. When Washington announced the sale of 66 F-16V fighters in 2019, it marked the first time since 1992 that the United States approved fighter jet sales to Taiwan.[24] The F-16 sale, along with a sale of Abrams tanks approved in the same year, represented a significant shift in Washington's approach to arms sales in recent years, as the United States had not offered major new weapons platforms in recent packages.[25] Moreover, both the George W. Bush and the Barack Obama administrations had decided against selling more advanced F-16 jets to Taiwan, with the Obama administration offering instead an upgrade package for Taiwan's existing F-16A/B fighters.[26]

In sum, the quantity of U.S. arms sales to Taiwan—in dollar terms—has been relatively consistent over time, though there had been some drop-off in the years prior to 2019. On the other hand, the weapons packages offered in 2019 were substantial in dollar terms and suggested a greater willingness to sell more advanced capabilities to Taipei.

INTERACTIONS BETWEEN U.S. AND TAIWANESE OFFICIALS

Broadly speaking, interactions between officials have become more frequent and institutionalized over the past several decades. In this subsection, I briefly discuss three manifestations: high-level, publicly announced meetings; Taiwan presidential visits to the United States; and more routine, lower-profile interactions.

High-level meetings

In the years after U.S.-PRC normalization, Washington placed strict limits on public, high-level interactions between U.S. and Taiwanese officials. Perhaps mostly notable, U.S. government guidelines did not allow cabinet-level officials to visit Taiwan. This policy changed in the 1990s, however. The George H. W. Bush administration sent Carla Hills, the U.S. trade representative, to attend a conference in Taiwan in 1992, and in 1994 the Bill Clinton administration formalized a policy change to allow cabinet-level officials in economic and functional agencies to visit Taiwan.[27] Four different cabinet-level officials visited Taiwan during the Clinton administration. But after Secretary of Transportation Rodney Slater's trip in June 2000, only one cabinet-level official visited Taiwan in the subsequent twenty years: Gina McCarthy, the administrator of the Environmental Protection Agency during the Obama administration in 2014.[28]

The Trump administration remained quite cautious about public, high-level meetings and visits during its first two years in office. For instance, there was some speculation that the United States would send a high-ranking official—such as a cabinet official or National Security Advisor John Bolton—to attend 2018 ceremonies for the opening of the new building housing the American Institute in Taiwan. Yet the United States instead sent the assistant secretary of state for educational and cultural affairs, a decision widely seen as an effort to avoid creating additional turbulence in U.S.-China relations.[29] Public, higher-level interactions became more frequent, however, beginning in 2019. In May Taiwan's national security chief David Dawei Lee and Bolton met in Washington, the first time that the two sides had acknowledged an in-person meeting of their respective national security advisors since 1979.[30] In August 2020 Secretary of Health and Human Services Alex Azar traveled to Taiwan; Azar was the first U.S. cabinet-level official to visit since 2014 and was the highest-ranking cabinet official to go there since 1979.[31] Shortly after Azar's visit, Under Secretary of State Keith Krach traveled to Taiwan to attend Lee Teng-hui's funeral.[32]

Taiwan presidential visits

Since 1994 U.S. policy has been to allow top Taiwanese leaders (including the president) to visit the United States via "stopovers" while en route to Taiwan's diplomatic allies, provided that these visits eschew public activities.[33] The destination cities of these stopovers (i.e., whether the stopover occurs in a major city such as New York), along with the expansiveness of technically private activities during the visit, can serve as a barometer of bilateral relations. For instance, consistent with a generally "pro-Taiwan" policy during the early George W. Bush administration, the United States was willing to allow relatively high-profile stopovers: Chen Shui-bian visited New York twice during his first term in office. However, the United States downgraded the nature of Chen's approved stopovers during his second term in office, a time when Washington was increasingly critical of some of Chen's initiatives that were viewed as unnecessarily provocative. In 2006 the United States declined a request to stopover in San Francisco and New York, and Chen refused the U.S. counteroffer of Anchorage and Honolulu (choosing not to stop in the country at all). In his final two years in office, Chen twice had to settle for refueling stops in Anchorage.[34]

Between 2008 and 2020 Taiwanese presidents averaged about two stopover visits within the contiguous United States per year (including a total of sixteen by Ma Ying-jeou and eight during Tsai Ing-wen's first term in office).[35] Both Ma and Tsai secured multiple visits to high-profile cities such as New York and San Francisco, and both frequently met a range of dignitaries during their visits, such as members of Congress and state governors. Tsai's visits, moreover, have tended to include more high-profile events than was the case during Ma's stopovers. For instance, Tsai visited NASA in Houston, which represented the first visit to U.S. federal government facilities by a Taiwan president since 1979.[36] Tsai also gave a public address at the Reagan Library in 2018.

Routine interactions

Routine, lower-profile interactions between U.S. and Taiwanese officials have clearly increased and have become more institutionalized over time. For instance, from 1979 until 2003, Foreign Service officers went on leave when serving in Taiwan; since 2003 they no longer need to do so (and Defense Department officials also started serving in Taiwan in 2003).[37] Meanwhile, in a recent report, Bonnie Glaser et al. outline a range of regular dialogues and channels that the United States and Taiwan maintain to discuss security issues and note that several other mechanisms (mostly not publicized) are used to discuss numerous other issues. They further note that "the mechanisms and channels used to manage the relationship have not evolved considerably in recent decades, but the breadth of issues addressed within them has broadened by orders of magnitude."[38] In short, behind the scenes, the United States and Taiwan have extensive routine interactions, which have generally expanded over time.

Summary of official interactions

General patterns in U.S.-Taiwan official interactions, then, point to a relationship that has been getting closer. This has generally been a long-term trend, as reflected in routine interactions and presidential stopovers. The more recent increase in public, high-level interactions starting in 2019 may indicate further strengthening in this regard.

U.S. NAVAL TRANSITS THROUGH THE TAIWAN STRAIT

The U.S. Navy has announced numerous transits through the Taiwan Strait over the past few years, including several by guided missile destroyers; these high-profile transits could also indicate some strengthening of U.S.-Taiwan security ties.[39] The frequency of transits has varied considerably over time, however, and long-term trends (at least over the past decade and a half) are ambiguous. Transits occurred on average 5.5 times per year from 2007 to 2010, increased to nearly 10 per year from 2011 to 2016 on average, and dropped to 4 per year from 2017 to 2018, before increasing sharply in 2019 and 2020.[40] On the other hand, the recent uptick in transits is notable, and it is worth highlighting as well that U.S. officials have begun to announce these transits on a regular basis—whereas in the past they typically went unannounced.[41]

CONGRESSIONAL ENGAGEMENT

Since normalization of U.S.-PRC relations, Congress has at times been highly involved in the Taiwan issue, including most obviously the passage of the Taiwan Relations Act in 1979. Over the past several years, there has been some uptick in congressional involvement in Taiwan. For instance, several bills seeking to strengthen U.S.-Taiwan relations have been introduced in Congress. Some of these bills have been passed into law, including the Taiwan Travel Act (signed into law in 2018), which encourages high-level visits between U.S. and Taiwanese officials;[42] the Asia Reassurance Initiative Act (signed into law in 2018), which notes that it is U.S. policy to "support the close economic, political, and security relationship between Taiwan and the United States"; the Taiwan Allies International Protection Enhancement Initiative (TAIPEI) Act (signed into law in 2020), which encourages support for Taiwanese participation in international organizations and calls on the U.S. government to help Taiwan strengthen its diplomatic relationships; and the Taiwan Assurance Act (signed into law in 2020 as part of a broader appropriations bill), which, among other things, requires a review of the State Department's guidelines on relations with Taiwan and expresses the view of Congress that such relations should be deepened.[43]

Furthermore, several recent National Defense Authorization Acts (NDAAs) have called for closer defense cooperation with Taiwan. As Shirley Kan writes, Senator John Cornyn led an effort to direct the secretary of defense to undertake an assessment of Taiwan's air force in the FY2010 NDAA conference report, and Taiwan has featured more prominently in the legislative process of these acts since then.[44] More recently, the NDAA of 2017 encourages exchanges of senior military officers between the United States and Taiwan, and the act passed in 2018 expresses the sense of Congress that the United States should invite Taiwan to participate in military exercises, should increase training exchanges between the U.S. and Taiwan militaries, should conduct bilateral military exercises with Taiwan, and should consider reestablishing port-of-call exchanges between the U.S. and Taiwan Navies. The 2018 act also to some degree normalizes the U.S.-Taiwan arms sales process by requiring the Department of Defense to submit a report to Congress within 120 days of an arms sales request from Taiwan.[45] And the NDAA of 2019 expresses support for closer U.S.-Taiwan military relations in a variety of ways and mandates that the Department of Defense conduct a comprehensive assessment of Taiwan's military forces and force readiness.[46]

U.S. OFFICIAL STATEMENTS AND WRITINGS CONCERNING THE COMMITMENT TO TAIWAN

Earlier in this chapter I outlined the broad contours of U.S. official policy relating to Taiwan that emerged as and after the United States normalized relations with the PRC. Here I briefly consider whether recent official statements remain generally consistent with these broad contours, or whether there is evidence of increased commitment to Taiwan.

In the immediate aftermath of Donald Trump's election in 2016, long-standing pillars of U.S. policy in the Taiwan Strait appeared to be in flux. In addition to taking the unusual step of talking with Taiwan's president, Tsai Ing-wen, by phone, Trump also questioned directly whether the United States needed to be bound by a "one China" policy in dealing with the PRC.[47] Once in office, however, Trump administration statements on Taiwan appeared more in line with longstanding U.S. policy: Trump told Xi Jinping in a February 2017 phone call that the United States would continue to "honor" its one China policy.[48] Vice President Mike Pence likewise noted that the United States would "continue to respect" that policy in his otherwise hawkish Hudson Institute speech on China in 2018.[49] And, as noted earlier, U.S. statements issued during times of tense interactions—such as when the PRC sent fighter jets across the Taiwan Strait midline in 2019—retained a considerable level of ambiguity concerning the U.S. commitment to Taiwan.

There are some more recent changes that warrant attention here. For instance, Taiwan features more prominently in recent strategic documents, including the *National Security Strategy of the United States* (2017) and the Defense Department's *Indo-Pacific Strategy Report* (2019). The latter also indirectly refers to Taiwan as a "country" (U.S. policy statements typically avoid characterizing Taiwan in this way).[50] Still, the actual policies outlined in these reports are largely consistent with past

U.S. policy. The *Indo-Pacific Strategy Report* emphasizes, for instance, that "the objective of [U.S.] defense engagement with Taiwan is to ensure that Taiwan remains secure, confident, free from coercion, and able to peacefully and productively engage the mainland on its own terms. The Department [of Defense] is committed to providing Taiwan with defense articles and services in such quantity as may be necessary to enable Taiwan to maintain a sufficient self-defense capability."[51]

The Biden administration has also appeared to signal stronger U.S. security interest in Taiwan in its official policy statements. For instance, the State Department referred to the U.S. commitment to Taiwan as "rock-solid" in January 2021 and then reaffirmed this position in April 2021.[52] Moreover, the administration worked to include references to shared interests in stability in the Taiwan Strait in the joint statements that emerged from President Biden's summits with both Japanese prime minister Yoshihide Suga and South Korean president Moon Jae-in in 2021.[53] On the other hand, after Biden himself appeared to suggest a stronger U.S. commitment in a town hall event, the White House quickly clarified that "the President was not announcing any change in our policy and there is no change in our policy."[54] U.S. commitments, in short, have remained ambiguous.

DISCUSSION

Taken together, the dimensions of U.S. policy toward Taiwan discussed in this section suggest a U.S.-Taiwan security relationship that got closer starting around 2018. In particular, arms sales packages in 2019 represent the most significant (quantitatively and qualitatively) approved sales to the island in many years; the United States has begun to make announced transits of the Taiwan Strait; there has been a recent uptick in high-level public interactions between U.S. and Taiwanese officials; Congress has become more active in passing Taiwan-relevant legislation; Taiwan has featured more prominently in U.S. strategic writings; and official U.S. statements relating to the commitment to Taiwan have gotten stronger. Furthermore, along several dimensions, U.S.-Taiwan relations have shown signs of steady improvement over a longer time frame. This is seen most clearly in the range of interactions between officials from the two sides, but also in increased congressional activism via the NDAAs. Meanwhile, U.S. naval transits of the Taiwan Strait are not new, and U.S. arms sales—in terms of dollar value—have remained fairly steady over time (once a moving average is used).

More broadly, the basic contours of longstanding U.S. policy in the Taiwan Strait remain unchanged as I write this chapter. The United States continues to base its one China policy on what Richard Bush refers to as a set of "sacred documents," including the three U.S.-PRC joint communiqués, the Taiwan Relations Act, and the Six Assurances.[55] There is little evidence, in short, that the United States is moving toward "abandoning" Taiwan or even noticeably reducing its security commitment to the island; rather, that commitment appears to be getting stronger, at least along the margins. On the other hand, that longstanding policy remains in place also means the U.S. commitment continues to be to a considerable degree informal, ambiguous, and conditional.

CONCLUSION: CLOSER, BUT STILL AMBIGUOUS, U.S.-TAIWAN SECURITY RELATIONS

Likely U.S. behavior in a cross-strait military conflict is a critical factor that would shape both how such a conflict would play out and, indeed, whether such a conflict would occur in the first place. As the likelihood of a strong U.S. intervention increases, a conflict becomes both more costly and riskier for Beijing. Yet Washington faces significant dilemmas in its approach to Taiwan and has thus chosen to tread cautiously in its security commitments to Taipei. U.S. security commitments remain informal, meaning that there is no alliance treaty, interactions occur on an unofficial basis, and the United States eschews stationing troops on Taiwan or undertaking major bilateral military exercises with Taiwan. U.S. commitments are also ambiguous, meaning that there exists some uncertainty concerning how—or even whether—the United

States would intervene in the event of a cross-strait conflict. And commitments are at least somewhat contingent on policy decisions in Taiwan, meaning that Washington has at times signaled reduced support for Taiwan when U.S. policymakers have concluded that actions in Taiwan are primarily to blame for an increased risk of a cross-strait military conflict.

But even as these general features of the U.S. commitment to Taiwan remain in place, U.S.-Taiwan security ties have also grown stronger in recent years. Moreover, Beijing clearly believes that such ties are improving, and PRC analysts and officials have expressed considerable alarm about these trends in meetings with U.S. officials.[56] As I discuss at greater length in later chapters, pessimism in the PRC about trends in the Taiwan Strait can increase the risks of conflict under certain conditions. In this case, while increased U.S. commitments could foster stability by improving the credibility of deterrence, they could also backfire if they convince Beijing that the United States is essentially green lighting what is seen in the PRC as revisionist behavior in Taipei. Beijing worries, in short, about precisely the sort of moral hazard problems—outlined earlier—that have helped to motivate an ambiguous U.S. commitment to Taiwan in the first place.

4

DOMESTIC DYNAMICS IN CHINA AND TAIWAN

For several decades after the end of the Chinese Civil War, the PRC government in Beijing and the ROC government in Taipei adopted symmetrical positions regarding Taiwan. Each viewed itself as the sole, legitimate government of China. Both viewed Taiwan as a part of China. And both viewed Taiwan's unification with mainland China as an important goal. More recently, however, this symmetry has broken down. Although the PRC government continues to view itself as the rightful government of China, and to view Taiwan as a part of China that must be unified with the rest of the country, the Taiwan government has drifted away from its "one China" principle of the martial law era. As emphasized in the introduction, to an increasing degree Beijing and Taipei do not see eye to eye on fundamental sovereignty issues.

This divergence has been driven by political changes and shifting public opinion on both sides of the Taiwan Strait—especially in today's democratic Taiwan. In recent years, most Taiwanese have not even self-identified as Chinese in major surveys conducted on the island; even fewer view unification with the PRC as a desirable outcome. And the rise of the DPP as a powerful force in Taiwan politics—the party has now won four of the last six presidential elections—means that Taiwan is often governed by a party that does not accept the idea that Taiwan is part of China in principle. Meanwhile, some studies find evidence of increasing nationalism in the PRC, even as current president Xi Jinping appears to be less patient on the Taiwan issue than his immediate predecessors. Domestic dynamics, then, appear to be both contributing to diverging views on underlying sovereignty issues and increasing the stakes of the cross-strait dispute as the Taiwan issue becomes relatively more important in China.

In this chapter I provide a basic overview of domestic trends on both sides of the Taiwan Strait. I focus in particular on a few major factors that are likely to have especially large implications for the future prospects for conflict and peace in the Taiwan Strait: views on sovereignty and identity issues in Taiwan; popular nationalism and foreign policy hawkishness among PRC citizens; and shifting views on Taiwan among China's top leaders. The first part of the chapter focuses on politics and public opinion in Taiwan, as I consider how these have changed over time and how they might evolve in the future. The second part considers domestic dynamics in the PRC.

POLITICAL AND SOCIAL TRENDS IN TAIWAN

As discussed briefly in this book's introduction, the KMT presided over a highly authoritarian political system for decades after retreating to Taiwan at the end of the Chinese Civil War. The ROC constitution had been suspended in the late 1940s, and the Nationalist government imposed martial law in Taiwan. Space for political dissent was limited. Although non-KMT members could run for local office, they had to do so as independents (*dangwai*, or outside the party), and opposition parties were banned. Opponents of the regime risked arrest and sometimes execution, particularly during the early years of KMT governance on Taiwan. And the upper echelons of government were dominated by mainlanders. Chiang Kai-shek—who hoped to re-establish ROC authority on mainland China—remained in power until his death in 1975 and was succeeded by his son, Chiang Ching-kuo. In this authoritarian political environment, advocacy of Taiwan independence was strictly prohibited, not only because it contradicted a core goal of the Chiang regime, but more fundamentally because it called into question the legitimacy of KMT rule on Taiwan: advocating for an independent Taiwan implied that the Nationalist government was in essence a foreign occupation. Thus the official position of the ROC government concerning Taiwan's status continued to mirror the PRC position even as the ROC became ever more marginalized internationally and as the goal of reestablishing ROC governance on the mainland became ever more divorced from reality.

Taiwan, however, underwent major political changes during the 1980s and 1990s. Opposition parties were tolerated after *dangwai* activists formed the Democratic Progressive Party in 1986, and martial law was lifted in 1987. When Chiang Ching-kuo died in 1988, his vice president, Lee Teng-hui, became the first native Taiwanese president of the ROC. Political reforms accelerated under Lee. The suspension of the ROC constitution was lifted in 1991, and in the early 1990s popular elections were held for both the National Assembly (now defunct) and the Legislative Yuan. In 1996 Taiwan held its first direct presidential election (Lee won in a landslide), and since then Taiwan has generally been viewed as a democracy. Freedom House, for instance, has categorized Taiwan as "free" in its Freedom in the World index since 1996.[1] Taiwan's democratization, in turn, has had enormous implications for cross-strait relations. Although Taiwan's relationship to China was contested even under martial law, democratization opened the door to open debates in this regard. By the 1990s, advocates of Taiwan independence no longer risked arrest by publicly championing this cause, and political candidates sometimes campaigned on this issue; indeed, in the early 1990s the DPP—which had by then established itself as the major opposition party—embraced formal Taiwan independence.

In democratic Taiwan, as in any democracy, politicians compete over a range of issues, and in election campaigns Taiwan's complex relationship with China is often overshadowed by domestic issues such as economic performance, rooting out corruption, and spending on social programs. Consider, for instance, Tsai Ing-wen's second inaugural address in May 2020. Tsai, not surprisingly, focused the first part of her speech on the most pressing issue at the moment—the coronavirus pandemic and her government's successful management of the crisis. But when she turned to plans for her second term in office, national security and cross-strait relations were the third topic she discussed; telegraphing where her priorities lay, she first talked at length about economic development strategies before moving on to health and social safety net spending programs.[2] At the same time, however, Taiwan's relationship with China always looms large as an issue in Taiwan's presidential elections, and all presidential inaugural addresses since 1996 have included extensive discussion of cross-strait relations. Indeed, some political scientists contend that the cross-strait relationship is ultimately the single most important issue in Taiwan politics. Nathan Batto argues, for instance, that "Taiwan's relationship with China, broadly conceived, is more important" in Taiwan politics than all other issues put together.[3]

In the remainder of this section, I begin with a discussion of national identity trends in Taiwan, perhaps the most widely used indicator of what Batto describes as the "China cleavage" in Taiwan politics.[4] Over time, a greater percentage of respondents in public opinion polls have self-identified as "Taiwanese" rather than either "Chinese" or both "Chinese and Taiwanese." Next, I consider more broadly public opinion relating to cross-strait relations—particularly relating to Taiwan's sovereign status. Here I highlight both declining interest in unification with mainland China and continued pragmatism in terms of policy preferences relating to cross-strait relations. Finally, I consider evolving views on cross-strait sovereignty issues among the two main political parties in Taiwan, the KMT and the DPP. I conclude this section with comments on broader implications of these trends for the cross-strait relationship.

INCREASING TAIWAN-CENTRIC IDENTITY

During the martial law era, the ruling KMT aimed to legitimize its monopoly on power in Taiwan by promoting what Dafydd Fell calls a "KMT Chinese nationalism."[5] As noted earlier, KMT legitimacy ultimately rested on Taiwan being an integral part of China, and the Nationalists representing the rightful rulers of China. From the standpoint of the Nationalist government, then, it was important for Taiwan's people to think of themselves first and foremost as Chinese. Fell observes that the KMT government adopted numerous policies to try to inculcate a Chinese-centric identity among Taiwan's citizens, ranging from promoting Mandarin (and requiring its use in schools), to mandating that schools teach a China-centric curriculum that emphasized Chinese history and culture, to promoting traditional Chinese culture and even renaming major streets after Chinese leaders and concepts. At the end of the day, however, these policies had only partial success in constructing a KMT Chinese nationalism in Taiwan; as Shelley Rigger notes, by the 1970s and 1980s a Taiwan culture movement had emerged, with growing interest in all things Taiwanese.[6] And as political liberalization accelerated into the 1990s, it became possible to reject KMT Chinese nationalism without risk of persecution.

Against this backdrop, Taiwan's first two democratically elected presidents, Lee Teng-hui and Chen Shui-bian, advocated for alternative new forms of nationalism in Taiwan. As Rigger puts it, Lee advanced a vision of civic nationalism centered on his concept of a "New Taiwanese consciousness," where all Taiwanese—"regardless of when they or their forbearers arrived on Taiwan"—"share a common destiny" that puts Taiwan's interests first.[7] Lee was suggesting an inclusive nationalism where all people of Taiwan, including both mainlanders (whose ancestors had arrived after 1945) and native Taiwanese (whose ancestors had arrived earlier), would take pride in Taiwan's economic and political development. But Chen, Rigger argues, pursued a form of ethnonationalism, highlighting not only Taiwan's political distinction from China (as Lee did), but also its cultural distinctiveness; in this formulation, Taiwan was neither politically nor culturally Chinese.[8] As Rigger observes, Chen's efforts in this regard were politically divisive in Taiwan and ultimately may have contributed to the DPP's landslide defeat in 2008. But even more telling were surveys, ubiquitous in Taiwan by the 2000s, asking individuals whether they think of themselves as Taiwanese, Chinese, or both. While the percentage of respondents choosing just Taiwanese rose quickly in the 1990s, it leveled off during the 2000s. And although the percentage of respondents identifying as solely Chinese dropped to very low levels, most respondents during the Chen years identified as both (see figure 4.1). Rigger observes that this finding suggests that many Taiwanese continued to "recognize their Chinese cultural heritage" even as they identified geographically (and politically) with Taiwan. Meanwhile, China's rise effectively "strengthened the association between 'China' and 'People's Republic of China,'" thus making it less likely that most Taiwanese would identify as solely Chinese.[9]

In the years since 2008, however, those identifying as solely Taiwanese have emerged as the clear majority of respondents in surveys on Taiwan self-identification (see again figure 4.1). According to surveys conducted by National Chengchi University's Election Study Center, by 2014 over 60 percent of respondents self-identified as solely Taiwanese, compared with 32.5 percent identifying as both Chinese and Taiwanese (and only 3.5 percent identifying as solely Chinese). The Taiwanese-only percentage dropped slightly in subsequent years but then skyrocketed again starting in 2019; in 2020 over 64 percent of respondents self-identified as solely Taiwanese, with less than 30 percent self-identifying as both Chinese and Taiwanese. The spike in 2014 occurred during the large protest movements (the Sunflower Movement) that reflected, in part, backlash against some of Ma's cross-strait policies (such as the Service Trade Agreement). The more recent surge in Taiwan-centric identity likely reflects a combination of intensified PRC coercive activities directed against Taiwan and the Hong Kong protest movement in 2019 and subsequent crackdown by Beijing. Still, even in the absence of these spikes, the longer-term trends are unmistakable, and most of Taiwan's citizens now identify as solely Taiwanese.

This shift has occurred broadly across Taiwan society; even among mainlanders (those who came to Taiwan from the mainland after 1945 and their descendants), the percentage self-identifying as solely Taiwanese has steadily increased since the 1990s.[10] And it is a trend that has characterized both major political camps in Taiwan: the vast majority of pan-green supporters identify as solely Taiwanese, and even though

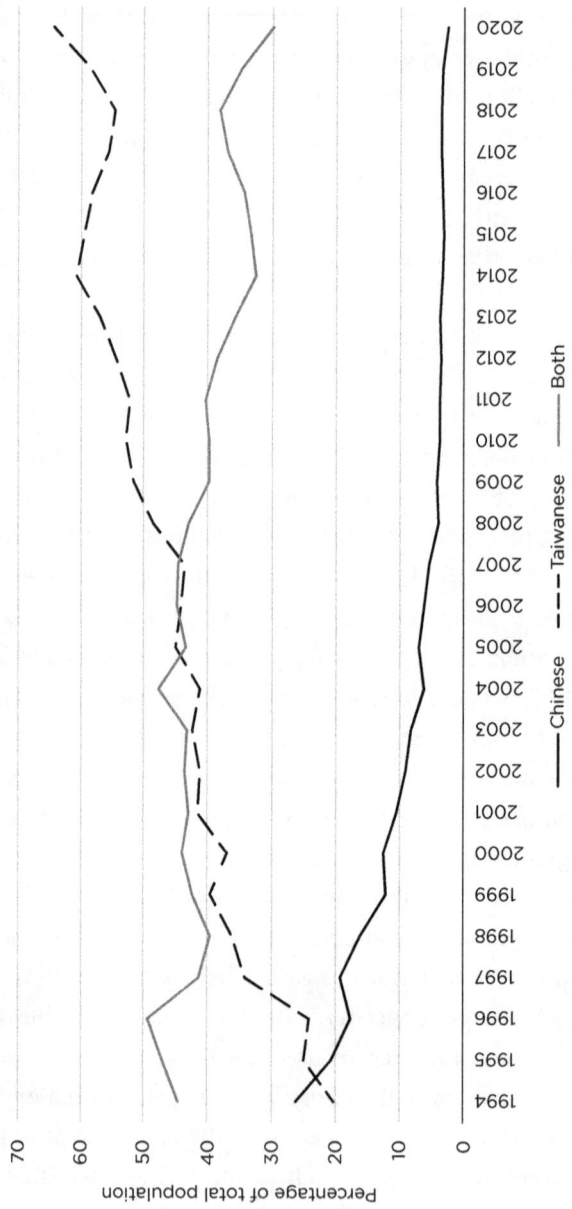

FIGURE 4.1 Self-identification in Taiwan, percentages over time.

Data from "Changes in the Taiwanese/Chinese Identity of Taiwanese as Tracked in Surveys by the Election Study Center, NCCU (1992–2020/12)," https://esc.nccu.edu.tw/upload/44/doc/6961/People202012.jpg.

a majority of pan-blue supporters still identified as both Taiwanese and Chinese as of 2012, the percentage of sole-Taiwanese identifiers among pan-blue supporters has also steadily increased. Wang argues that those self-identifying as solely Taiwanese have tended to take a "primordial view of being 'Taiwanese.'"[11] Simply put, these respondents have tended to explain in follow-up interviews that they consider themselves Taiwanese because they live in Taiwan, or because they were born and raised in Taiwan.

As Rigger argued with respect to earlier shifts, these trends appear to reflect the reality that the PRC has essentially monopolized what it means to be "China" in today's world.[12] Yang Zhong, for instance, shows that most Taiwan citizens will self-identify as Chinese in some way if given the option of self-identifying as a "member of the Chinese nation" (*zhonghua minzu yifenzi*). In his surveys, Zhong found that 54 percent of respondents self-identified as a member of the Chinese nation, 3 percent as "Chinese" (*zhongguo ren*, the same term used in the polls discussed earlier), and 25 percent as both Chinese and a member of the Chinese nation. On the other hand, a large majority of respondents disagreed with the suggestion that, since Taiwan's official name is the Republic of China, people living in the ROC should be called Chinese. Zhong interprets these findings as suggesting that most of Taiwan's citizens no longer consider themselves Chinese nationals because that term increasingly is synonymous with PRC nationals in today's world; but at the same time, most continue to identify as culturally and ethnically Chinese.[13]

DECREASING INTEREST IN UNIFICATION, BUT CONSIDERABLE PRAGMATISM

Since the percentage of Taiwan's citizens who self-identify either as both Taiwanese and Chinese or solely Chinese has dropped sharply since the 1990s, and since scholars often interpret this as reflecting the PRC's increasing monopolization of "China" as a political entity, it is perhaps not surprising that interest in unification with mainland China has also declined in Taiwan. Indeed, analysts of Taiwan public opinion have emphasized that there is a high correlation between the identity patterns just described and individual views on unification or independence. Chen Rou-lan, for instance, disaggregates national identity in Taiwan into two dimensions: a primordial dimension (which captures whether individuals self-identify as Taiwanese or Chinese, whether they view Taiwanese and Chinese as different, and so forth) and a political dimension (which captures individual views on future national status questions). Chen finds that the two dimensions are distinct but nonetheless highly correlated with each other.[14] Simply put, those who identify as solely Taiwanese tend to be much less supportive of unification as a goal and indeed are much more likely to view Taiwan and China as two independent states.[15]

The Election Study Center at National Chengchi University has conducted surveys on this topic since the early 1990s. The surveys give respondents six possible outcomes to choose from, including unification as fast as possible; maintaining the status quo for now, unification later; maintaining the status quo for now and deciding at a later date; maintaining the status quo indefinitely; maintaining the status quo for now, with independence later; and independence as fast as possible. To keep things simple, figure 4.2 draws from these surveys in collapsing outcomes into three categories: those that reveal support for independence (either now or in the future); those that reveal support for unification (either now or in the future); and those that are supportive of the status quo with no revealed preferences over independence/unification. The surveys show, first, that there appears to be declining interest in unification among Taiwan's public: support for unification, even as a long-term goal, has dropped from above 20 percent in the 1990s to under 10 percent in the past two years (with a short-term increase in 2018 that likely reflected general dissatisfaction at the time with the Tsai Ing-wen administration). Among unification supporters, the vast majority favor this as a long-term outcome; in recent years usually fewer than 2 percent of respondents favored reunification as soon as possible (and in 2020 this number stood at 1 percent). Second, support for independence hovered near 20 percent for roughly fifteen years before increasing sharply since 2019 (and in 2020

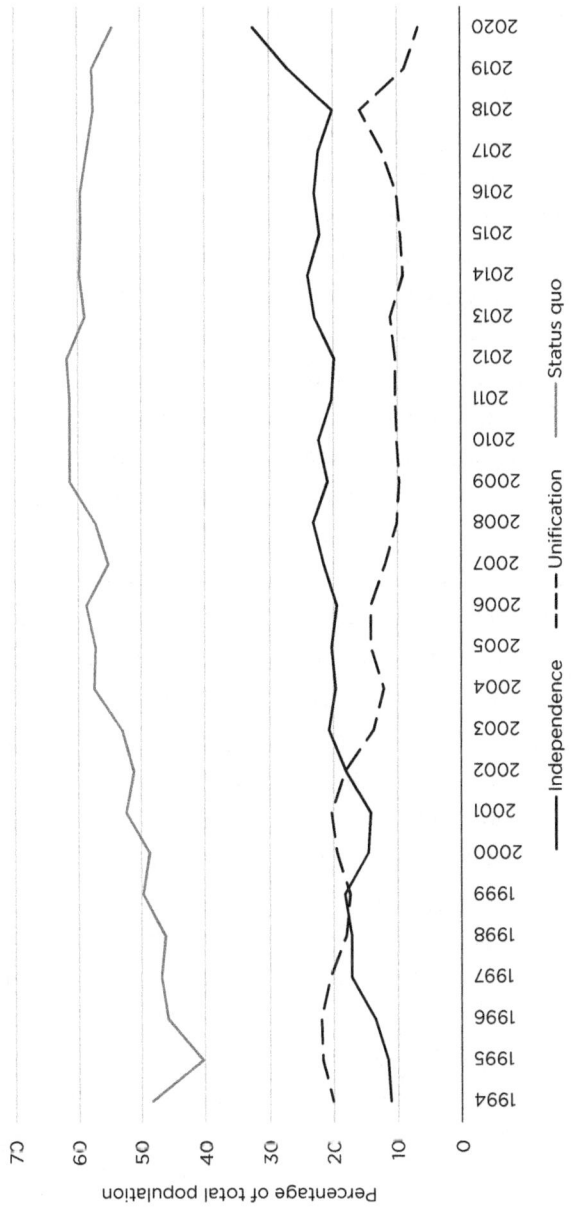

FIGURE 4.2 Support for independence/unification in Taiwan, percentages over time.

Data from "Changes in the Unification-Independence Stances of Taiwanese as Tracked in Surveys by the Election Study Center, NCCU (1994–2020/12)," https://esc.nccu.edu.tw/upload/44/doc/6963/Tondu202012.jpg.

stood at greater than 30 percent). As with the recent spike in Taiwan-centric identity, this increase is likely in response to the PRC's recent actions in Hong Kong and increased displays of military force in the Taiwan Strait. Finally, for the past two decades a majority of respondents have not revealed even a long-term preference on unification/independence, favoring maintaining the status quo indefinitely or maintaining the status quo for now and making a decision later.

The large number of respondents favoring the status quo in the Election Study Center surveys suggests on the surface a high level of pragmatism among Taiwan's voters when it comes to Taiwan's sovereign status, and many scholars have probed this finding at greater length. Several important studies published during the 2000s showed that the views of Taiwan citizens on final status issues were conditional on the circumstances under which independence or unification might come about. Chu Yun-han, for instance, uses survey data from the 1990s and early 2000s that asks respondents whether they (a) would support independence if it could be achieved peacefully and (b) would support unification if the social, political, and economic conditions in mainland China were to become comparable to Taiwan. In Chu's schema, principled independence supporters would agree with the first possibility and disagree with the second. Principled unification supporters would do the opposite, and what he terms "open-minded rationalists" would support both hypotheticals. He found that by the late 1990s and early 2000s, principled independence supporters tended to represent slightly more than 20 percent of survey respondents; principled unification supporters slightly less than 20 percent; and open-minded rationalists, who could support either unification or independence under the right circumstances, represented between 22 percent and 35 percent of respondents.[16] Along similar lines, Emerson Niou found that, as of 2003, a majority of respondents could support either independence or unification under the right conditions. Roughly 64 percent of respondents favored unification if Taiwan and mainland China were to become similar, while 72 percent supported independence if it could be achieved peacefully. On the other hand, only 19 percent favored unification if the two sides remained different from each other, and only

26 percent supported independence if it could not be realized peacefully.[17] Taken together, these studies suggested a highly pragmatic Taiwan public, where (a) support for independence was high, but only if could be obtained peacefully; (b) people remained open to unification if it the PRC were to become politically, economically, and socially similar to Taiwan; and (c) people generally opposed change to the status quo that involved high costs to Taiwan—either a war caused by an independence declaration or unification with an untransformed PRC.

Since the mid-2000s, however, support in Taiwan for unification—even under favorable conditions—has declined quite sharply. The Taiwan Election and Democratization Study's survey in 2012 found that only 35 percent of respondents favored unification if economic, political, and social conditions were to become the same in mainland China and Taiwan, while 51 percent opposed unification even under these favorable circumstances.[18] By 2020 this same survey found that support for unification under favorable conditions dropped to 27 percent of respondents, while 64 percent opposed unification even if mainland China and Taiwan were to become similar.[19] The Taiwan National Security Survey (TNSS) in 2020 likewise found only 26 percent of respondents supported unification under favorable conditions, while 64 percent were opposed.[20] Moreover, support for the PRC's proposed one country, two systems formula has generally been quite low in Taiwan.[21] It is worth noting as well that the vast majority of Taiwan's citizens believe that Taiwan (or the ROC) is currently a sovereign state.[22] Still, support for formalizing independence remains highly conditional on its likely costs. Although the 2020 TNSS found that 71 percent of respondents would favor independence if it would not lead to a PRC attack against Taiwan, only 37 percent supported independence if it were to trigger a PRC attack. Thus public opinion remains quite pragmatic in Taiwan. While most Taiwanese support independence in principle (if it could be achieved peacefully), view Taiwan and/or the ROC as a sovereign state, and oppose unification with mainland China even under favorable circumstances, most Taiwanese also oppose formalizing independence if doing so were to trigger a military conflict with China.

PARTY DIFFERENCES AND PARTISAN TURNOVER

The previous two sections highlighted a number of changes in how Taiwan's citizens have approached key facets of what Batto terms the "China cleavage" in Taiwan's politics.[23] This cleavage closely overlaps with Taiwan's party system.[24] Simply put, the KMT and its allied parties (the pan-blue coalition) have tended to draw more support—relative to the DPP and its allied parties—from those who self-identify as Chinese (including dual identifiers) and those who either support eventual unification or are at least open to the idea under favorable circumstances. And the DPP and allied parties (the pan-green coalition) have tended to draw more support from those self-identifying as solely Taiwanese, those who are opposed to unification even under hypothetical favorable circumstances, and those who are more willing to support independence even if it leads to conflict with China. Indeed, the China factor is the best overall predictor of party identification in Taiwan.[25] In turn, party identification tends to be a very strong predictor of individual views on most China-related issues. For instance, Alexander Tan and Karl Ho show that DPP voters tended to view the ECFA as harming Taiwan's economy even as most KMT voters believed ECFA was beneficial to Taiwan's economy.[26]

Given the importance of the China cleavage in Taiwan's politics and its close overlap with the party system, it should come as no surprise that the two major camps have clear differences in their approach to cross-strait relations. Although neither party supports unification with the current PRC government, the KMT supports a version of a one China principle (in the form of the 1992 consensus) while the DPP does not. Furthermore, the Taiwan public has consistently viewed the pan-blue coalition as relatively pro-unification and the pan-green coalition as relatively pro-independence.[27] Of course, the cross-strait policies of both parties have evolved considerably over time. Consider the DPP, which has yo-yoed between outspoken commitment to formal Taiwan independence and moderation meant to assure voters that it could be trusted not to start a war with China: the party endorsed formal independence in the early 1990s; downplayed the stance after performing poorly in elections to the now-defunct National Assembly in 1991; nominated an outspoken pro-independence candidate for president in 1996; again downplayed the need to declare independence in the lead-up to the 2000 election; was led by a president—Chen Shui-bian—who became increasingly outspoken on sovereignty issues during his tenure in office in the 2000s; and is now led by a president who has sought to signal moderation in her cross-strait policies. The KMT, for its part, has swung from a clear goal of restoring ROC governance on mainland China during the martial law era, to Lee Teng-hui's walking away from a one China principle in the 1990s, to the party's current embrace of a weak version of a one China principle in the form of the ambiguous 1992 consensus.[28] Still, despite this variation within each camp over time, it is clear that over the past two decades the KMT has been more supportive than the DPP of unification as an end-goal, and more willing than the DPP to endorse the idea that Taiwan is part of China in principle. In turn, we have seen a clear partisan cycle to cross-strait stability emerge, where relations have been less stable during periods of DPP governance (as DPP presidents pursue policies that are more at odds with Beijing on sovereignty issues), and more stable during periods of KMT governance (i.e., the Ma administration).

DISCUSSION

The societal and political trends discussed in this section have potentially large implications for cross-strait relations. Consider first some of the broad patterns in Taiwan public opinion relating to China. In today's Taiwan, a declining percentage of citizens think of themselves as Chinese, and support for unification—even under hypothetical favorable circumstances—has dwindled in recent decades. Meanwhile, a growing majority of Taiwan's citizens now self-identify as solely Taiwanese, and most would support formal Taiwan independence if it could be achieved peacefully. Still, most Taiwanese appear to be relatively pragmatic on sovereignty issues, as most oppose formal independence if it were to trigger war with China. These trends create as set of challenging dilemmas for a PRC that hopes to achieve formal unification with Taiwan. The declining interest in unification among Taiwan's people—especially in a democratic setting where leaders are elected and accountable to Taiwan's voters—should in principle give the PRC reason to double down on efforts to improve its image on the island, and to pursue policies, like those described in chapter 1, that seek to win the hearts and minds of Taiwan's voters. But Beijing's approach to Taiwan in recent years has, to the contrary, relied heavily on coercive signaling—including most obviously the extensive military exercises China has undertaken near Taiwan. This approach most likely further undercuts the PRC's image in Taiwan and likely makes unification an even less attractive prospect to most Taiwanese. So why take such an approach? The answer likely lies—at least in part—in the very pragmatism among Taiwan's voters just summarized. Simply put, given that most Taiwan citizens would prefer independence if it could be achieved peacefully, PRC military deterrence is critical to preventing this outcome. Unfortunately for Beijing, that deterrence likely further erodes interest in unification among Taiwan's citizens and thus makes the goal of peaceful unification less achievable.

Given the importance of the China cleavage in Taiwan's politics, declining interest in unification among Taiwan voters also presents challenges to a KMT that remains committed to the principle that Taiwan is part of China. The KMT's interpretation of the 1992 consensus allows the party considerable room to maneuver here, and Ma Ying-jeou was clear that he viewed the ROC as a sovereign state. Yet as more of Taiwan's citizens self-identify as solely Taiwanese, and as fewer view unification as a desirable future outcome, the fact that Taiwan voters themselves view the KMT as the pro-unification party could become a serious liability to the KMT moving forward.[29] And, indeed, the KMT appears to be in serious political trouble as I complete this book. The NCCU tracking poll for December 2020, for instance, found that only 17 percent of respondents supported the KMT, compared to 34 percent supporting the DPP (with about 40 percent answering no party or no response, and the rest supporting minor parties). The KMT had similar levels of support during the early Chen administration, but at that time support for other pan-blue parties (most important, James Soong's

People's First Party) meant that the pan-blue alliance was still on equal footing with the pan-green alliance. Today the KMT and its allied parties appear to be in a much less favorable position.[30]

To be clear, it is far too early to declare the demise of the KMT. The party as recently as 2018 performed very well in local elections in Taiwan, and KMT support during most of the Ma administration—not exactly ancient history—was consistently much higher than DPP support. If the China cleavage continues to evolve as it has in recent years, however, the KMT will need to adapt if it wishes to remain competitive in national elections. What does this mean for the future of Taiwan's cross-strait policies? One possibility, of course, is that some of the societal trends we have seen in recent years will change course: perhaps intensifying tensions in cross-strait relations will lead to renewed pragmatism among Taiwan voters and greater willingness to accept formulations—such as the 1992 consensus—that could open the door to renewed dialogue with Beijing. A second possibility is that the KMT will adapt to the new trends by downplaying its commitment to unification, including perhaps by jettisoning (or modifying its interpretation of) the 1992 consensus. If this were to occur, the partisan cycle in cross-strait policy would likely be attenuated to some degree, especially if the DPP remained committed to Tsai's pragmatism. But cross-strait relations would likely remain tense regardless of which party were in power in such a scenario. A third possibility is that the KMT will simply become less relevant as a political force in Taiwan, at least for the near term; in turn, PRC pressure on Taiwan would likely continue.[31]

DOMESTIC POLITICAL DYNAMICS IN CHINA

Taiwan, of course, is only one party to the cross-strait relationship, and ultimately the degree of convergence or divergence in cross-strait views on the Taiwan sovereignty issue will also be informed by domestic trends in the PRC. In this section I consider two especially salient domestic factors that will likely help to shape the PRC's approach to Taiwan in the years ahead, and that will help to determine how much of a priority the Taiwan issue will be for Beijing (relative to other goals). I begin with a discussion of the role of public opinion and nationalism in China. Although the PRC's authoritarian political institutions mean that the country's leaders have only limited direct accountability to China's citizens, the CCP's legitimacy is ultimately grounded—in part—in a nationalist narrative that emphasizes that party's role in constructing a strong and unified country. Taiwan, in turn, is an integral part of this narrative. Second, I consider the preferences of top Chinese leaders, noting that different leaders have approached the Taiwan issue differently over time.

NATIONALISM, PUBLIC OPINION, AND TAIWAN

Although the PRC has long claimed Taiwan as rightfully part of China and has threatened to fight a war to prevent Taiwan's formal independence, why Beijing should place such high importance on Taiwan's status is not obvious. As Alan Wachman wrote in a major study exploring Chinese interest in Taiwan: "One cannot explain the fiery commitment to sacrifice all that the PRC has gained in the past decades of material growth and international respectability in terms of the presence on Taiwan of any rich archaeological, architectural, religious, or cultural sites that trigger among the 'Chinese people'—in whose name the PRC leadership claims to act—fervent sentiments of national pride or yearning. Taipei is *not* China's Jerusalem."[32] Wachman argues that PRC interest in Taiwan is ultimately grounded in strategic concerns. Most directly, the PRC is made more vulnerable by a Taiwan that has close security ties with the United States; on the other hand, a Taiwan that is under PRC control ensures much easier access to the Pacific Ocean for the PLA Navy.[33]

Yet China's interest in Taiwan clearly goes beyond geostrategic considerations. Foreign corporations and entertainers, for instance, sometimes face the wrath of Chinese netizens if they depart from or contradict the PRC's official stance on Taiwan. In one recent example, a popular South Korean television show faced criticism for filming a board game that included the ROC flag. In recent years foreign corporations (such as airlines that fly to Taipei) have faced pressure to label Taiwan as a part of China, and Hollywood has generally accommodated the CCP on the Taiwan issue so as to avoid complicating access to the PRC's lucrative movie market.[34] Taiwan, simply put, is a deeply nationalistic issue in China. Even though it is typically state entities that pressure foreign corporations to alter their depictions of Taiwan, when they do so it appears to resonate widely with China's citizens.

Thomas Christensen outlines two broad pathways through which nationalism helps to shape China's interest in Taiwan. The first is what he refers to as "sincere nationalism."[35] Many in the PRC, including within the Chinese leadership, sincerely believe that Taiwan is rightfully part of China. Taiwan had been incorporated into the Qing Empire and then was lost to Japan during the "century of humiliation." Returned to the ROC after the end of World War II, the island was separated from rest of China again when Chiang's KMT forces retreated there as the newly formed PRC consolidated control on the mainland; U.S. intervention, moreover, helped to keep it separate. For many in China, writes Susan Shirk, "the 'century of humiliation' will not end until China is strong enough to achieve reunification."[36] Taiwan, in essence, remains unfinished business from a time when China was weak. As such, Taiwan remains an important national interest, and perceived foreign interference relating to Taiwan—foreign actions that appear to undercut prospects for unification—can elicit a strong and emotional response in the PRC.[37]

The second way in which nationalism helps to shape the PRC's interest in Taiwan concerns regime legitimacy. Since the onset of the post-Mao economic reforms in China, the Chinese Communist Party has been forced to rely more on nationalism for legitimacy—as Christensen writes, the "baldly capitalist reform program" has "gutted any other ideological justification" for continued CCP rule.[38] Given Chinese feelings of sincere nationalism relating to Taiwan, there is widespread belief in China that any government that "lost" Taiwan—by "allowing" it to become formally independent—would lose the support of the Chinese people.[39] Moreover, in part because regime legitimacy depends on nationalism, leaders who appear weak on Taiwan run the risk of having the issue used against them in internal political struggles, particularly during times of leadership transition when a new leader is still consolidating power.[40] Thus popular nationalism is sometimes framed as a double-edged sword for the CCP, where, on the one hand, it is cultivated and used by the party to enhance regime legitimacy, but, on the other hand, it can act as a constraint on issues like Taiwan that touch directly on past national humiliations.[41]

To be clear, popular nationalism is hardly a new phenomenon in China; to the contrary, as Jessica Chen Weiss writes, "resistance to foreign domination has been a central tenet in Chinese political discourse since the mid-nineteenth century," and antiforeign demonstrations were common during the Mao years.[42] But to the degree that popular nationalism is increasing in China or public views regarding Taiwan are hardening, it could potentially limit the ability of PRC leaders to be patient on the Taiwan issue.

As Alastair Iain Johnston notes, it has become a conventional wisdom that nationalism in China has indeed been increasing since the 1990s. Johnston's own findings, however, call into question the validity of this meme. Rather, using time-series survey data from Beijing that dates back to the 1990s, and drawing on responses to a range of survey questions that focus on national pride (such as, "China is a better country than most") and questions that assess whether Chinese respondents view Chinese people as inherently different from Japanese people or Americans, he finds evidence of increasing nationalism until 2009, and then some attenuation.[43] On the other hand, as Weiss observes, feelings of national pride or superiority do not necessarily correlate directly with hawkish foreign policy views. And, indeed, Weiss finds in her own analysis—drawing on several different surveys conducted in the PRC—that Chinese public opinion is generally quite hawkish. For instance, respondents are generally more likely to favor increased rather than decreased military spending, and to believe that China relies too little rather than too much on military strength. Furthermore, younger respondents tended to be more hawkish than older respondents.[44]

Since Taiwan is a sensitive political topic in China, there is a dearth of reliable public opinion data relating to cross-strait relations, particularly in comparison to public opinion data available in Taiwan. But one recent study—drawing on surveys conducted in 2013—does explore public attitudes toward Taiwan in ten major Chinese cities.[45] The authors find that most respondents would like to see the separation of mainland China and Taiwan resolved as soon as possible but also that the vast majority of respondents prefer negotiations over the use of force as a means to resolve the issue. Still, it is worth emphasizing that the survey was conducted at a time when cross-strait relations were characterized by détente during the Ma Ying-jeou years, and indeed the authors find that a large majority of respondents believed that most Taiwanese favored unification. This suggests, in turn, that mainland Chinese respondents likely were at least somewhat confident in the efficacy of negotiations for resolving the Taiwan issue. Moreover, it is worth noting that the survey questions were framed as how best to "resolve" Taiwan's separation from mainland China; by favoring negotiations over force, respondents appeared to be reluctant to use force as a means to compel unification. On the other hand, Elina Sinkkonen finds that survey respondents in 2007 overwhelmingly favored using military force in the event of a Taiwan declaration of independence.[46] And Peter Gries and Tao Wang argue—based on more anecdotal evidence—that support for "forceful reunification" has been increasing in the PRC (both among elites and the general public) since the election of Tsai Ing-wen as Taiwan's president in 2016.[47] In sum, public opinion data on the Taiwan issue is quite limited in the PRC, but available evidence suggests the mainland Chinese public wishes to see progress on unification with Taiwan; has tended to favor negotiations over use of force as a means for achieving unification, although support for use of force may be increasing; and strongly supports the use of force in the event of a Taiwan declaration of independence.

Nevertheless, even if the PRC public holds relatively hawkish foreign policy views in general, and even if hawkishness on the Taiwan issue in particular is increasing, it still begs the question: In authoritarian China, how much of a constraint is such hawkishness on the PRC's approach to Taiwan? Although it has become almost conventional wisdom to view

the PRC leadership as increasingly boxed in by a hawkish and nationalist public, there are reasons to think that Chinese leaders likely retain
considerable flexibility in their approach to the Taiwan issue. Obviously,
PRC leaders are not directly accountable to PRC citizens, and the PRC
state retains substantial capacity to limit protests when it wishes to do
so.[48] But some recent studies suggest that the PRC government is also
able to manipulate public opinion in important ways that help to reduce
its susceptibility to audience costs in foreign policy decision making.
Audience costs represent the penalty—in terms of reduced popular
support—that a leader pays for making a threat and then backing down
in an international dispute; in essence, they are the costs a leader pays
for being called on a bluff. In an important study undertaken in the
United States, Michael Tomz has shown that leaders tend to lose popular support when they take a strong stand but ultimately back down in
international disputes, and Xiaojun Li and Dingding Chen use a survey
experiment in China to show that these findings apply there as well.[49]
On the other hand, Kai Quek and Alastair Iain Johnston in one article,
and Jessica Chen Weiss and Alan Dafoe in another, show—also using
survey experiments—that audience costs can be greatly reduced depending on how the decision to back down is described to Chinese citizens.[50]
For instance, Quek and Johnston find that Chinese leaders can reduce
the public opinion costs of backing down in a crisis if they emphasize
the costs of conflict or China's identity as a peaceful country, and Weiss
and Dafoe find that emphasis on future success can increase support for
near-term restraint in a crisis.[51] Thus Chinese leaders might actually have
considerable leeway to back down in a dispute over Taiwan if they choose
to do so.

In sum, nationalism is clearly a key reason that the PRC views
Taiwan as an important national interest. Moreover, although there is
reason to be skeptical that nationalism is on the rise in China, PRC citizens tend to hold quite hawkish foreign policy views in general, and
hawkishness on Taiwan in particular may also be increasing. But PRC
leaders likely retain considerable flexibility in their approach to Taiwan,
both because of limited direct accountability to PRC citizens and also
because of the ability to frame a particular approach as advancing the
ultimate cause of unification.

LEADERSHIP AND THE PRC'S CHANGING APPROACH TO TAIWAN

Even though PRC leaders since Mao Zedong have viewed Taiwan as rightfully part of China and have embraced unification with the island as an important national goal, the PRC's approach to Taiwan—as noted in this book's introduction—has changed over time. Indeed, just as there is a clear "leader effect" on Taiwan's approach to cross-strait relations that goes beyond simple partisanship (compare, for instance, Tsai Ing-wen's relatively pragmatic approach with that of Chen Shui-bian), there also appears to be a leader effect in the PRC. Simply put, some preeminent leaders have been more cautious and patient in their approach to Taiwan than others.

Most notably, some scholars have argued that Jiang Zemin was relatively impatient on the Taiwan issue, especially after the mid- to late 1990s. Susan Shirk writes that Jiang "dreamed of going down in the history books as the Chinese leader who reunified China," and that he started in 1998 "to talk about timelines for reunification."[52] Shirk further writes, based on comments by a "well-connected insider," that Jiang himself insisted on adding to the PRC's White Paper on Taiwan in 2000 that indefinite delay by Taiwan's government on negotiating reunification would be a legitimate reason for use of force against Taiwan.[53] Chien-kai Chen likewise concludes that Jiang was impatient on the Taiwan issue and points to other episodes such as a 1999 interview in which Jiang appeared to suggest that unification with Taiwan should be accomplished by the middle of the 21st century.[54] Chen argues, on the other hand, that Jiang's successor, Hu Jintao, was more patient on the Taiwan issue: he appeared to be less interested in timetables than Jiang had been, and Chen interprets key Hu initiatives—such as his "six-point" proposal in 2008—as revealing a willingness to wait to make progress on unification.[55]

Current Chinese president and CCP general secretary Xi Jinping appears, in turn, to be less patient on Taiwan than Hu, and possibly Jiang as well. As noted in the introduction, Xi insisted even during the Ma Ying-jeou administration that the Taiwan issue could not be passed down "from generation to generation," and he reiterated this view in his speech on Taiwan in 2019.[56] Xi has also on multiple occasions indicated that national unification is a necessary part of what he terms the Chinese dream of national rejuvenation,[57] and he has highlighted 2049—the centenary of the PRC—as the year by which that dream should be realized.[58] Xi has echoed past policy statements—including the White Paper in 2000 and the Antisecession Law of 2005—in suggesting that indefinite delay on reunification would constitute legitimate reason to use force against Taiwan.[59] More generally, Xi's approach to Tsai Ing-wen appears more broadly coercive than was Hu Jintao's approach to Chen Shui-bian, even though external observers tend to view Tsai as more moderate and pragmatic than Chen in her approach to cross-strait relations.

Still, even if we accept that different Chinese leaders have seen the Taiwan issue differently, it can nevertheless be hard to separate leader effects from the broader environment in which they operate. Jiang's impatience, for instance, may have been mostly a reflection of pessimism arising from perceived unfavorable trends in Taiwan (such as Lee Teng-hui's policies and then the election of Chen Shui-bian), while Hu's greater patience likely reflected optimism arising from Chen's declining support in Taiwan and later the rise of Ma Ying-jeou.[60] Meanwhile, core tenets of Taiwan policy tend to change quite slowly in China, and once the CCP embraces a key stance such as the one China principle or one country, two systems, future leaders tend to formulate Taiwan policy within the parameters of those principles.[61] Xin argues that Chinese leaders have consistently prioritized development and modernization over reunification in any event; even for Xi, reunification is viewed as the consequence, rather than the cause, of national rejuvenation.[62]

CONCLUSION: DOMESTIC DYNAMICS MAGNIFY CROSS-STRAIT DIVERGENCE

Increased divergence in cross-strait views on sovereignty issues is, to a considerable degree, a consequence of domestic political dynamics in both China and Taiwan. In Taiwan, a growing number of citizens self-identify as solely Taiwanese and not Chinese, and support for unification with China—even as a distant goal under favorable conditions—has declined considerably over the past two decades. Taiwan's two main political camps have diverging views on sovereignty issues, including their willingness to accept—even in weak form—the idea that Taiwan is in principle part of China. This means, in turn, that the degree of stability in cross-strait relations has varied depending on which party is in power in Taiwan. In China, meanwhile, commitment to national unification is rooted deeply in nationalism, and there is a widely shared view that leaders would pay high political costs were they to suffer clear losses relating to Taiwan (such as, most obviously, an inability to prevent a formal Taiwan declaration of independence). Domestic dynamics, in short, act as both a driver of divergence and a constraint on finding common ground.

II

ASSESSING THE PROSPECTS
FOR CONFLICT AND PEACE

5

MODELING CROSS-STRAIT
RELATIONS

I n part I of this book I highlighted several trends and features of the cross-strait relationship that obviously have large implications for stability in the Taiwan Strait. Taiwan and China have become closely intertwined economically, which in turn can be stabilizing (by increasing the costs of war) but might also increase PRC influence in Taiwan. PRC military capabilities have increased rapidly, which potentially increases Beijing's coercive leverage over Taiwan. The role of the United States is critical to assessing the balance of power in the Taiwan Strait, but U.S. resolve to intervene has remained ambiguous. And domestic political dynamics in both China and Taiwan are contributing to diverging preferences between Beijing and Taipei on Taiwan sovereignty issues.

The purpose of part II is to analyze how these different trends and features of China-Taiwan relations collectively shape the prospects for war and peace in the Taiwan Strait. I begin by constructing a simple model of the cross–Taiwan Strait relationship, which draws directly from the bargaining theories of conflict that international relations scholars commonly use to analyze conflict more generally. The model serves as a baseline that I then use in the following two chapters to explore how two types of conflict might emerge in the Taiwan Strait: a conflict that is rooted in efforts by Taiwan to alter the status quo in a way that conflicts with Beijing's preferences on sovereignty issues (chapter 6); and a conflict that is rooted in efforts by the PRC to impose its preferred sovereignty solution on Taiwan (chapter 7). The conclusion discusses how these scenarios might be avoided.

WHY CONSTRUCT A MODEL OF CROSS-STRAIT RELATIONS?

Before turning to the model itself, it is worth discussing why modeling the cross-strait relationship might be a useful exercise in the first place.[1] As will become clear, the model that I outline greatly simplifies what is in reality a highly complex relationship. In constructing a simplified version of the relationship, I am not denying this complex reality. Indeed, in my many years of studying and following China-Taiwan relations, I have come to appreciate the many nuances of the relationship—the different versions of a one China principle; the quasi-official dialogue; the importance of symbolism and rhetoric that seeps into all aspects of the relationship. So, why abstract away from this reality?[2]

To put it bluntly, it is the very complexity of cross-strait relations that has motivated me to develop a simplified model. To see why, consider a map. As Kevin Clarke and David Primo observe in their insightful discussion of models in political science, maps are useful precisely because they greatly abstract away from complex reality.[3] Indeed, the more closely a map replicates that which it aims to represent, the less useful it typically becomes. A subway map, for instance, becomes less helpful if it is cluttered with detailed information on every twist and turn of each line, and even less useful if crowded with information on above-ground roads and bus routes. My motivation in constructing a model of cross-strait relations parallels this logic because I believe that it is easy to get lost in the nuances of cross–Taiwan Strait relations, to lose, that is, the forest for the trees. My hope, in other words, is to construct a model that will prove useful in the same way that a subway map is useful for riders: because it abstracts away from complex realities and focuses on a few important pieces of information (such as the ordering of stations on each line and the identification of transfer stations).

The next obvious question is: Useful for what? To continue with the map metaphor (and to continue borrowing from Clarke and Primo), different types of maps are more or less useful depending on what the user hopes to accomplish. A subway map is useful for someone riding the subway, but not at all useful for someone driving across town. A trail map is useful for someone going for a hike, but not at all useful for most other purposes. Simply put, the sort of information that is most useful in a map is obviously contingent on the underlying purpose of the map. In my case, I hope to use my model of cross-strait relations for two purposes. The first purpose is organizational.[4] In part I, I described a number of different trends that are clearly salient when thinking about the prospects for conflict and peace in the Taiwan Strait. But it is not clear how these trends fit together or interact with each other. One of my aims in building a model of cross-strait relations is to provide a framework that might allow an analyst to think through how these different trends fit together.

Second, the model is meant to serve a predictive function: to assess the prospects for conflict and peace in the Taiwan Strait. To be clear, I am not trying to assess who would "win" such a war, nor am I trying to pinpoint precisely when such a conflict might occur. I am also not aiming to predict specific strategies that the PRC or Taiwan might use in such a conflict.[5] Rather, I hope to better understand how worried interested observers should be about a cross-strait conflict arising in the first place. To get to that point, I believe it is critical to have a clear understanding of the fundamental underlying causal processes that could lead to conflict in the Taiwan Strait, and I believe that a simplified model is likely to be useful in uncovering those processes.

DRAWING INSIGHT FROM BARGAINING MODELS OF CONFLICT

The model that I develop draws heavily from bargaining models of international conflict and builds in particular on the model presented in James Fearon's seminal article.[6] As David Lake observes, the bargaining model has become the "workhorse model" of war in the international relations literature.[7] Bargaining models of war are grounded in an important insight about armed conflict that is sometimes overlooked: because war is always costly for all participants, there should always be bargains available that all participants would prefer over actually fighting the war.[8] In the Taiwan Strait, Beijing has explicitly threatened to fight a war and indeed has warned that it is prepared to "pay any costs" in doing so, in order to prevent Taiwan's formal independence. As I emphasized in this book's introduction, if such a war were to occur, it would have potentially catastrophic costs for both sides. Whether or not the PRC could successfully invade and occupy Taiwan, it is without question that China possesses the capacity to inflict tremendous damage on the island, its people, and its military. In undertaking such a war, China would also be exposing itself to substantial risk—not only of the direct costs that could be imposed by Taiwan's military, but the possibility that China's broader economic linkages to the global economy will be threatened and that war could escalate to conflict with the United States, the country possessing the world's most powerful military. Surely, it would seem, there should be peaceful outcomes that both sides would prefer to the war outcome.

Yet this same observation holds true more generally, and nevertheless costly wars are a recurring feature of the international system. In fighting the Iraq War, for instance, the United States paid by some estimates several trillion dollars in direct and indirect costs.[9] More than four thousand U.S. service members lost their lives in this war, and tens of thousands were wounded. The war ultimately became a major drag on the Republican Party and probably undercut the ability of the George W. Bush administration to accomplish other goals as Bush's popularity dropped in his second term. Although the war resulted in the successful removal of Saddam Hussein from power, it led to a prolonged insurgency, and it is unclear whether future Iraq governments will be on friendly terms with Washington. And, needless to say, the war was even more costly for Saddam and his regime. It seems, in short, that bargains should have been available that would have left both the United States and Iraq better off than the actual war outcome that we observed.

Understanding why wars occur in general, and why a cross-strait war might occur in particular, requires analysts to grapple with the reality that wars are an inefficient means to resolve disputes, and that in principle outcomes should exist that leave all disputants better off than the war outcome. The bargaining model literature asks why disputants are unable to find these outcomes instead of resorting to costly fighting. Theorists working in this literature have highlighted two broad causal explanations in this regard. First, wars can arise as a consequence of information problems. Leaders, for instance, are unlikely to have a perfect understanding of their adversary's military capabilities and resolve to pay the costs of fighting a war, and obtaining credible information in this regard is difficult. Second, wars can arise as a consequence of commitment problems, where leaders may recognize bargains that are preferable to war in principle, but where they doubt the credibility of other leaders to uphold those bargains in practice.

To be clear, rationalist bargaining models of war should be recognized for what they are: highly simplified representations that, like all models, capture only some elements of complex reality. Indeed, theorists working in this tradition are often quite explicit that the model ignores a range of factors that could serve as explanations for war, such as the possibility that individual leaders could make decisions that are irrational and impulsive, or that a society might glorify rather than abhor the violence and destruction of war.[10] Likewise, despite generally working within the rationalist paradigm in his own work, Lake has observed a number of shortcomings that arise when using a bargaining model framework to explain the Iraq War.[11] Despite these shortcomings, I have decided to build my analysis around the bargaining model because I am making, as Lake and Robert Powell put it, a "methodological bet" that such a model will prove useful in serving the predictive and organizational functions outlined in the previous section.[12]

First, although key studies such as Fearon's abstract away from factors such as domestic political dynamics,[13] the bargaining model is actually quite flexible in what it can accommodate. In particular, numerous factors outlined in the first part of this book—such as U.S.

resolve to intervene in a cross-strait conflict, or the rising costs of conflict due to economic integration—can be incorporated into a bargaining model framework. Economic integration, for instance, affects the costs of war. U.S. resolve also affects the costs of war, as well as expectations in both Beijing and Taipei about the likely war outcome. Even domestic political factors, such as nationalism in China, can be incorporated into the framework; nationalism, for instance, might serve to increase the value of Taiwan relative to other PRC interests. I am thus making a bet that the bargaining model will serve as a useful organizational framework that I can use to consider simultaneously how a variety of factors shape the prospects for conflict and peace in the Taiwan Strait.

I am also betting that the major simplifying assumptions I need to make in applying a bargaining framework to cross-strait relations will be worth it from the standpoint of insights gained. The model requires that I abstract away from a considerable amount of nuance in cross-strait relations; for example, one simplifying assumption I make is that Taiwan's status can be conceptualized as residing on a continuum, and where it sits on that continuum represents the key issue in dispute between Beijing and Taipei. Things are obviously more complicated, and some scholars have questioned whether it makes sense to think of Taiwan's status as a continuous good, as I note later on.[14] I am betting that these simplifications will pay off by enabling me to highlight and analyze more clearly a series of strategic problems that could give rise to war in the Taiwan Strait. Of course, the reader may disagree that my bets are in fact paying off. If nothing else, I hope that at least the analysis that follows will spur further consideration of the processes through which conflict could arise in the Taiwan Strait, even if future studies effectively debunk the arguments I make.

Thus the remainder of this chapter draws from the bargaining model of war to construct a simple model of armed conflict in the Taiwan Strait. More specifically, the model contextualizes insights from the bargaining model—drawing especially heavily on Fearon—to the Taiwan Strait in particular.[15] The model is not formalized, although I do utilize some simple figures to help illustrate key processes and insights.

ASSUMPTIONS

The model makes several assumptions about the nature of the cross–Taiwan Strait relationship, the relevant actors, and their preferences.

TAIWAN'S SOVEREIGN STATUS IS
THE KEY ISSUE IN DISPUTE

To begin, I assume that the key issue in dispute in the Taiwan Strait centers on Taiwan's sovereign status. More specifically, the two sides differ on whether Taiwan's current government is sovereign, whether Taiwan is, or should be, part of China, and what "China" means. As discussed in chapter 4, these questions are also contentious within Taiwan, with some holding views that are less in conflict with Beijing's preferences than the views held by others.

TAIWAN'S SOVEREIGN STATUS CAN BE
CONCEPTUALIZED AS A CONTINUUM

A second key assumption of the model is that Taiwan's sovereign status can be thought of as a continuum, ranging from formal unification under a unitary PRC government, on one extreme, to a formally independent Republic of Taiwan, on the other.[16] The status quo, where Taiwan enjoys de facto independence but lacks international legal recognition, and where the ROC government name and constitution remain effective, lies somewhere between the two extremes. Figure 5.1 illustrates this.

In the figure, the PRC's proposed one country, two systems framework lies close to the unification end of the continuum; here, unification would occur under a unitary central government, where autonomy—but no residual sovereignty—would be granted to Taiwan. A federal arrangement would imply Taiwan surrendering a considerable amount of sovereignty to Beijing and hence lie quite far to the right on the

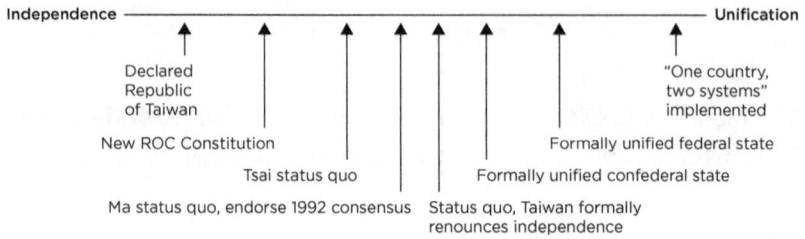

FIGURE 5.1 Taiwan's sovereign status as a continuum: examples of possible outcomes. The precise positioning of different outcomes on this continuum is obviously subjective.

continuum as well. A confederal arrangement lies farther to the left, but still to the right of the status quo. Here each side would hold sovereign status, but some sovereign authority would be pooled into a higher-level government or organization. Near the middle of the continuum lie different variants of the current broad status quo where Taiwan enjoys de facto sovereignty but has not sought to formalize independence in the form of a Republic of Taiwan. Toward the right of this status quo range lies a hypothetical scenario where a Taiwan government formally renounces independence. Farther left might reside the Ma Ying-jeou version of the status quo, where Taiwan endorsed a weak version of a one China principle in the form of the 1992 consensus. Farther left still is Tsai Ing-wen's version of the status quo, where Taiwan refuses to accept even a weak version of a one-China principle, but still accepts the ROC and is open, in theory, to future political integration as a negotiated and mutually agreed-on outcome. Finally, toward the left side of the continuum reside actions Taiwan could take to formally establish itself as an independent Republic of Taiwan, including implementing a new constitution and formally declaring independence.

CHINA AND TAIWAN ARE THE MAIN ACTORS BARGAINING OVER TAIWAN'S STATUS

I assume that China and Taiwan are the primary actors bargaining over Taiwan's status. Clearly, other states are relevant, including, most important, the United States; later I explain in more detail how I conceptualize the U.S. role.

Bargaining between China and Taiwan usually occurs tacitly. Often this tacit bargaining takes the form of Taiwan's government adopting some sort of stance on sovereignty-related issues (Ma's endorsement of the 1992 consensus, Tsai's willingness to signal continued commitment to a Republic of China government but unwillingness to accept the 1992 consensus, etc.), and Beijing reacting either positively (engaging in direct talks, etc.), or negatively (military threats, etc.). And tacit bargaining also takes the form of the PRC signaling its own position on sovereignty issues (such as Xi Jinping's speech on Taiwan in 2019), and the Taiwan government reacting in some way (such as Tsai's criticism of that speech). In other words, the two sides frequently signal their preferences on sovereignty issues, as well as their resolve to pursue those preferences.

THE PRC PREFERS OUTCOMES CLOSER TO THE UNIFICATION END OF THE CONTINUUM

Although Beijing's policies toward Taiwan have changed over time (such as the shift from a focus on "liberating" Taiwan during the Mao era to the focus on "peaceful reunification" in the Deng Xiaoping era), broad contours of that policy have been consistent in recent decades. Briefly, the PRC's policy on Taiwan is that the island is part of Chinese territory; that there is only one rightful government of China (including Taiwan), and that is the PRC; that Taiwan's de facto separation from the rest of China must end in formal unification; that the terms of unification are negotiable and would involve considerable autonomy for Taiwan under the one country, two systems framework; and that efforts by Taiwan to formalize its de facto independence from China are cause for war.

Furthermore, Taiwan is an important priority for Beijing, and the PRC has clearly signaled a willingness to fight a war to prevent highly unfavorable outcomes (such as formal Taiwan independence). PRC leaders have framed Taiwan as a "core" national interest, and China has for decades signaled—often in very costly ways—the island's importance to

Beijing.[17] These signals include military exercises and a willingness to risk crises (such as the Taiwan Strait crisis in 1995–1996); extensive investment in military capabilities designed with a Taiwan contingency in mind; and willingness to pay diplomatic costs (such as a delay in normalization in relations with Washington to obtain preferred outcomes in U.S. Taiwan policy), among others. In short, the PRC clearly prefers an outcome close to the unification end of the continuum, where Taiwan holds a subordinate status within a formally unified China, and the PRC views the Taiwan issue as an important national priority.

TAIWAN'S PREFERENCES DEPEND ON WHICH PARTY IS IN POWER

During the martial law era, the ROC government's official policy largely mirrored the PRC's: there was only one rightful government of China, and that was the ROC; Taiwan is part of China, and its de facto separation must end in formal unification. However, there was always a range of views on the island concerning Taiwan's sovereign status, and since democratization and the end of martial law, these views are openly expressed and embraced by different political parties and interest groups in Taiwan (as discussed in the previous chapter). Simply put, Taiwan's sovereign status is a contentious political issue in Taiwan; the two main political parties, the KMT and the DPP, have different positions on the issue; and those positions themselves change over time and contain ambiguities. Briefly, in recent years the KMT has endorsed a weak version of a one China principle in the form of the 1992 consensus; it views the ROC as sovereign, though its governing authority extends only to Taiwan and the other islands it controls; and it has opposed formal Taiwan independence.[18] Meanwhile, the DPP charter has since 1991 called for the establishment of an independent Republic of Taiwan, although more recently the party has framed its position as follows: Taiwan already is a sovereign and independent country that is named the ROC; thus a declaration of independence is unnecessary.[19] The DPP has refused to accept even a weak version of a one China principle, although Tsai

Ing-wen has adopted a somewhat more ambiguous stance on the 1992 consensus (not endorsing but not fully rejecting).[20]

Given these differences, I assume, in the context of the simple continuum sketched out in figure 5.1, that the KMT and the DPP have different ideal points with regard to Taiwan's status. I assume—again in the context of my stylized model—that the DPP would prefer (in an ideal world) an outcome near the independence end of the continuum: a formally independent Taiwan that enjoys international recognition. And the KMT's ideal point lies somewhere closer to the middle of the continuum—where the basic status quo is preserved, unification remains on the table, but there is little interest in entering into a unification agreement with the current government of the PRC.

THE STATUS QUO

I assume the contemporary status quo in the Taiwan Strait lies somewhere near the middle of the continuum sketched out in figure 5.1, far away from the two extremes of formal unification and formal independence. Clearly the status quo changes over time, as the discussion earlier made clear. The status quo under Ma Ying-jeou (a weak version of a one China principle), for instance, lay closer to the unification end of the continuum than the status quo under Tsai Ing-wen (who does not endorse a one China principle).

What I am assuming here, in other words, is that Taiwan—or more specifically, Taiwan's government at any particular time—has a considerable amount of agency in setting the status quo. To be certain, Taiwan's choices in this regard do not occur in a vacuum. Taiwan is under constant threat from the PRC, and choosing options closer to the independence end of the continuum carry substantial risk for the island. Likewise, certain features of the contemporary cross-strait relationship are obviously driven primarily by actions taken in Beijing, such as stepped-up military coercion directed against Taipei, or efforts to squeeze Taiwan's international space. But Taiwan has the ability to define its status in a way that more closely resembles formal independence (though doing so could trigger a military response, as I discuss in the next section), Taiwan can choose to accommodate Beijing by embracing a one China principle, and Taiwan ultimately would need to consent to any negotiated bargain over unification.

THE WAR OUTCOME

If China and Taiwan were to fight a war, Taiwan's status at the end of the war would still lie somewhere on the continuum outlined in figure 5.1. I have labeled this outcome as "W" (for war outcome) in figure 5.2. Note that this placement is arbitrary, and the logic of my discussion does not hinge on the precise location of W.

There are two ways to think about the war outcome in the model. First, it can be conceptualized as an implicitly or explicitly negotiated end to fighting. Figure 5.2 places the war outcome somewhat closer to the unification end of the continuum, which suggests that in this scenario, war ends with Taiwan agreeing (implicitly or explicitly) to be relatively accommodating on sovereignty issues. For instance, perhaps the war would end with Taiwan agreeing to accept a version of a one China principle, or formally renouncing independence. A second way of conceptualizing the war outcome is as a probabilistic outcome, where there is some probability that the war would end with China imposing its preferred outcome of formal unification (presumably by successfully occupying Taiwan). The higher that probability, the closer W would lie to the unification end of the continuum. The W outcome, in short, represents

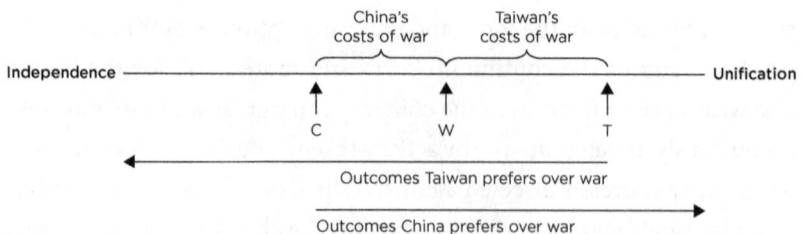

FIGURE 5.2 A model of cross-strait conflict.

Taiwan's expected level of sovereignty after the conclusion of fighting. The greater the probability that war would end on terms favorable to China, either via a negotiated settlement or via occupation, the farther to the right on the continuum W lies.

As I discussed earlier, one of the central assumptions of bargaining models of conflict is that war is costly for all countries that fight the war, regardless of its eventual outcome. Thus war is an inefficient way of resolving disputes, and the central puzzle of war is why states are unable to locate bargains peacefully that all should prefer to the war outcome.[21] If China and Taiwan were to fight a war in the Taiwan Strait, both sides would clearly incur substantial costs. Obviously there would be direct costs, including casualties to soldiers and civilians, the destruction of military hardware, and possibly extensive damage to civilian infrastructure. But beyond these direct costs, a war would have vast indirect consequences for both sides. Extensive economic ties across the Taiwan Strait would be threatened and possibly destroyed. Taiwan's civilian leaders would risk arrest and possible death in a PRC attack. A war, if it were to go poorly for China, could put the CCP's hold on power at risk. Were China to be widely viewed as the instigator of conflict, the international reputational damages to Beijing might be substantial, even if the war were to end on favorable terms for the PRC. Other countries, such as the United States, might impose economic sanctions on China. And so forth.

Thus I assume that the actual utility that Taiwan and China get from the war outcome lies not at point W but at some point farther away from their respective ideal points of independence and unification, once the costs of war are factored in. Thus in figure 5.2 Taiwan's war utility lies at point T, and China's war utility lies at point C. The higher China's costs of war, relative to the value it places on the Taiwan issue, the farther to the left C will lie; likewise, the higher Taiwan's costs of war, relative to the value it places on the sovereignty issue, the farther to the right T will lie (holding constant the expected outcome of war at W).

In other words, because war is costly, Taiwan would prefer to negotiate peacefully a bargain at point W, rather than fight a war to obtain that outcome. China likewise would prefer to negotiate a bargain at point W, rather than fight a war to obtain that same outcome. Indeed, the costs of fighting a war imply that both China and Taiwan would prefer a range of negotiated settlements over fighting a war. Because China's war utility lies at point C, China should prefer all points to the right of C over fighting a war, since all points to the right of C lie closer to Beijing's ideal point of unification. And, if we assume for now a Taiwan government that has an ideal outcome close to the independence end of the continuum, Taiwan prefers all outcomes to the left of point T over fighting a war, since all points to the left of T lie closer to that ideal point than the war outcome. As such, all outcomes between T and C leave both sides better off than the war outcome. In turn, as long as the status quo lies somewhere between T and C, both China and Taiwan should prefer that status quo over fighting a war.

THE ROLE OF THE UNITED STATES

The United States is clearly a critical actor in the Taiwan Strait. Washington has intervened in past Taiwan Strait crises, and expectations about its future behavior cast a long shadow over decision making in Taipei and Beijing. Even if we abstract away from likely U.S. actions in a cross-strait conflict, initiating a cross-strait military conflict would be a risky undertaking for Beijing; the possibility of U.S. involvement, in turn, greatly magnifies those risks. Likewise, the possibility that Washington might sit on the sidelines in the event of a cross-strait war magnifies the risks Taipei faces when it takes actions that are viewed in Beijing as provocations. Even in peacetime, the United States looms large in shaping the prospects for conflict in the Taiwan Strait. Arms sales to Taiwan, for instance, affect the cross-strait military balance of power, and extensive U.S. economic ties with China potentially increase China's expected costs of conflict.

In my stylized model of cross-strait conflict, I conceptualize the U.S. role as affecting different model parameters. For instance, I assume that the expected behavior of the United States in a cross-strait war has direct implications for the location of W. As the likelihood of direct and substantial U.S. intervention grows, W resides farther to the left on the continuum summarized in figure 5.2 (meaning war is less likely to end on terms favorable to the PRC than if the United States were to be uninvolved). Likewise, the possible involvement of the United States should affect each side's anticipated costs of war. For China, those costs would almost certainly increase were the United States to become involved; U.S. intervention, on the other hand, would likely help to limit Taiwan's expects war costs, at least on the margins.

In sum, I incorporate U.S. behavior, and expectations about its future behavior, into the model indirectly (rather than directly including the United States as a strategic player). Doing so helps to keep the model simple, though of course it means the model abstracts even more from the complicated cross-strait relationship.

UNCERTAINTY, COMMITMENT, AND PROSPECTS FOR WAR IN THE TAIWAN STRAIT

Thomas Christensen has written that the Taiwan issue is primarily about "coercion and political identity" rather than about territorial conquest.[22] The simple model that I have sketched out is largely consistent with such a characterization. I have assumed a Taiwan that can define its identity, but in the shadow of a possible PRC military response. Presumably, if a war were ever to occur in the Taiwan Strait, it would not be Taiwan that would initiate fighting. Thus, in the context of my simple model, war should be avoided so long as Taiwan adheres to a status quo that resides to the right of point C in figure 5.2; the utility that China derives from such a status quo would then exceed its war utility, which resides at point C. In short, we can think of point C as China's reservation value, the least favorable bargain (from its standpoint) that it will accept rather than initiating war to try to achieve something better. In the context of this model, to understand why war would occur in the Taiwan Strait, we need to understand what keeps the two sides from settling on a status quo that resides between C and T. As I noted briefly earlier in this chapter, bargaining model theorists have highlighted two types of problems that can contribute to states' inability to settle on peaceful outcomes that should leave all better off than the war outcome.

First, uncertainty can complicate bargaining. Although states have some understanding of the capabilities of other states, that understanding is necessarily incomplete. States, for instance, go to great lengths to keep some of their military plans and capabilities secret, so as to preserve possible tactical advantages on the battlefield. Likewise, state leaders are likely to have only limited understanding of the resolve of other leaders. Resolve can be thought of as the willingness to pay costs to achieve desired ends; it captures how much a leader really cares about obtaining a favorable bargain over the issue in dispute. Meanwhile, not only is it difficult to gauge capabilities and resolve, but leaders often have strategic incentives to misrepresent these characteristics. Leaders sometimes want to feign stronger capabilities and greater resolve than they really possess so as to obtain a better bargain by bluffing. On the other hand, leaders sometimes want to feign weakness to achieve tactical success on the battlefield. Wars, then, can arise because leaders have private information about capabilities and resolve, and strategic incentives to misrepresent that information.[23]

Second, credible commitment problems can make it difficult to avoid conflict even if state leaders in principle would be willing to accept peaceful solutions. Some scholars, for instance, have framed the problem of preventive war as a credible commitment problem.[24] Here, an established power initiates war to prevent a rising power from overtaking it. The rising power might recognize that it would lose such a war with devastating consequence and so should, in principle, prefer some negotiated settlement instead, such as a commitment to respect the established power's interests even as the rising power becomes stronger. The established power, however, could view such a commitment as lacking credibility: once the rising power becomes strong, it will be in a position where it can renege on its agreement and infringe on the established power's interests with impunity. Scholars have identified a number of different credible commitment problems like this that could complicate bargaining between states and potentially lead to war.

Both types of problems—private information with incentives to misrepresent, and the difficulties of making commitments credible—loom large in the Taiwan Strait. Consider first information problems. If we return to the simple model sketched out in figure 5.2, imagine that a Taiwan government has an ideal point of formal Taiwan independence, if it could be achieved peacefully. Recognizing that war with China would have devastating consequences, such a Taiwan government should claim a level of status just to the right of China's reservation value (point C). Doing so yields an outcome that provides Taiwan with the highest level of status that China would accept over the war outcome.

Identifying point C is quite complicated, however, even in the context of this highly stylized model: to assess where C lies requires an understanding of China's expectations about the likely war outcome, China's expectations about its likely war costs, and how those costs compare to the value China places on the Taiwan issue. All these values are private information held by Beijing, and each is shaped by numerous factors—including trends highlighted in part I of this book. For instance, Beijing's expectations about the war outcome will be informed by its assessment of the cross-strait balance of military power, its assessment of Taiwan's resolve, and its assessment of U.S. capacity and resolve to intervene on Taiwan's behalf. Furthermore, Beijing has obvious incentives to overstate its resolve. Because the PRC's ideal point is unification, it wants Taiwan's government to believe that C lies as far right as possible. Thus even though there should exist a range of outcomes that both Taiwan and the PRC prefer over war, locating those outcomes is likely to be complicated by information problems.

Likewise, a number of credible commitment problems lurk in cross-strait relations and could undermine efforts to maintain peace. Most obviously, it is difficult for the PRC's authoritarian government to make credible promises concerning Taiwanese autonomy under its proposed one country, two systems framework. The erosion of autonomy in Hong Kong illustrates clearly that Beijing will have a hard time tolerating genuine dissent in a Taiwan that has entered into a unification agreement.

The next two chapters explore, at much greater length, how information and credible commitment problems could trigger war in the

Taiwan Strait. I reference the simple model sketched out in this chapter throughout, and I organize my analysis around two broad conflict scenarios: The first scenario, the subject of chapter 6, is rooted in efforts by Taiwan to construct a sovereign status that lies closer to formal independence. The PRC has long tried to deter Taiwan from undertaking policies that—from Beijing's perspective—have the effect of making Taiwan appear more like a sovereign and independent country today, or that could lead to this outcome in the future. War, in this scenario, arises because PRC deterrence fails; that is, the PRC is unable to deter what is sometimes termed *Taiwan revisionism*. I argue that information problems are especially salient for this broad type of war scenario, but commitment problems are also relevant and can contribute to deterrence failure.

The second scenario, the subject of chapter 7, is rooted in PRC efforts to advance its goal of unification with Taiwan. Both Taiwan and the United States have long aimed to deter Beijing from pursuing unification coercively using military force. War in this scenario arises because Taiwan/U.S. deterrence fails; that is, Taipei and Washington are unable to deter what might be termed *Chinese revisionism* on the Taiwan issue. I argue again that both information and credible commitment problems can contribute to this type of deterrence failure, emphasizing in particular that a fundamental and dangerous credible commitment problem looms over the cross-strait relationship if current trends—including, most important, the shifting balance of military power in China's favor—continue into the future.

6

THE PROBLEM OF
TAIWAN REVISIONISM

I n 2001, during the second year of the Chen Shui-bian administration in Taiwan and the first year of the George W. Bush administration in the United States, the documentary series *PBS Frontline* ran an episode called "Dangerous Strait: Exploring the Future of U.S.-China Relations and the Long Simmering Issue of Taiwan." It explored whether the Taiwan Strait should be thought of as a flashpoint for conflict and included interviews with several experts and officials in China, the United States, and Taiwan. The general sentiment of these interviews was that the Taiwan issue was indeed dangerous, with some suggesting that the Taiwan Strait was among the most volatile flashpoints in the world. And for several of the interviewees, war—were it to occur in the near term—would most likely be triggered by what might be termed *Taiwan revisionism*.[1]

Simply put, a number of trends, events, and policies—including the growth in Taiwan-centric identity; the election of a DPP president for the first time; Chen Shui-bian's rejection of a "one China" principle and insistence that Taiwan was a sovereign and independent country (consistent with his party's charter)—implied the construction of a new cross-strait status quo that resided farther from Beijing's ideal point of unification. And many in Taiwan, including probably President Chen himself, hoped to both consolidate this new status quo and to push it even closer to formal independence. Thus in the PBS documentary prominent U.S. China expert David M. Lampton emphasized the need "to deter Taiwan from engaging in such risky behavior that they precipitate an attack," noting further that the PRC would likely remain patient were Taiwan to eschew such behavior. *New York Times* Beijing bureau chief Erik Eckholm argued that "what the Chinese are most afraid of is a real movement toward independence. Which they have to stop." And PRC Foreign Ministry spokesperson Zhu Bangzao reiterated PRC official policy that "Taiwan independence means war."[2]

The views expressed in the *Frontline* episode reflected an assessment of the cross-strait relationship widely shared by regional experts at the time. In this assessment, the cross-strait relationship was tense and conflict-prone; PRC leaders cared deeply about the Taiwan issue and viewed unification as a long-term goal but were generally reluctant to risk war in the near term; Taiwan, particularly during the Lee Teng-hui and Chen Shui-bian administrations, was redefining its relationship with China and potentially would pursue more radical changes in the future (such as formal Taiwan independence); and, despite PRC patience on unification, Beijing would not (or, in some formulations, could not) accept formal Taiwan independence and would initiate war to try to stop it regardless of cost. Consequently, the key potential source of instability or war in the Taiwan Strait—at least in the near term—resided in potential Taiwan efforts to redefine its status to look more like a formally independent country.[3] Although analysts today tend to give equal or greater weight to PRC revisionism as a potential trigger of a cross-strait military conflict (which will be the focus of the next chapter), many still view Taiwan revisionism as highly salient.[4] And the specter of Taiwan "separatism" continues to dominate PRC threats directed against Taiwan: like leaders before him, Xi Jinping has framed his refusal to renounce the use of force against Taiwan as directed at the "interference of external forces" and the "very small number of 'Taiwan independence' separatists and their activities."[5]

As emphasized in this book's introduction, however, it isn't obvious why war would ever emerge as a consequence of revisionist behavior by Taiwan. War would be enormously costly for Taiwan, regardless of how it plays out; even if the PRC could not successfully occupy Taiwan, the island would remain highly vulnerable to PRC attack. Furthermore, even in the most optimistic scenario where a revisionist Taiwan government—presumably with the aid of U.S. intervention—were to "win" a war and obtain its most preferred outcome of formal independence, it is worth emphasizing that this would amount to largely symbolic gains over the status quo of de facto independence.[6] Thus, as Steve Tsang has put it, no Taiwanese president would "intentionally announce a policy that will immediately cause China to attack Taiwan."[7] The war outcome would almost certainly leave Taiwan worse off than the status quo. Why, then, would Taiwan ever pursue policies so revisionist that they risked triggering a war with the PRC?

In this chapter, I show that Taiwan revisionism is potentially dangerous in the context of the information and credible commitment problems briefly discussed in chapter 5. Drawing from extant literature, I tease out two causal pathways through which Taiwan revisionism could potentially trigger conflict in the Taiwan Strait. In the first scenario, a revisionist Taiwan government crosses PRC bottom lines on sovereignty issues, triggering a military response. I contend that such a scenario, if it were to occur, would primarily arise as a consequence of information problems. I further argue, however, that it has been relatively straightforward for the United States, China, and Taiwan to manage these information problems and thus avoid a major military confrontation arising as a consequence of this sort of scenario. And I argue as well that major trends in the cross-strait relationship are making this scenario less likely.

The second causal pathway is one that I have elsewhere somewhat inelegantly labeled a "pessimistic trends analysis scenario."[8] Here, it is the potential for *future* revisionist Taiwan behavior that could lead to a cross-strait conflict. In this scenario, war could occur if two conditions hold. First, Beijing becomes pessimistic about long-term trends in the Taiwan Strait, believing, for instance, that U.S. support for Taiwan is likely to increase, or that support for independence in Taiwan will continue to grow. Second, Beijing believes that use of military force in the short term could help to arrest or reverse those trends. I will show that this second scenario is ultimately grounded in a credible commitment problem analogous to the problems that rising challengers face when trying to assuage the concerns of established powers. Finally, I will maintain that this scenario remains a source of some concern, particularly in light of societal trends in Taiwan and trends in the U.S.-Taiwan and U.S.-China relationships.[9]

TAIWAN REVISIONISM, PRC RED LINES, AND PRIVATE INFORMATION

One straightforward scenario for a cross-strait military conflict involves a revisionist Taiwan government implementing policies, such as (but not necessarily limited to) a formal declaration of Taiwanese independence, that cross PRC red lines and trigger a military response from China. As the interviews in the *Frontline* episode suggest, analysts of cross-strait relations—particularly during the 1990s and 2000s—often had this sort of scenario in mind when thinking about how war could occur in the Taiwan Strait. And with good reason: the scenario captured key features of the cross-strait relationship at the time. The Lee Teng-hui and Chen Shui-bian administrations pursued clearly revisionist policies and actions relating to Taiwan's sovereign status, and Beijing often warned Taiwan at the time that these policies risked a PRC military response. In this section, I tease out the logic of what I will call a "red-line conflict" scenario and show that China, Taiwan and the United States have generally done a reasonably good job of managing the risks associated with this type of scenario. I suggest, therefore, that the likelihood of a red-line conflict has always been relatively low. Finally, I argue that long-term major trends in cross-strait relations have made the red-line conflict scenario even less likely, although I hedge my arguments here by drawing attention to a few worrisome recent trends.

THE RED-LINE CONFLICT SCENARIO

During the Lee Teng-hui and Chen Shui-bian administrations, crisis bargaining in the Taiwan Strait often took the form of a revisionist

Taiwan testing China's red lines and the PRC responding with military threats. As noted in chapter 4, after Taiwan transitioned to a fully democratic country in the 1990s, longstanding ROC government orthodoxy on sovereignty issues was increasingly at odds with mainstream views in Taiwan society. As president, Lee Teng-hui aimed, on the one hand, to align himself and the KMT with these mainstream views and, on the other hand, to foster the development of a new Taiwan identity grounded in the island's many accomplishments, including both economic development and democratization. His speech at Cornell University in 1995 highlighted both a deep dissatisfaction with the current status quo of an internationally marginalized Taiwan and a determination to alter that status quo. As he put it in the speech: "Frankly, our people are not happy with the status accorded our nation by the international community. . . . Some say that it is impossible for us to break out of the diplomatic isolation we face, but we will do our utmost to 'demand the impossible.' "[10]

In this book's introduction, I summarized some of the concrete policies and statements outlined by both Lee and Chen that challenged the idea of a one China principle and that highlighted Taiwan's otherness from China. Examples included Lee's description of cross-strait relations in 1999 as "state-to-state relations, or at least special state-to-state relations"; Chen's characterization of relations as "one country on each side of the strait"; his renaming of state entities to emphasize their Taiwaneseness rather than their Chineseness; his pursuit of a new constitution more "suitable to Taiwan"; and his pursuit of a national referendum endorsing Taiwan's entry into the UN under the name "Taiwan." Beijing often responded to these policies with bellicose threats. Most notably, after Lee's Cornell speech, the PRC launched a series of military exercises in the Taiwan Strait that triggered what is often described as the third Taiwan Straits crisis, and which culminated in PRC missile tests near Taiwan's major ports in 1996. Beijing was signaling to Taiwan, and Washington, that it was resolved to fight a war to prevent formal Taiwan independence.[11]

Thus, the dynamics of cross-strait relations during the Lee and Chen administrations suggested a clear pathway to a cross-strait military conflict, where revisionist policies in Taiwan trigger a PRC military attack aimed at halting formal Taiwan independence. In the context of the simple model summarized in figure 5.2, this scenario can be conceptualized as a revisionist Taiwan government redefining the status quo in cross-strait relations to be closer to the independence end of the continuum. If that redefined status crosses to the left of point C, then the PRC prefers to initiate war rather than accept that new status quo. Point C, as noted in the previous chapter, thus represents the PRC's indifference point between accepting a particular status quo and initiating a war to try to redefine that status quo; it can be thought of as China's red line on sovereignty issues.

As mentioned earlier, no Taiwan government would willfully cross China's red line, given the high costs of war. If Taiwan could know with certainty where China's red line lies, it should choose a level of sovereign status just to the right of that line. The problem, however, is that Taiwan cannot know with certainty where the line sits. Not only are China's expectations about the war outcome and China's expected costs of war private information, but the PRC has clear incentives to bluff: to overstate its resolve to fight a war so as to make any moves toward independence risky for Taiwan. Indeed, Beijing is quite ambiguous about the location of its red line: although the PRC has been clear that a formal declaration of independence would trigger a military response, it has been less clear about what steps short of formal independence would trigger such a response.[12] Thus war occurs in this scenario because it is hard for Taiwan to know with certainty the location of Beijing's red line on sovereignty issues; a revisionist Taiwan government could, in turn, unintentionally cross this line, triggering a military response.

The information problem at the root of the red-line conflict scenario mirrors a problem that has helped to trigger numerous past military conflicts: what is sometimes called "overconfidence" or "overoptimism" or "false optimism" about the likely war outcome.[13] Indeed, Stephen Van Evera asserts that "at least some false optimism about relative power preceded every major war since 1740," while Alex Weisiger suggests that "overoptimism on at least one side about the probability and ease of victory is easily the most common feature of the start of war."[14] If we return to figure 5.2, the red-line conflict war scenario ultimately occurs because the PRC is overly optimistic about its likely war payoff and sets its red line (C) too far to the right (so that even a Taiwan government that accurately forecasts the likely outcome of war might stumble across it); or because Taiwan is overly optimistic about PRC expectations of its likely war payoff and thus assumes that the PRC's red line lies farther left than it really does; or both. And, because the PRC has incentives to misrepresent C's location, PRC statements about its bottom lines on sovereignty issues don't necessarily resolve the problem: Taiwan, and especially an overconfident Taiwan, could take these statements as bluffs.[15]

Consider, for instance, the near crisis that erupted after Lee Teng-hui articulated his "special state-to-state relations" formulation in 1999. The new formula for cross-strait relations appeared to be a rejection of a one China principle and from Beijing's standpoint represented an effort to redefine the cross-strait status quo closer to formal independence. Beijing, not surprisingly, was highly critical and threatening in its response. A Foreign Ministry spokesperson warned Lee and his government "not to underestimate the Chinese Government's firm determination to uphold national sovereignty, dignity and territorial integrity . . . don't underestimate the courage and force of the Chinese people to oppose separatism and Taiwan independence."[16] The Lee government, on the other hand, was openly dismissive of that "determination." Lee, citing China's own problems, asked "where is the means to willy-nilly take action against Taiwan,"[17] while ROC defense minister Tang Fei asserted that Chinese use of "force would be a last resort, because they are concerned about international pressure and economic growth."[18] The episode, of course, did not lead to war. However, the clear danger of this particular near crisis—and the danger of Taiwan revisionism more generally—is that this sort of optimism could have been misplaced. Had Lee in fact been overoptimistic at the time about China's reluctance to use force, then his statements might, in retrospect, have echoed European soldiers' August 1914 promises to return home for Christmas, or Saddam Hussein's confident belief that the United States lacked the resolve to invade Iraq.[19]

MANAGING THE RISKS OF A
RED-LINE CONFLICT SCENARIO

The statements and actions undertaken by the Lee Teng-hui and Chen Shui-bian governments suggest that analysts at the time were right to be worried about the risks of a red-line conflict scenario. Of course, although at times characterized by considerable tension, the Taiwan Strait nevertheless averted war throughout both administrations. I argue in this section that this outcome was not simply the result of luck. Rather, I suggest that two factors have made the red-line conflict scenario a relatively straightforward strategic problem, and that consequently the United States, China, and Taiwan have been able to manage the risks of a red-line conflict scenario relatively easily and successfully to date. First, because an information problem lies at the root of the red-line conflict scenario, the risks of this type of conflict can be managed via costly signaling. As I will elaborate on below, even though talk might be cheap, the PRC has a range of options at its disposal to signal its commitment to the Taiwan issue more credibly. Second, the nature of the good in dispute—Taiwan's sovereign status—is such that Taiwan revisionism entails taking concrete risks to obtain primarily symbolic gains. In turn, Washington has tended to discourage Taiwan revisionism, and Taiwan governments themselves generally have strong incentives to tread cautiously when contemplating what might be viewed in Beijing as revisionist policies.

Avoiding the red-line conflict scenario requires that Beijing successfully deter revisionist Taiwan governments from crossing its red line on sovereignty issues. As we have seen, the PRC has issued numerous explicit threats in this regard. Less clear, however, is whether these threats are credible, since Beijing has incentives to overstate its resolve. However, the PRC can—and has—partially overcome this problem through costly signaling, where Beijing incurs some costs in making threats or imposing costs on Taiwan. Demonstrating a willingness to incur costs should, in turn, increase confidence in Taipei that the pursuit of revisionist policies means risking conflict because it eliminates the possibility that China is simply a paper tiger unwilling to take any serious action against

Taipei.[20] In the case of cross-strait relations during the Lee and Chen administrations, China signaled in a variety of ways, including tough rhetoric (as noted earlier), which both put Beijing's reputation on the line and at times could be unnerving to international investors; provocative military exercises and maneuvers that had the potential to poison relations with the United States and countries in East Asia; its military modernization and in particular its deployment of systems capable of striking Taiwan (as discussed in chapter 2); and occasional economic sanctions directed against Taiwan (as noted in chapter 1). Although uncertainty about the precise location of Beijing's red line remains, these types of costly signals have effectively enhanced the credibility of PRC deterrence and induced a greater level of caution in Taipei than might otherwise have been the case. As Ross persuasively argues, Beijing after the 1995–1996 Taiwan Strait crisis had credibly established that it was prepared to fight a war to prevent Taiwan independence.[21]

Of course, even though costly signaling helped to reduce the severity of the information problem lying at the root of the red-line conflict scenario, the problem was not obviated entirely. While Beijing credibly established that Taiwan independence was a casus belli, less clear was what steps short of that extreme might lead to war. Beijing's 2005 anti-secession law, for instance, asserts that "major incidents" of Taiwan independence were cause for war without identifying precisely what might count as "major." Yet a second factor has helped to further mitigate the likelihood of the red-line conflict scenario: that Taiwan revisionism entails risking concrete losses to advance mostly symbolic gains.

Taiwan, of course, already enjoys de facto independence: leaders are democratically elected, and the PRC government has no authority to make decisions in Taipei. We have already seen that, even though different Taiwan governments have conceptualized the status quo in different ways, all have done so in a way that characterizes the Taiwan government (whether they call it Taiwan or the ROC) as sovereign. Taiwan revisionism on sovereignty issues does not change the basic reality of a functionally independent state; rather, it seeks to change what the state is called (Taiwan versus the ROC), the symbols associated with the state (such as changing the flag or removing memorials that glorify

Chiang Kai-shek), and the way that people in Taiwan think about themselves (identifying as Taiwanese rather than Chinese) and the future (such as whether unification is even considered a possible long-term outcome). Thus, to the extent that Taiwan revisionism risks a PRC military attack, it means that Taiwan governments pursuing revisionist policies are risking concrete losses to people's lives and livelihoods (and possibly to Taiwan's de facto independence itself) in order to advance these mostly symbolic gains.[22] This feature of Taiwan revisionism, in turn, helps to mitigate the risks of a red-line conflict scenario through two mechanisms.

First, the symbolic nature of gains from Taiwan revisionism has tended to intensify U.S. criticism of revisionist Taiwan initiatives. Given U.S. interests in Taiwan's security (as discussed in chapter 3), the United States clearly wishes to deter PRC attacks against the island. Less clear, however, is how the United States benefits from revisionist Taiwan actions that push the status quo from de facto independence toward formal independence. In fact, as I emphasized in chapter 3, the United States has in the past signaled that it does not view the symbolic gains that might be obtained from revisionist policies as worth the heightened risk of conflict. The George W. Bush administration in particular was at times quite critical of Chen Shui-bian for some of his revisionist policies, including his decision to hold a referendum on UN membership at the same time as the presidential election in 2008. Then deputy assistant secretary of state Thomas J. Christensen explained U.S. criticism in a speech in 2007: "As much as we oppose Beijing's threat to use force, we also take it seriously, and Taipei cannot afford to do otherwise. It is for this reason that Taiwan's security is inextricably linked to the avoidance of needlessly provocative behavior. This does not mean that Taipei should or can be passive in the face of PRC pressure. But it means that responsible leadership in Taipei has to anticipate potential Chinese red lines and reactions and avoid unnecessary and unproductive provocations."[23] In short, the United States has tended to criticize Taiwan revisionist behavior as unnecessarily provocative because it increases the risk of conflict to obtain mostly symbolic gains. U.S. criticism could be politically costly to a Taiwan president whose country depends heavily on the United States for security, but it also increases the downside risks of conflict for Taiwan by raising the possibility that the United States might be less enthusiastic about intervening in a conflict seen in Washington as triggered by Taiwan provocations.

Second, the primarily symbolic nature of gains from Taiwan revisionism helps to undercut its allure to Taiwan's domestic audience. To be certain, symbolism and identity are important, and the mostly symbolic nature of the potential gains associated with actions such as name changes does not mean that their pursuit would never lead to real conflict. Disputes over sites that have religious significance, for instance, can be especially prone to conflict.[24] And disputes can become more intractable if one or both sides adopt a discourse that frames the dispute as all-or-nothing (such as a PRC discourse that frames any outcome short of formal unification as unacceptable, or a discourse in Taiwan that frames any outcome short of formal independence as unacceptable).[25] Nevertheless, as shown in chapter 4, Taiwan's electorate is quite pragmatic on sovereignty issues. For instance, although most support independence in principle, most do not support independence if it means the PRC will attack. In turn, Taiwan presidents risk domestic political backlash if cross-strait relations (and U.S.-Taiwan relations, as noted) appear to worsen as a consequence of mostly symbolic efforts to assert Taiwan's separate identity. This isn't to say that advocating revisionist policies is always politically counterproductive. For instance, Chen Shui-bian won reelection in 2004 after launching a national referendum law, advocating for a new constitution, and framing cross-strait relations as "one country on each side of the Taiwan Strait," among other things. After his relatively moderate approach to cross-strait relations early in his first term failed to produce any breakthroughs with Beijing on issues like direct links, Chen may have concluded that his only path to reelection was to make sovereignty the key issue dimension and to pursue a "rally the base" strategy. On the other hand, the political dividends of Chen's revisionist policies appeared to decline over time, and his UN referendum gambit did not stave off a landslide defeat for the DPP in the 2008 presidential and legislative elections. While other factors—including the corruption scandals that came to dominate Chen's second term in office—were obviously relevant (and probably more important), the Chen presidency does suggest that clearly revisionist policies can become a political liability to the degree they appear to trigger worsening cross-strait relations.

COULD A RED-LINE CONFLICT SCENARIO STILL HAPPEN?

Some of the broad trends outlined in part I of this book have worked to further reduce the likelihood of the red-line conflict scenario, even beyond the factors just outlined that have helped to make the scenario a relatively manageable strategic problem.

First, the trends in Taiwanese public opinion on sovereignty issues discussed in chapter 4 for the most part continue to reward relative moderation in cross-strait policies. Even though there is very little interest in unification in Taiwan, and even though a large majority of the island's population now identifies as exclusively Taiwanese, it nevertheless remains the case that the Taiwan public is still relatively pragmatic on sovereignty issues. Support for independence drops precipitously if it is expected to lead to a conflict with China, and most Taiwanese continue to support the status quo in cross-strait relations. Tsai Ing-wen's lopsided win over challenger William Lai in the DPP presidential primary of 2019—at a time when Tsai's popularity was tenuous and her party had recently suffered a sharp rebuke in local elections in 2018—appeared to confirm that moderation continued to pay, even within the DPP. Lai, who once called himself a "political worker for Taiwan independence," was supported by traditionalists within the DPP, including many who advocated for a stronger stance on sovereignty issues. But Lai ultimately refrained in the primary campaign from advocating cross-strait policies that diverged markedly from Tsai, perhaps recognizing that advocacy of formal Taiwan independence was unlikely to be a winning political platform.[26]

Furthermore, the broad trends described in chapters 1 and 2— including deepening cross-strait economic integration and a shifting balance of military power—have the combined effect of further reducing the attractiveness of revisionist policies from Taiwan's perspective. Increased cross-strait economic ties should have the effect of increasing the costs of military conflict for both China and Taiwan (since war would put many of these ties at risk).[27] If we return to figure 5.2, increasing costs of war suggest that deepening cross-strait economic ties over the past few decades have the ceteris paribus effect of pushing China's red line (C) to the left, and Taiwan's expected war payoff (T) to the right. These shifts are summarized in the lighter arrows in figure 6.1. Meanwhile, the shifting cross-strait military balance of power should mean that, if war occurs, it will end on terms increasingly favorable to China (in figure 5.2, point W shifts right). In turn, the ceteris paribus effect of the shifting balance of power is to push China's red line (C) to the right, while also pushing Taiwan's expected war utility (T) to the right. These effects of a shifting balance of military power are summarized in the darker arrows in figure 6.1.

Thus, although deepening economic ties reduce the attractiveness of the war outcome for both sides, the shifting military balance of power has opposite implications for the two sides, reducing the attractiveness of the war outcome for Taiwan but increasing the attractiveness of the war outcome for Beijing. Taken together, the trends suggest that Taiwan's war utility has been getting unambiguously worse: both a shifting military balance and deepening economic ties have the effect of pushing Taiwan's war payoff, T, to the right (toward the unification end of the continuum). But the trends have contradictory, and hence ambiguous, effects on China's war utility (C, China's red line). The net effect,

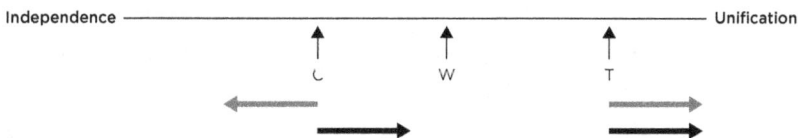

FIGURE 6.1 Economic ties, a shifting balance of power, and the red-line conflict scenario. Dark arrows represent effects of a shifting balance of military power. Light arrows represent effects of economic integration.

then, is to increase the risks of Taiwan revisionism. Since trends have ambiguous impact on China's red line, Taiwan has no reason to think it has more leeway to maneuver toward independence. On the other hand, the downside risks of pushing too far—and triggering a military response—are unambiguously growing for Taiwan (as its war payoff T continues to worsen). Thus major structural trends over the past few decades encourage moderation in Taiwan's policies, where the potential benefits of revisionism are increasingly outweighed by the risks associated with it.

LOOKING TO THE FUTURE

My analysis to this point suggests that the risk of a red-line conflict scenario has always been relatively limited because of the nature of the strategic problem, and that broad trends over the past few decades have made the scenario even less likely to occur. Still, just because the scenario may be unlikely does not mean that it could not realistically occur. To the contrary, I conclude this section by drawing attention to several factors that could increase the relevance of the red-line conflict scenario in the years ahead.

First, even though domestic political dynamics in Taiwan have largely rewarded caution on cross-strait relations in recent years, the fact remains that there is a sizable base in the pan-green coalition that would like to see stronger actions on sovereignty-related issues. Although William Lai lost his primary challenge to Tsai in 2019, there is no guarantee that a candidate advocating a more robust agenda on sovereignty issues— and from the PRC perspective more revisionist—won't capture a future DPP primary. To the extent that the DPP were to move again toward a more a more revisionist agenda, the PRC would likely have itself to blame, at least in part. Beijing's relentless pressure on Tsai despite her relatively cautious approach to cross-strait relations could easily lead future DPP politicians to conclude that caution does not pay: it still leads to unflinching hostility from the PRC. And, given the recent troubles of the KMT—which has polled extremely poorly since fall 2019 and has now lost two landslide presidential elections in a row—it is clearly quite possible that a more avowedly revisionist DPP candidate could be elected president of Taiwan in the future.

Second, in contrast to the Chen Shui-bian administration, when both the PRC and the United States were highly critical of Chen's revisionist foreign and domestic policies, the two countries do not see eye-to-eye on Tsai Ing-wen. In Washington, there is widespread agreement that Tsai has generally been much more cautious in her cross-strait policies compared to Chen, and that Beijing is consequently primarily to blame for the recent increase in cross-strait tension. But PRC analysts generally do not share this assessment of Tsai and view her as quite revisionist in her own right.[28] In turn, unlike the mid-2000s, when Washington and Beijing were sending the same message to Taipei (to cool it), today they are sending mixed messages. As China turns the screws on Taiwan, Washington, as discussed in chapter 3, has been building closer security ties with Taiwan and indeed often frames those ties as a consequence of increasing PRC pressure. Beijing, in turn, today views Taiwan's efforts to improve ties with Washington as one of Tsai's greatest transgressions, and if China concludes that U.S. support is effectively green-lighting what it sees as revisionist Taiwan behavior, it could conclude that a stronger response is needed.

Third, Beijing's red line itself may be changing, meaning that Beijing is becoming less willing to tolerate outcomes it might have tolerated in the past. Consider several recent trends, including a continuing shift in the military balance of power; a recent slowing in cross-strait economic integration (noted in chapter 1, and which could become more pronounced in a postpandemic world); and a worsening U.S.-China relationship (which might give China less to lose from a war). All these recent trends have the impact of reducing China's war costs or increasing its likelihood of prevailing in a conflict; all, in other words, improve China's expected war utility and consequently should make Beijing less tolerant of Taiwan revisionism. In chapter 7 I discuss the implications of a shifting PRC red line at much greater length, as a shifting line opens the door to growing PRC revisionism as an underlying cause of war. But here it is worth noting that a shifting line can also contribute to the red-line conflict scenario teased out in this section. The problem here arises in part from government turnover in Taiwan. When Tsai Ing-wen entered office, she changed the status quo in the Taiwan Strait (relative to the Ma government) by refusing to endorse the 1992 consensus; this shift, although strongly criticized in Beijing, was insufficient to trigger a military conflict in the Taiwan Strait. Now imagine that a future KMT government (perhaps one that comes to power in 2024) reaffirms some version of a one China principle that resembles the 1992 consensus. Presumably a successor DPP government would again, like Tsai, walk away from a formula that remains anathema to core DPP principles; such a government, moreover, would presumably assume it could safely do so having already observed Tsai walk away from the 1992 consensus. If PRC red lines are shifting, however, then it may be that a future shift to a DPP government—even one espousing relatively moderate policies like the current Tsai government—could potentially trigger a serious crisis in the Taiwan Strait.

Finally, although the PRC has a range of options at its disposal through which to signal the location of its red lines, there are reasons to expect it to rely especially heavily on military signaling in the future. Economic sanctions, for instance, can signal resolve, but they also can be counter-productive, hurting the very constituencies in Taiwan (those with a business stake in stable cross-strait relations) that are least supportive of Taiwan independence to begin with.[29] Moreover, because Taiwan is already relatively isolated in the international arena, the marginal impact of further diplomatic sanctions is probably declining as well. And, in fact, the PRC (as noted earlier) has frequently signaled using various military activities since Tsai Ing-wen became Taiwan's president in 2016. Military signaling, of course, carries its own risks, including most obviously that an accident could occur—either as Taiwanese jets scramble to intercept PRC jets operating near Taiwan, or as the United States engages in its own signaling by publicizing naval transits through the Taiwan Strait. While the likelihood that an accident would lead to unintended war is low,[30] a midair collision or an incident at sea could easily trigger a crisis, and some analysts have pinpointed this risk as especially worrisome in recent dialogues involving Taiwan experts from the United States and China.[31]

PESSIMISM IN BEIJING AND THE RISKS OF PREVENTIVE WAR TO KEEP TAIWAN FROM SLIPPING AWAY

During the Chen Shui-bian administration, Thomas Christensen published a series of articles warning about the dangers of pessimism in Beijing about long-term trends in the Taiwan Strait.[32] He argued that such pessimism could lead even a defensively minded PRC government to initiate military force, particularly if Beijing perceived a "closing window of opportunity" to prevent Taiwan independence.[33] PRC pessimism was especially strong immediately after Chen Shui-bian's narrow reelection as Taiwan's president in 2004, when there also appeared to be a realistic chance that the DPP could capture the legislature in year-end elections.[34] Beijing feared that a DPP with unified control of Taiwan's political system would institute changes relating to sovereignty issues (such as constitutional reform meant to redefine Taiwan's status) that would be difficult to reverse.

In the end, the DPP failed to win a majority in Legislative Yuan elections of 2004, and Chen was unable to undertake constitutional reforms; PRC pessimism waned as the DPP's popularity dropped sharply during Chen's second term. Yet the dynamic that Christensen warned about in the mid-2000s is relevant again today, with unified DPP governance and back-to-back landslide presidential victories. In this section, I describe a scenario for conflict rooted in pessimism in Beijing about *future* Taiwan revisionism. I show that such a scenario derives from a credible commitment problem akin to the type of commitment problem that sometimes emerges as a consequence of changes in the balance of power between countries. And I argue that although some of the long-term trends described in part I of this book help to mitigate against this type of scenario, others—including, most important, changes within Taiwan—give reason for concern.

TAIWAN REVISIONISM AS A
COMMITMENT PROBLEM

In chapters 3 and 4 I outlined several trends that the PRC views with deep concern. For example, support for unification in Taiwan has declined over time and is dropping even more sharply as the PRC undercuts one country, two systems in Hong Kong. Taiwan's citizens increasingly self-identify as solely Taiwanese, rather than as Chinese or as both Chinese and Taiwanese. Younger Taiwanese, moreover, are especially likely to share these views—suggesting as well that these trends could become even more pronounced over time. More recently, the KMT has suffered major electoral setbacks, and its level of support is low. And several indicators suggest a deepening U.S.-Taiwan security relationship even as the broader U.S.-China relationship appears as though it could drift into a new cold war. These trends, in turn, have led some observers to suggest that China may be at risk of losing Taiwan for good.[35] To the degree that elites in Beijing share this assessment, it opens the door to a war scenario that resembles the logic of preventive war.

Existing literature on preventive wars suggests they are most likely to occur in the context of a power transition. If a powerful country, A, fears that a weaker country, B, will grow stronger in the future, then A might try to stop B's rise while it still has the capability to do so. This will especially be the case if A expects that B, once it is strong, will act in ways that are contrary to A's interests. Of course, wars are costly, and so both countries would presumably benefit from some sort of agreement whereby B promises to act with restraint as it grows stronger in exchange for a promise by A not to attack. The problem, however, is that such promises are unlikely to be credible: once B becomes powerful, it will have the capacity to simply walk away from previous commitments. A commitment problem thus lies at the root of preventive wars, and a number of scholars have argued that the problem can be difficult to resolve and has led in the past to protracted and destructive wars.[36]

In the Taiwan Strait, the logic of prevention centers not on a shifting balance of power, but rather on political trends in Taiwan and the nature of U.S.-Taiwan relations. Nevertheless, the basic logic of the underlying credible commitment problem is similar to that which occurs during power transitions. If Chinese leaders are pessimistic about long-term political trends in Taiwan, or they believe that the United States is likely to move in the future toward an unconditional commitment to Taiwan's security, it can be difficult to assuage these concerns today. As we saw with the Ma administration's embrace of the 1992 consensus, for instance, commitment by a Taiwan government to a particular conceptualization of Taiwan's sovereign status is not credible over the long term: ultimately if such a conceptualization is unpopular in democratic Taiwan, it is unlikely to be embraced by future governments. Likewise, even if a current U.S. president commits to a one China policy and accommodates PRC interests on Taiwan to some degree, future U.S. presidents are not bound to pursue similar policies.

Still, even if PRC leaders are pessimistic about long-term trends in Taiwan and in Taiwan-U.S. relations, and even granting that Taiwanese and U.S. leaders can't make credible commitments today about Taiwan's future status and U.S.-Taiwan relations, it still begs the question: Why would initiating military conflict help to solve these problems? In a power transition, an established power might rationally consider launching a preventive war against a potentially revisionist rising power if it believes (a) that time is not on its side, and as such it faces a closing window of opportunity to halt the upstart power's rise (at some point it will be too weak, relative to the rising state, to do so), and (b) that the war will actually solve the problem by arresting the rise of the upstart state.[37] For a similar logic to play out in the Taiwan Strait as a consequence of possible future Taiwan revisionism, then, two analogous conditions would appear necessary: (a) PRC leaders believe that time is not on their side and that they consequently face a closing window of opportunity to prevent Taiwan's permanent (or long-term) separation from China; and (b) PRC leaders believe that initiating military conflict now would alter the long-term trends that they find worrisome.[38] Absent a belief that time isn't on China's side, it isn't clear why PRC leaders would believe they need to act sooner rather than later to halt

Taiwan revisionism. And absent a belief in the efficacy of force, it isn't clear why war would be viewed as a viable means to address a closing window of opportunity. Below I briefly elaborate on both points in assessing the severity of a commitment problem relating to possible future Taiwan revisionism.

ASSESSING THE SEVERITY OF A TAIWAN REVISIONISM COMMITMENT PROBLEM

Some of the trends noted in chapter 4, including strong recent DPP performance in Taiwan's elections, low and decreasing interest in unification among Taiwan's citizens, and a deepening sense of Taiwan-centric identity (especially among younger generations), are potentially worrisome from Beijing's perspective in part because they can lead to changes that will be difficult to unwind later. Indeed, even the KMT has considered changing its approach to sovereignty issues, because doing so is increasingly critical to the party's viability in a democratic Taiwan, given broader societal changes.[39] Likewise, the more entrenched DPP power appears to be, the greater the ability to undertake policies that potentially reinforce Taiwan-centric identity, such as educational reforms that treat Chinese history as separate from Taiwan history. In this environment, Beijing could conceivably worry that the longer it waits to resolve the Taiwan issue, the worse things will get from its perspective.

These types of concerns are present in the recent writings of some PRC-based Taiwan experts. Qiang Xin writes, for instance, that the PRC has come to view the long-term "perpetuation of Taiwan de facto independence" as its "foremost concern" with respect to cross-strait relations. Xin points to three worrisome trends in particular. The first is the growing tendency by Taiwanese leaders—including Tsai Ing-wen—to emphasize that Taiwan is already sovereign and independent, and that the ROC is Taiwan. As Xin puts it, "General recognition of such a political stance will make it impossible for Taiwan to willingly accept reunification at any time, in any form, for any reason." Second, Xin highlights the continued efforts by the DPP to pursue desinicization, including educational reforms, which will further weaken identification with China. Finally, Xin points to Taiwan's deepening political and security ties with the United States as a source of concern, as these could further encourage the perpetuation of de facto Taiwan independence.[40] Other PRC-based analysts have outlined similar concerns.[41]

Social and political trends in Taiwan also call into question whether extensive cross-strait economic ties are actually helping to advance Beijing's unification goals—as has long been hoped. As discussed in chapter 1, the PRC has viewed economic exchanges across the Taiwan Strait as potentially helping to increase influence in Taiwan, and during the Ma administration a number of PRC analysts were generally optimistic about the political and security implications of cross-strait economic exchange.[42] But the Sunflower Movement and Tsai Ing-wen's landslide win in 2016 called into question assumptions about the long-term political and social implications of cross-strait economic integration. As Xin puts it, the PRC shifted strategy in response, from placing hope on the Taiwan people to "placing more hope on the mainland itself."[43] In sum, echoing some of the pessimism that Christensen documented in the early 2000s, there is clearly some concern in China about long-term trends in the Taiwan Strait.

Meanwhile, a number of scholars have shown that the PRC historically has had a tendency to use force or coercion to try to alter unfavorable trends relating to key foreign policy interests. For instance, Christensen shows that PRC leaders have frequently used military force when they perceive either a closing window of opportunity or an opening window of vulnerability. Importantly, PRC leaders have sometimes resorted to force even if they are not confident about "winning" a military campaign in a traditional sense—they might do so because they believe the consequences of inaction would be even worse.[44] Taylor Fravel likewise argues that China is most likely to use force in territorial disputes when leaders sense that the PRC's bargaining power is declining, leading in turn to a need both to signal resolve and— sometimes—to seize territory preventatively.[45] And Ketian Zhang argues that China has been more likely to use coercion in South China

Sea disputes when PRC leaders believe that China's resolve is in doubt.[46] The reemergence of pessimism in Beijing about long-term trends in the Taiwan Strait, then, is potentially quite dangerous.

Still, it is important to emphasize a distinction between possible PRC use of military force to signal resolve in response to current trends in the Taiwan Strait, on the one hand, and PRC initiation of preventive war to arrest these trends, on the other. Many of the trends that I highlighted earlier reflect policy choices in Taipei and Washington: whether, for instance, Taiwan should continue with curriculum reform; how leaders in Taiwan describe the ROC; what steps the United States takes to improve security coordination with Taiwan, and so forth. Although the PRC doesn't have particularly effective methods at its disposal to alter societal trends in Taiwan, such as shifting identity, it has in the past demonstrated a willingness to take actions to try to change policy trends by signaling a willingness to impose costs on both Taipei and Washington. In this regard, pessimism over trends that reflect primarily political decisions in Taipei and Washington should, I believe, be viewed as a subset of the red-line conflict scenario previously outlined. The risk of military conflict primarily revolves around the possibility that (a) Beijing is highly resolved to prevent, for instance, further institutionalization of the U.S.-Taiwan security relationship or educational reforms that further desinicize Taiwan, and (b) Washington and Taipei fail to fully appreciate that resolve, thereby triggering a military response to activities Beijing views as crossing its red lines. In this scenario, Beijing's goal would not necessarily be to unify Taiwan by force, but rather to create a new understanding in Taipei and Washington about the risks involved in current policy decisions.

On the other hand, societal trends in Taiwan—including reduced interest in unification and more widespread Taiwan-centric identity—potentially create a more fundamental credible commitment problem. Unlike policy decisions, leaders in Washington and Taipei have limited ability to shape these trends, and Taiwanese leaders cannot credibly promise to alter the future trajectory of things like Taiwan identity or the amenability of the Taiwan people toward unification. These trends would be especially concerning to Beijing to the extent PRC leaders believe that they have the effect of making unification increasingly difficult or unlikely. Beijing might fear, for instance, that these trends will make a negotiated unification agreement increasingly unlikely. Or the PRC might worry that these trends will make Taiwan more difficult to govern even if Beijing were able somehow to maneuver Taiwan into unification through coercion or occupation. This type of thinking would suggest a perceived closing window of opportunity of the sort that in the past has precipitated PRC use of force.

Nevertheless, short of an invasion and occupation of Taiwan, it is unclear how the initiation of armed conflict would ameliorate these societal trends. To the contrary, the use of military force against Taiwan would potentially reinforce what Beijing views as unfavorable societal trends by further alienating Taiwan's citizens. Moreover, although the balance of power has clearly shifted in Beijing's favor, attempting to seize and occupy Taiwan would still represent a highly risky and costly undertaking that might fail spectacularly. Indeed, China's continued rise and military modernization gives Beijing good reason to believe that time remains on Beijing's side, even as using military force in the near term to arrest unfavorable societal trends in Taiwan risks military disaster and consequently the further slipping away of Taiwan. In turn, some recent PRC analysis suggests a calculus that still, on balance, views long-term trends as favoring Beijing and hence suggests that Beijing is likely to act with (or should act with) restraint in the shorter term. For instance, even though Xin, as noted, argues that Beijing is concerned about several cross-strait developments, he nevertheless emphasizes that Beijing remains patient so long as Taiwan is deterred from pursuing de jure independence. As he puts it: "Beijing understands clearly that reunification should be the consequence, instead of the cause, of its progress" toward national rejuvenation. In other words, Xin suggests that Beijing views modernization and development as conducive to long-term unification with Taiwan. On the other hand, launching a war today to achieve unification would put more fundamental development goals at risk.[47]

In sum, pessimism in Beijing is potentially dangerous. But it is important to differentiate between pessimism about trends in policy

decisions in Taipei and Washington and pessimism about more fundamental structural trends in cross-strait relations (such as expectations
about the balance of power) and in Taiwan's politics and society (such
as the growth in Taiwan-centric identity and the increased power of the
DPP). Although pessimism about policy decisions in Washington and
Taipei could lead the PRC to use force, doing so would primarily reflect
an effort to signal resolve on the Taiwan issue with the aim of altering
those policy trends (such as increased U.S.-Taiwan security cooperation). War in this type of scenario occurs primarily due to an information problem (insufficient understanding of PRC resolve in Taipei and
Washington) and thus is subsumed by the red-line conflict scenario
outlined earlier. Pessimism over more fundamental structural trends,
on the other hand, could potentially give rise to more intractable commitment problems and the possibility of preventive war. Yet two factors
appear to help mitigate the likelihood of preventive war. First, some
trends—including most clearly the shifting balance of military power—
appear to be moving in Beijing's favor, and many in China recognize
this. In turn, Beijing has some reason to believe that time remains on its
side. Second, using military force as a preventive measure to arrest
social and political trends in Taiwan would carry enormous risks for
Beijing. The limited use of force could backfire by reinforcing negative
views of the PRC in Taiwan, while any effort to seize Taiwan would risk
catastrophic failure. As such, until Beijing is confident that it can invade
and occupy Taiwan in a way that would not put more fundamental
development goals at risk, the likelihood of a preventive war remains
relatively low.

SUMMARY

How worried should analysts be, then, about a war triggered by actual
or potential Taiwan revisionism? In this chapter, I have argued that the
likelihood of such a conflict is relatively low. The PRC has—in this
author's view—signaled quite clearly a willingness to use force if Taipei

and Washington cross certain red lines, and for the most part the United States and Taiwan have in turn respected those lines. Moreover, major trends in cross-strait relations over the past few decades have greatly magnified the downside risks to Taiwan associated with testing PRC red lines. And although the PRC has some reasons to be pessimistic about long-term structural trends in the Taiwan Strait, it also has reasons for optimism and continued patience.

Still, even if the scenarios for war outlined in this chapter are unlikely, they remain real possibilities, particularly in a world in which Taiwan politics and society appear to be drifting ever farther from Beijing's orbit; where U.S.-Taiwan security relations get stronger on the surface but uncertainties remain about actual U.S. commitments; and in which Beijing becomes more confident in its ability to use force efficaciously. Indeed, as PRC power continues to grow, the scenarios outlined in this chapter could potentially reemerge in more dangerous forms, as I discuss in the next chapter.

7

THE PROBLEM OF PRC REVISIONISM

Xi Jinping's January 2, 2019, speech on Taiwan suggested to some a growing impatience with the cross-strait status quo. Echoing a phrase he had used in the past, Xi described the Taiwan issue as one that should not be passed down from generation to generation, even as he declined to rule out the use of force in the Taiwan Strait. Xi's speech, combined with stepped-up diplomatic and military pressure directed against Taiwan, led a number of analysts in Taipei and Washington to conclude that the PRC leader was "eager to take unification with Taiwan as a matter of higher urgency,"[1] and that he was "anxious for movement on Taiwan."[2] Against the backdrop of a modernizing PLA, many of these analysts warn that growing PRC impatience is dangerous and could lead Beijing to consider launching a war to unify Taiwan by force. Such a war would be grounded not in Taiwan revisionist behavior, but rather in PRC dissatisfaction with the current status quo in the Taiwan Strait—or what might be termed *Chinese revisionism*.[3]

In the previous chapter I suggested that several factors have helped to lower the likelihood of a war triggered by Taiwan revisionism. I argue in this chapter, however, that some of the same trends are also increasing the long-term danger of a conflict rooted in PRC revisionism. In particular, as PRC military power continues to grow, there could come a time when leaders in Beijing believe they have the capacity to use military force to achieve unification at acceptable cost. As was the case with the Taiwan revision scenarios examined in chapter 6, both information and credible commitment problems are likely to loom large in a world where the PRC is increasingly unhappy with the cross-strait status quo. I argue that these information and commitment problems are potentially more intractable than those that could arise as a consequence of Taiwan revisionism, pointing in particular to a number of serious credible commitment problems that are likely to accompany a continued shift in the cross-strait balance of power.

CROSS-STRAIT TRENDS AND PRC RED LINES

In chapter 6 I argued that revisionist policies are becoming riskier for Taiwan because long-term trends in the Taiwan Strait are making Taiwan's expected war payoff unambiguously worse: improving PRC military capabilities, combined with Taiwan's economic dependence on China, mean that war would be catastrophic for the island. The impact of long-term trends on China's war utility, on the other hand, has been more ambiguous (as suggested by figure 6.1). Although economic integration with Taiwan—and with the world more broadly—increases Beijing's expected costs of conflict, other factors, including the shifting balance of military power, work in the opposite direction.

More recently, however, the net impact of long-term trends on China's war utility is becoming less ambiguous. On the one hand, China's military modernization continues, and the balance of power in the region continues to shift toward the PRC. In turn, the likely war outcome (denoted W in figure 6.1) is becoming more favorable from Beijing's perspective. On the other hand, it is less clear that China's expected costs of war are still on the rise; indeed, if anything, they appear as though they may be falling. As noted in chapter 1, for instance, economic integration across the Taiwan Strait—after growing rapidly for several decades—has been leveling off in recent years. Meanwhile, as noted earlier, a number of analysts believe that Xi Jinping is more determined to make tangible progress on unification than his predecessors, and—as discussed in chapter 4—there is some evidence of increasing hawkish-ness among the Chinese public. In turn, to the degree that China places more value on the Taiwan issue than before, it implies that, ceteris pari-bus, China's costs of war are declining (relative to the value of a better outcome on the Taiwan sovereignty issue).

These trends suggest, in short, that China's expected utility for fight-ing a cross-strait war is almost certainly increasing. This does not mean that leaders in the PRC want war, nor does it imply that the PRC is not still deterred by the very high costs a war would entail. To the contrary, as I noted in the previous chapter, some recent commentary suggests that many PRC analysts continue to view the risks and likely costs associ-ated with an invasion and occupation of Taiwan as unacceptably high.[4] Here I am making the simpler—and I think relatively uncontroversial—point that recent trends imply that Beijing likely views war as *less unattractive* than before. In the context of the simple model outlined in chapter 5, China's war utility—its expected payoff from fighting a war, denoted C in figure 5.2—is shifting to the right.

In the Taiwan revisionism scenarios outlined in chapter 6, war ulti-mately occurs because of deterrence failure—in this case, PRC failure to deter present or potential future Taiwanese steps toward indepen-dence. But to the degree that current trends are making war less unat-tractive to China, we then face an increased risk of a war rooted in China's own deeply revisionist preferences with regard to Taiwan sov-ereignty. In figure 5.2, if C ever moves so far to the right that it crosses the status quo, then the PRC is in a position where it views war as preferable to a continuation of that status quo. Here, war occurs because of compellence failure—PRC failure to get Taiwan to accom-modate China by yielding ground on sovereignty issues. How worried should analysts be about this type of conflict?

ACCOMMODATING A MORE POWERFUL CHINA?

I noted in the previous chapter that Taiwan has strong incentives to avoid crossing China's red lines on sovereignty issues: war would have potentially devastating consequences for the island, and those costs are increasing. As such, Taiwanese leaders have generally avoided actions likely to provoke a PRC military response. But the trends just described suggest that China's red lines themselves are changing, and that at some point Chinese leaders could conclude that they will obtain a better outcome from fighting a war than they obtain in the current status quo. Still, even if such a situation ever arises, it is important to begin by observing that war remains an extremely unattractive outcome for both sides. A PRC that "won" a war and successfully occupied Taiwan would still likely pay very steep costs in achieving that outcome. And obviously the costs to Taiwan would be catastrophic.

Thus, for the same reasons that Taiwanese leaders have generally avoided pursuing highly revisionist policies that might cross China's red lines, it would seem that leaders in Taipei would also have strong incentives to accommodate a PRC whose reversion point is drifting toward the status quo. Consider figure 7.1, which reproduces the simple model of war presented in figure 5.2. Here, as China's expected war utility improves, C shifts to the right (as denoted by the dark arrow). Again, C is shifting to the right in part because China's costs of war may be declining, but also because the likely outcome of war (W) is becoming more favorable to China as the balance of military power changes in Beijing's favor. If C were to cross the status quo, then China is in a position where it prefers war over maintaining that status quo. But the war outcome for Taiwan is terrible, lying far to the right at point T. Taiwan thus has clear incentive to accommodate Beijing to avoid war, by redefining the status quo closer to the unification

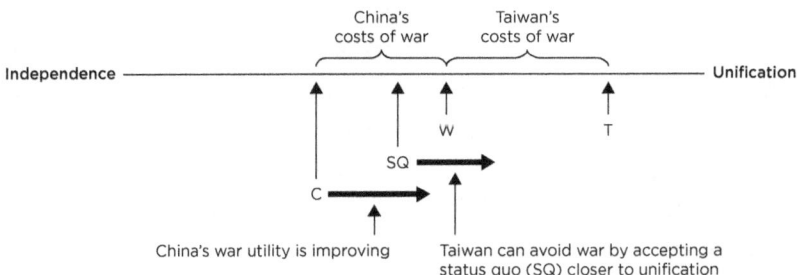

FIGURE 7.1 Taiwanese accommodation in the face of shifting PRC red lines.

end of the continuum. In other words, Taiwan ends up with a better outcome than war if it continues to adjust the status quo to lie just to the right of C. And as long as the status quo continues to reside to the right of C, PRC leaders should likewise prefer that outcome to actually fighting a war.

And, indeed, a number of observers of the cross-strait relationship have argued in recent years that current trend lines—including, most important, the shifting balance of military power in the region—imply that Taiwanese accommodation on sovereignty issues is becoming virtually inevitable. John Mearsheimer, for instance, writes: "If China continues its impressive rise, Taiwan appears destined to become part of China." As Chinese power continues to grow, Taiwan is likely to find it increasingly difficult to deter a PRC attack. Mearsheimer thus expects that ultimately Taiwan will likely be forced to pursue a "Hong Kong strategy," where "Taiwan accepts the fact that it is doomed to lose its independence and become part of China" and so "works hard to make sure that the transition is peaceful and that it gains as much autonomy as possible from Beijing."[5] Along similar lines, Robert Sutter has noted that "China's economic, military, and diplomatic leverage over Taiwan increasingly constrains Taipei to follow a path leading to accommodation of and eventual reunification with China."[6] Bruce Gilley, recalling Finland's strategic accommodation of Soviet interests during the Cold War, argues that "Taiwan is moving in the direction of eventual Finlandization."[7] Chas Freeman contends that the United States is "engaged in a futile effort to maintain a military balance that is now turned against us and could turn even more against us . . . if there were ever a case where we should be encouraging a political, diplomatic, or negotiated solution, this is it."[8] Charles Glaser argues that the best way for the United States to deal with the rise of China is to pursue a grand bargain with Beijing, which would combine U.S. accommodation on Taiwan (meaning ending U.S. security ties with the island) with a PRC promise to peacefully resolve regional disputes and to accept a continued U.S. presence in the region.[9] And, before becoming the KMT's presidential candidate in 2020, Han Kuo-yu warned in early 2019 that "Taiwanese people have less and less time to avoid discussing a peace treaty" with China, since the "dynamics of cross-strait relations are becoming more and more volatile."[10]

Unsurprisingly, these sorts of arguments have not gained much traction with most Taiwanese voters. Accommodation on sovereignty issues implies moving closer toward formal unification with China, and, as we have seen, there is very little support for unification in Taiwan. Indeed, perhaps recognizing where public opinion stands on the issue, Han Kuo-yu later clarified that he would not sign a peace treaty with the PRC unless Beijing first renounced the use of force against Taiwan.[11] Still, if key trends—including, most important, a shifting balance of military power—continue to move in Beijing's favor, the alternatives to accommodation seem likely to be even worse for Taiwan. A war to unify Taiwan would undoubtedly devastate the island, and should Taiwan end up losing such a war, it would face a grim future of occupation and the likely crushing of dissent.[12] Simply put, although accommodation on sovereignty issues is an extremely unattractive option from the perspective of most in Taiwan, it would seem—on the surface at least—preferable to the alternatives if China's reversion point were to cross the status quo.

Nonetheless, just as information and credible commitment problems could potentially lead to a war rooted in Taiwan revisionism, such problems also stand in the way of peaceful accommodation of shifting PRC red lines—potentially leading to war rooted in PRC revisionism. Indeed, efforts by Beijing to advance unification are likely to generate information and credible commitment problems that are much more severe and intractable than those associated with Taiwan revisionism described in the previous chapter. In the remainder of this chapter, I elaborate on these problems.

SHIFTING PRC RED LINES, INFORMATION, AND ACCOMMODATION

Should Beijing come to believe that it can get a better outcome from fighting a war than it obtains in the present status quo, it would presumably like to be able to signal this conviction credibly to Taiwan, so as to convince the island to yield ground on sovereignty issues peacefully. However, just as Beijing has incentives to overstate its resolve to use force in response to revisionist Taiwan behavior, it also has incentives to overstate its resolve to unify Taiwan by force, because regardless of China's true resolve to fight a war, it would always like to see Taiwan yield ground on the sovereignty issue. Indeed, the information problems associated with a revisionist China trying to compel Taiwan accommodation are likely to be even more vexing than the information problems associated with deterring Taiwan independence, for several reasons.

First, scholars have long suggested that deterrence tends to be easier than compellence, an observation that could be rooted—at least partly—in human psychology.[13] In trying to deter Taiwan independence, the PRC is warning Taipei that it is risking very high costs (including war) in order to obtain additional—largely symbolic—gains. As I noted in chapter 6, since Taipei would be risking tangible harm to obtain those gains, it has good reason to be cautious. This is especially so in light of the predictions of prospect theory, which suggests that people tend to eschew risk-taking behavior in order to gain more than they already have.[14] On the other hand, prospect theory also suggests that people tend to be more willing to take risks to protect what they already have. In this case, as we saw in chapter 4, most Taiwanese view Taiwan (or the ROC) as already being sovereign and independent; accommodating China on sovereignty issues would, in turn, imply losing some of that sovereignty. Prospect theory suggests, then, that Taiwanese people should be more willing to accept risks to avoid this outcome (relative to the risks they are willing to assume to gain more sovereign status).

To see what this means in practice, consider a simple example. Suppose the PRC were to warn Taiwan that if it moves forward on some hypothetical reform—such as changing the official name of the ROC to just Taiwan—that it would be risking war. Even if Taiwanese leaders believed that the PRC is unlikely to carry out this threat (assume they view it as a 20 percent probability), they might still be deterred, believing the downside risks of war—even if unlikely—aren't worth the symbolic gain of renaming the country. Now imagine that PRC leaders are warning that Taiwan is risking war if it does not reaffirm a one China principle and commence political negotiations with Beijing. Were Taiwan to accommodate this demand, it would likely be viewed by most Taiwanese as a major concession to Beijing, and one that would suggest relatively unambiguously that Taiwan is drifting closer to Beijing's orbit. In turn, Taiwanese leaders would likely be more reluctant to accommodate such a demand unless they were quite sure that the threat was credible. In other words, to get accommodation, the signaling bar is much higher for Beijing.

Second, a Beijing seeking to compel Taiwan to give ground on sovereignty issues must deal with the reality that it has until now been willing to acquiesce to Taiwan not yielding such ground. Taiwan's status quo sovereign status did not trigger a PRC attack yesterday, and it has not today; yet somehow Beijing must convince Taiwan that this same status quo will be unacceptable tomorrow and will trigger an attack. Clearly the PRC has been signaling disapproval of the status quo since Tsai Ingwen became Taiwan's president in 2016. The growing coercion aimed at the island, including provocative military maneuvers and increased diplomatic pressure, could be an effort to signal a future willingness to use force unless that status quo changes. These actions might also represent an effort to reduce the value of the status quo to Taiwan—perhaps with the aim of making the Taiwan public indifferent between maintaining the current status quo or acquiescing to some formula closer to unification (such as unambiguous acceptance of a one China principle). But it is one thing to pressure Taiwan and another thing entirely to launch a military attack—even if limited—against the island. Convincing Taiwan that Beijing is prepared to do just that, given its past unwillingness, is likely to be a daunting challenge for a revisionist China.

Finally, because Taiwan is a democracy in which leaders are ultimately accountable to the public, Beijing faces the additional challenge of convincing not only Taiwan's leaders of its resolve, but also the Taiwan public. The problem here, of course, is that accommodation on sovereignty issues is likely to be extremely unpopular among Taiwan's citizens—given public opinion trends outlined in chapter 4, especially the lack of widespread interest in unification with China. To be sure, as discussed in the introduction, Ma Ying-jeou was able to pursue a policy of détente with the PRC by embracing the ambiguous 1992 consensus, which represented a weak version of a one China principle. Although this sort of ambiguous formulation was acceptable to most Taiwanese at the time, it also became clear during the Ma presidency that there was little appetite for further accommodation of China on sovereignty issues. For instance, Ma faced heavy criticism when he raised the possibility of a cross-strait peace agreement in 2011 (in the lead-up to the 2012 presidential election), even though the proposal was, as Alan Romberg writes, "heavily caveated from the beginning." Facing attacks from DPP candidate Tsai Ing-wen, Ma was forced to add further caveats, such as a promise that an agreement would require the consent of the Taiwan people in a national referendum.[15] Broaching a peace agreement was seen as an unforced error that hurt Ma's reelection campaign, and the episode suggests that any Taiwan government contemplating significant accommodation on sovereignty issues would likely face fierce public opposition.

In short, should PRC leaders reach a point where they believe they can successfully fight a war against Taiwan at acceptable cost, they will find it difficult to communicate this information credibly. Beijing has obvious incentives to overstate its resolve on Taiwan; a truly resolved Beijing thus needs to distinguish itself from a Beijing that is merely bluffing. Doing so, in turn, is likely to be especially difficult in a situation where the PRC is trying to compel Taiwan to back away from a status quo that, until now, China has been willing to live with peacefully.

AN OVERLAPPING TANGLE OF CREDIBLE COMMITMENT PROBLEMS

The information problems outlined in the previous section suggest that Beijing will face daunting difficulties in convincing a Taiwan government to accommodate on the sovereignty issue, even if Chinese leaders are truly resolved to initiate war absent such accommodation. Yet even if China were to surmount these problems and figure out a way to convince Taiwan of PRC resolve, more serious barriers—rooted in several credible commitment problems—would likely stand in the way of a peaceful settlement that Chinese leaders would prefer to fighting a war. At the most basic level, Taiwan has obvious reasons to doubt PRC commitments to Taiwanese autonomy in the context of a more formally unified China. But, as I explain in this section, the commitment problems associated with finding a peaceful solution closer to Beijing's ideal point of unification run much deeper.

WHY YIELDING GROUND ON SOVEREIGNTY IS POTENTIALLY DANGEROUS FOR TAIWAN

To begin, let us assume we are in a world in which Chinese leaders have come to believe that they have the capability to successfully invade and occupy Taiwan at acceptable cost, and they prefer to pursue this option rather than continue to live under the current status quo of de facto Taiwan independence—in other words, C has crossed to the right of the status quo in the simple model presented in figure 7.1. Further assume that both the United States and Taiwan recognize this reality—meaning that the information problems outlined in the previous section have been surmounted. In this hypothetical scenario, Taiwan and Washington face a choice: try to reach some sort of accommodation with Beijing to avoid a war, or fight the war in the hopes that they can repel Beijing's efforts to forcibly occupy Taiwan.

Of course, if C is indeed shifting to the right, what is sufficient today to accommodate the PRC and avoid war may become insufficient in the future. If, hypothetically, C were to cross to the right of the status quo this year, then a return to the Ma Ying-jeou approach to cross-strait relations—including endorsement of the 1992 consensus—might be sufficient accommodation to avoid war. But if C continues to drift right into the future, then future Taiwan governments would presumably need to offer greater accommodations—such as negotiating and entering into some sort of formal unification agreement—to avoid the war outcome. Conversely, were trends to shift and were C to reverse its rightward drift, then Taiwan would again have more room to maneuver. So, were Taiwan to choose a path of accommodation, it would likely be a dynamic process, where Taipei calibrates its concessions based on its evaluation of China's evolving war utility.

That such accommodation would be a process—rather than a one-off event—should not, in itself, imply that the accommodation path is infeasible. To the contrary, states and individuals must often adjust expectations as facts on the ground shift over time. I might today agree to give the school bully half of my lunch money per day as a price to avoid being attacked, but I enter into this bargain recognizing that the bully's calculus might shift in the future. Perhaps the bully spends afternoons in the weight room and in a few months will be in a position to demand even more of my lunch money. The fact that I might need to renegotiate in the future is regrettable but doesn't change my calculus today: I'm still better off keeping half of my lunch money each day than risk losing all of it and getting attacked in the process. In other words, that China might not be able credibly to promise to honor its current commitments in the future (a point I come back to later) should not, *in itself*, prevent Taiwan from making accommodations today to avoid war.

Accommodation becomes more dangerous for Taiwan, however, if accommodation itself can influence key trends in cross-strait relations, and hence the location of C. More specifically, if the future location of C is determined in part by the bargains that Taiwan reaches with China today, then China-Taiwan relations could be characterized by a dynamic commitment problem that resembles the problem of appeasement that James D. Fearon describes.[16] In the appeasement problem, a state might in principle be willing to make a concession—such as ceding a piece of territory—to a second state to avert war. But imagine that the piece of territory further adds to the second state's bargaining power: once ceded, the second state will be in a position to demand even more concessions from the first state. The second state might promise that it won't demand more later, but the promise is not credible given that it will have the capacity to break its promise once the territory is in its hands. There are at least three reasons why accommodation on sovereignty issues would likely give rise to a similar problem in cross-strait relations.

First, and most obviously, concessions on sovereignty could directly undercut Taiwan's ability to defend itself against PRC coercion. Relatively minor, symbolic concessions—such as agreeing to a one China principle—should not have this sort of direct effect, but major steps toward actual unification will likely entail significant compromises concerning Taiwan's armed forces. For instance, although PRC officials have previously suggested that Taiwan would be able to retain its armed forces after unification, Xi Jinping's more recent New Year speech on Taiwan omits such a promise.[17] Even if Taiwan were allowed to keep some of its military postunification, its ability to deter PRC coercion would undoubtedly decline sharply. It is hard to imagine, for instance, that Beijing would tolerate the continued presence of missiles in Taiwan that could target the mainland, or that it would allow Taiwan's military to undertake exercises meant to practice fighting the PLA. In short, if the island were to move into a formal unification agreement with China, even if the agreement promised very high levels of autonomy, Taiwan would still lose much of its deterrent capability.

Second, recall that a key determinant of China's war utility, C, is likely U.S. behavior in a war: as the likelihood of a U.S. military intervention increases, China's expected war costs increase and the likely war outcome (W) becomes less attractive from Beijing's perspective. Yet the likelihood of U.S. intervention is almost certainly (partially) endogenous to Taiwan's status. Consider as an extreme example what would happen if Taiwan were to seriously entertain a formal unification agreement with China, even one that formally guarantees a high level of Taiwan autonomy. It is hard to imagine that Washington would continue to maintain its currently robust informal military relationship with Taiwan once Taipei's interest in such an agreement becomes apparent, since the United States would naturally fear that such cooperation would end up helping Beijing.[18] Likewise, just as any U.S. military intervention in Hong Kong is virtually inconceivable even as the PRC undermines the one country, two systems framework in the former British colony, it becomes unlikely that the United States would intervene on Taipei's behalf once the Taiwan government enters into some sort of unification agreement with the

PRC, since doing so would then unambiguously constitute military intervention in another superpower's internal affairs.[19]

Even less extreme Taiwanese accommodation on sovereignty issues could risk undercutting U.S. support for the island. Consider, for example, the case of former U.S. member of Congress Dana Rohrabacher. Rohrabacher is a staunch conservative and was a long-time supporter of Taiwan in Congress, serving as one of the founding cochairs of the Congressional Taiwan Caucus. Yet in 2009, during the Ma Ying-jeou presidency in Taiwan, Rohrabacher indicated that he planned to resign as cochair of the caucus. Rohrabacher was upset that Ma was pursuing a policy of détente and reconciliation with Beijing, noting that his support for Taiwan was pointless if the island was working with China instead of fighting against it.[20] Although this position was relatively extreme, it does point to the reality that, for some in Washington, support for Taiwan is rooted primarily in what they see as a broader threat posed by a rising China. To the degree that some U.S. supporters of Taiwan view the island's value primarily in strategic terms—as a potential check against China—then a Taiwan that appears to be moving closer to the PRC becomes less valuable in their minds.[21] In short, accommodating China on sovereignty issues risks reducing U.S. support for and interest in Taiwan—which in turn has the potential to further undercut Taiwan's bargaining leverage with Beijing.

Accommodation could also undercut Taiwan's bargaining leverage with Beijing via a third channel: to the degree that political accommodation increases economic and social interactions across the Taiwan Strait, it could also increase PRC influence in Taiwan.[22] In chapter 1 I noted that evidence is mixed concerning the political implications of cross-strait economic ties. Despite this mixed evidence, at a minimum it is clear that economic integration does give Beijing more avenues through which to pursue coercion against Taiwan, as we have seen with the tourism sanctions imposed during the first Tsai Ing-wen administration. While, of course, it should be possible in theory for Taiwan to yield ground on sovereignty issues without acceding to increased economic integration with China, in practice I suspect that any cross-strait political understanding would incorporate economic dimensions such as a free trade agreement and a revived trade-in-services agreement. And to the degree that this is the case, it opens the door to increased PRC political leverage over Taiwan in the future.

Thus, if we return to figure 7.1, it seems plausible—even likely—that the location of China's war utility, C, is at least partly endogenous to Taiwan's willingness to pursue political accommodation. That is, by yielding ground on sovereignty issues today, Taipei is increasing China's long-term bargaining advantages over Taiwan even more than those advantages would otherwise be increasing as a result of cross-strait trends such as a shifting cross-strait balance of power. Accommodation potentially accelerates the rightward shift of C and increases the likelihood that Taiwan will be forced to make even greater accommodations in the future.

As noted earlier, Fearon persuasively frames the problem of appeasement as a credible commitment problem. When bargains that might avert war themselves change the bargaining power of the states involved, the country gaining an advantage must figure out a way to credibly promise not to use its enhanced bargaining power to demand even more from the second state in the future. If the state gaining the advantage cannot tie its hands in this way, the second state might prefer war to appeasement—preferring to roll the dice on the battlefield rather than make a concession that will leave it with progressively less bargaining power in the future. Fearon suggests that the Winter War between the Soviet Union and Finland can be explained in part by this dynamic, where Finland preferred to fight rather than yield to Soviet demands to cede some small islands in the Gulf of Finland that Moscow viewed as strategically important: here, Helsinki feared that ceding the islands would give the USSR more leverage to demand further concessions in the future, and Stalin presumably couldn't be trusted to honor a promise not to do so.[23] Leaders in Taiwan will likewise be reluctant to accommodate the PRC by yielding ground on the island's sovereign status, unless they can be confident that Beijing could be trusted to honor commitments not to take advantage of the increased bargaining power such accommodation would provide. Unfortunately, there are a number of reasons to doubt the credibility of PRC promises in this regard, as I discuss in the next section.

WHY THE PRC HAS DIFFICULTY MAKING CREDIBLE PROMISES TO TAIWAN

PRC officials over the past four decades have often made promises to Taiwan concerning the island's status and autonomy within the context of a unified China. In 1981 Ye Jianying outlined key parameters of what would become the PRC's one country, two systems proposal, promising that postunification, "Taiwan can enjoy a high degree of autonomy as a special administration region, and it can retain its armed forces. The central government will not interfere with local affairs in Taiwan."[24] Since then, high-ranking PRC officials have routinely repeated variations on these basic promises. For instance, Jiang Zemin, in his eight-point proposal of 1995, promised that "the lifestyles of our Taiwan compatriots . . . should be fully respected. All their legitimate rights and interests must be protected." Moreover, he emphasized that "on the premise that there is only one China, we are prepared to talk with the Taiwan authorities about any matter."[25] More recently, in 2019 Xi Jinping promised in a speech on Taiwan that postunification, "the social system and life styles of Taiwan compatriots will be fully respected . . . and the private property, religious beliefs, and legitimate rights and interests of Taiwan compatriots will be fully guaranteed."[26] These promises suggest that Beijing clearly recognizes that China must provide assurances to Taiwan in order to convince the island to move toward political unification with the PRC.

Unfortunately, it is extremely difficult for Beijing to make its assurances to Taiwan credible, for obvious reasons. Simply put, PRC political and legal institutions are in the service of the Chinese Communist Party and its top leaders.[27] Were Chinese leaders to conclude that violating some aspect of Taiwan's promised autonomy is in their interests, Taiwan would have little recourse within PRC institutions to stop them from doing so. Moreover, the PRC has a long track record of breaking promises concerning regional autonomy. Xinjiang, for instance, is formally an autonomous region. Yet not only does Xinjiang lack any real autonomy, the CCP under Xi Jinping has undertaken an extensive policy of repression in the region, which includes the arbitrary detention of at least one million Muslims in reeducation camps.[28] Likewise, China promised substantial autonomy to Tibet but has instead pursued what Allen Carlson describes as an "unrelenting assimilationist" strategy aimed at "Sinicizing" the region.[29] And China's 2020 passage of a national security law strips Hong Kong of much of the autonomy afforded to it under the one country, two systems framework. The new law gives Beijing broad latitude to interfere in Hong Kong's judicial system and schools and stations security officers in Hong Kong, among other things.[30] Although some Chinese analysts have emphasized that PRC policy toward Taiwan is completely separate from PRC policy in Hong Kong,[31] the undercutting of autonomy in Hong Kong sends an especially troubling signal to Taiwan given that Beijing also calls its proposed formula for Taiwan "one country, two systems."[32]

Finally, just as PRC leaders view dissent in Xinjiang or Tibet or Hong Kong as a threat to CCP rule, they will almost certainly view dissent in Taiwan as a threat. Beijing will likely see Taiwan's educational system as a breeding ground for dissent and lack of patriotism, just as it does in Hong Kong.[33] And just as the PRC is currently cracking down on those supporting Hong Kong independence, it will have every desire to silence those in Taiwan who have advocated for independence.[34] In short, the PRC has clear motive—rooted in Chinese leaders' conceptualization of the interests of the CCP and its continued rule in China—to intervene extensively in Taiwan politics and society if given the opportunity to do so. Indeed, the PRC already tries to influence political outcomes in Taiwan through a variety of channels.[35]

Thus not only do PRC institutions and past behavior make it difficult for the PRC to make credible promises to Taiwan, but Beijing also has clear incentives to intervene heavily in Taiwan politics and society to the extent it is able to do so. In this environment, Taiwan is likely to be extremely reluctant to pursue any sort of accommodation that could reinforce PRC bargaining power, as Taiwan has little reason to trust that PRC leaders will refrain from leveraging that increased bargaining power against Taiwan in the future.

INTENSIFYING U.S.-CHINA RIVALRY AND TAIWAN

Further complicating matters, Taiwan is but one of many contentious issues in a broader U.S.-China rivalry, one that has intensified sharply in recent years. Many scholars, often drawing on international relations theorizing about power transitions, have argued that military conflict between a rising China and a declining United States is becoming more likely.[36] While I do not wish to dwell on the broader risk of a war between the United States and China, the reality that Taiwan is perhaps the most intractable issue in an intensifying rivalry is important when thinking about the prospects for conflict and peace in the Taiwan Strait in particular. Indeed, a broader U.S.-China rivalry—and Taiwan's place within that rivalry—could add to the credible commitment problems described earlier through at least three channels.

First, recall from chapter 4 that, although nationalism and domestic politics are clearly important drivers of Chinese interest in Taiwan, the island is valuable to Beijing in part because of its strategic significance, especially the increased access to the Pacific that control over Taiwan would offer. This increased access, in turn, implies that unification would likely have implications for the U.S.-China naval balance of power.[37] Moreover, Taiwan has been a key focus of the PRC's military modernization; unification would mean that Beijing would have greater freedom to focus on other priorities. And Taiwan is widely seen as being strategically important for Japan, a close U.S. ally.[38] A Taiwan that is part of the PRC would give Beijing greater leverage over Tokyo in part because of the island's proximity to Japan's key trading routes.[39] In sum, PRC-Taiwan unification has the potential to affect the broader U.S.-China balance of power through multiple channels—by increasing PLAN access to the Pacific Ocean, freeing up resources, and harming the security of a key U.S. ally in the region. In turn, just as a dynamic commitment problem would likely complicate any consideration of accommodation in Taipei, a dynamic commitment problem is also likely to make Washington reluctant to accommodate on the Taiwan issue. U.S. policy makers are likely to fear that yielding on Taiwan—and accepting greater PRC control over the island—might reinforce long-term trends in the regional balance of power and hasten China's rise as a military power that can challenge U.S. superiority.

Second, in the context of a larger rivalry that includes numerous disputes on issues ranging from the South China Sea to trade to human rights, both the United States and China are likely to use Taiwan as a bellwether issue from which to draw inference about the other. Some in Washington have viewed PRC behavior in the Taiwan Strait as signaling broader Chinese intentions in the region. As the late senator Paul Simon put it during the 1995–1996 Taiwan Strait crisis: "If China should turn militaristic and seize Taiwan, that would be only the first acquisition . . . as we have learned from Hitler, dictators can always find some historic justification for further actions."[40] Yet China might also draw inference from U.S. behavior toward Taiwan, and some U.S.-based analysts have made this point explicitly with regard to possible accommodation on the Taiwan issue. Shelley Rigger, for instance, writes: "A change in U.S. Taiwan policy could raise China's expectations without making peaceful cross-strait unification any easier, further damaging U.S.–China relations."[41] Nancy Bernkopf Tucker and Bonnie Glaser similarly state that U.S. accommodation on Taiwan would lead Beijing to "conclude that a weaker United States lacking vision and ambition could be pressured and manipulated."[42] More generally, Daniel Drezner has shown that expectations of future disputes with a rival have a tendency to make it less likely that a country will make concessions to that rival on any given issue. As he argues, making concessions increases the risk of harming a country's future bargaining position while also encouraging the rival country "to expect acquiescence in the future as well, which will encourage future coercion attempts."[43] In this case, the United States could be reluctant to pursue accommodating policies on Taiwan—particularly in the face of growing PRC pressure on the island—because U.S. leaders might worry about acquiring a reputation for weakness that could carry over to Washington's many other disputes with China.

Finally, it is not just Beijing that has difficulties making credible assurances on Taiwan. Recent U.S. foreign policy behavior—especially during the Trump administration—demonstrates clearly that U.S. commitments likewise frequently lack credibility. These credibility issues can complicate any Washington effort to pursue a bargain with Beijing over Taiwan. Suppose, for instance, that the United States and China were to enter into a grand bargain along the lines that Glaser proposes (and that I noted earlier).[44] Given continued support for Taiwan in Washington at a time of intensifying U.S.-China rivalry, such a bargain would—even under the best of circumstances—provoke a great deal of controversy and opposition. Just as the Trump administration walked away from controversial agreements reached during the Obama administration, including the Iran nuclear deal and the Paris Climate Accord, it is quite possible that a future administration would ignore or abrogate a grand bargain with China were it to include accommodations relating to Taiwan. Moreover, even if such an agreement were to remain in place, it is far from clear that the United States would feel itself bound to it were conflict to erupt in the Taiwan Strait.

In sum, increasingly hostile U.S.-China relations create additional commitment problems that are likely to complicate bargaining over Taiwan's status in the shadow of a revisionist China.

CONCLUSION: AN INCREASINGLY DANGEROUS STRAIT

The PRC has a mix of status quo and revisionist preferences with regard to Taiwan, wishing both to prevent legal Taiwan independence (a status quo preference) and to accomplish formal unification (a revisionist preference). These competing preferences, in turn, suggest two very different logics for a cross-strait military conflict. In the first logic, war occurs as a consequence of PRC deterrence failure, the inability of Beijing to prevent a current or future revisionist Taiwan government from taking steps toward Taiwan independence. In chapter 6 I suggested that there is some reason to be at least somewhat optimistic that a war grounded in this sort of logic is unlikely, and that broad trends have, on balance, made it even more so. The focus of this chapter has been on the second logic, one grounded in the PRC's ultimately revisionist aims with regard to Taiwan. Here war occurs as a consequence of PRC compellence failure, the inability of Beijing to convince Taipei and Washington to pursue more accommodating policies even as Chinese tolerance for the status quo wanes.

In this chapter I have made three broad arguments. First, trends in the Taiwan Strait are increasing the relevance of a war rooted in PRC revisionism. Of course, this point probably seems obvious to many—perhaps most—U.S.-based observers of the cross-strait relationship. China's military capabilities continue to advance, and the balance of power in the Taiwan Strait has continued to shift in the PRC's favor. Chinese nationalism may be on the rise, and there is some evidence that Xi Jinping places considerable value on making tangible progress on unification. Cross-strait economic integration has leveled off and may decline in a postpandemic world. U.S.-China relations are at a historic nadir—certainly worse than at any point since normalization. These trends, in turn, imply (a) that China should have growing confidence that, if war occurs, it is likely to end on increasingly favorable terms to China; and (b) that China has less to lose from fighting a war than it did before. To be clear, I am not making the claim that China now or in the near future is likely to view war in the Taiwan Strait as an attractive possibility. I am making the more limited claim that war is becoming less unattractive than before, and that there could come a day when PRC leaders believe that the war outcome offers greater utility than a continued status quo of de facto Taiwan independence.

Second, I have emphasized that, should we enter a world in which Chinese leaders in fact come to believe that the PRC could win a war at acceptable cost—or, to be more precise, where they believe that Beijing's expected war outcome is preferable to continuing to tolerate the status quo—war itself is not the inevitable outcome. To the contrary, given the horrific costs a war would impose on Taiwan, Taipei should in principle prefer to reach a bargain with Beijing where it cedes ground on the sovereignty issue such that the PRC no longer prefers war. Similarly, given that war would also imply high costs for China, and given that the war outcome will inevitably be shrouded in some ex ante uncertainty, Beijing, too, would almost certainly prefer to reach a peaceful settlement with Taipei rather than actually fighting a war; indeed, this has been the basic premise of PRC policy toward Taiwan since the 1970s. In other words, Taiwanese accommodation should leave both China and Taiwan better off than they would be in the war outcome. A number of observers, moreover, have made this basic point: that shifting power realities in the Taiwan Strait will ultimately force Taiwan to accommodate Beijing on the sovereignty issue—at least to some degree.

My third argument, however, has been that a number of significant information problems and credible commitment problems are likely to stand in the way of peaceful Taiwanese accommodation; indeed, these problems are likely to be much more intractable than in scenarios rooted in Taiwan revisionism. PRC leaders are likely to find it very difficult to communicate, credibly, that Beijing is really prepared to pursue a military option if Taiwan does not yield ground on sovereignty issues. Moreover, Beijing will be demanding that Taiwan make concessions on something—sovereign statehood—that most Taiwan citizens believe that island already possesses. Because people are generally more willing to take risks to protect what they already have than they are to try to obtain something new (such as formal independence), Taiwanese leaders will be unlikely to yield to the PRC unless they are highly confident that Beijing is really prepared to fight a war. Finally, and perhaps most important, several interconnected and difficult to resolve commitment problems are likely to stand in the way of peaceful accommodation. Accommodation not only means that Taiwan will sacrifice some of its sovereignty today; it also means that Taiwan is likely to lose future bargaining power vis-à-vis China. But given its political system and past and current management of other formally autonomous regions, such as Tibet and Hong Kong, the PRC has a very difficult time making credible promises not to use that increased bargaining leverage in a way detrimental to future Taiwanese autonomy. And deepening rivalry in the broader U.S.-China relationship introduces additional commitment problems to the mix.

In sum, the arguments I have made in this chapter provide grounds for pessimism about the future prospects for peace in the Taiwan Strait. To be clear, I am not arguing that war is inevitable. Far from it. My arguments suggest, though, that if we reach a point where PRC leaders believe that war is preferable to the status quo, then finding a peaceful way out will be very difficult. The key to avoiding war, then, is to avoid getting to such a point in the first place. In the conclusion, I offer some thoughts about how to avoid a Taiwan Strait tragedy.

CONCLUSION

The Most Dangerous Place on Earth?

The May 1, 2021, cover of the *Economist* magazine shows an image of Taiwan at the center of a radar screen, flanked by the flags of China and the United States. The headline reads, ominously, "The Most Dangerous Place on Earth."[1] The cover received extensive attention in Taiwan media and drew a variety of responses on the island.[2] President Tsai Ing-wen cast a reassuring tone, writing on Facebook that although "Taiwan does face a real threat from China, I want to assure everyone that our government is fully capable of managing all potential risks and protecting our country from danger."[3] Some suggested the cover was a useful reminder of the need to be prepared in the face of a growing threat from China, while others suggested it was overly alarmist.[4] The magazine's grim headline drew considerable ridicule on some social media in Taiwan.[5]

The headline is indeed hyperbolic (there are, after all, plenty of places on Earth where devastating war and other forms of violence are a current fact of life, not a hypothetical danger), but it nevertheless points to an important truth: even though armed conflict in the Taiwan Strait would be a catastrophe, it is something that realistically could happen. Ultimately, to avoid a Taiwan Strait tragedy, it is important to have a clear understanding of how such a conflict could occur in the first place. My aim in writing this book, in turn, has been to think through the causal processes that could lead to a China-Taiwan conflict and to assess how complex trends in the Taiwan Strait are collectively shaping the likelihood of war. In this conclusion, I summarize some of the key arguments advanced in this study. I close by offering some thoughts about how war in the Taiwan Strait might be averted.

THE INTRACTABILITY OF THE CROSS-TAIWAN STRAIT SOVEREIGNTY DISPUTE

Were armed conflict to occur in the Taiwan Strait, at its root would be an intractable sovereignty dispute that has persisted since the end of the Chinese Civil War. In its current manifestation, the dispute centers on Taiwan's status: whether Taiwan should be considered part of China now, and whether it should be formally unified with mainland China in the future. The PRC views itself as the sole legal government of China, Taiwan as part of China in principle, and formal unification as an important national goal. While Beijing has embraced a policy of "peaceful reunification," it has refused to renounce the use of force and has explicitly threatened to go to war if Taiwan were to formally declare its independence from China, be occupied by foreign forces, or delay—indefinitely—negotiations over formal unification. In Taiwan, even though individuals have widely divergent views on cross-Strait policy, and even though the two major parties differ considerably in their approach to China, there nevertheless exists wide agreement that Taiwan (or the ROC) is a sovereign state, and there is very little support for near-term unification with the PRC. Absent a dramatic change in circumstances, then, there is little prospect for the two sides peacefully resolving the underlying dispute.

The underlying dispute over Taiwan's status is further complicated by the reality that each side holds a mix of status quo and revisionist goals with respect to Taiwan's sovereignty. In Taiwan, for instance, there is agreement across the political spectrum that unification in the near term should be avoided (a status quo goal), and both the Ma and Tsai governments have framed their cross-strait policies as upholding the status quo. But both political parties also advocate for more international space for Taiwan (which can be interpreted as revisionist), and some hold decidedly revisionist preferences—such as those advocating that Taiwan formalize its independence from China. Meanwhile, Beijing aims to prevent movement toward independence (a status quo goal) even as it hopes to accomplish unification with Taiwan (a clear revisionist goal). This mix of status quo and revisionist goals helps to feed a security dilemma in the Taiwan Strait. For instance, rapidly improving PRC military capabilities, combined with frequent PRC exercises near Taiwan, help to motivate efforts to improve Taiwan's security, such as via closer U.S.-Taiwan military cooperation. Yet these efforts, which both Taiwan and the United States view as reactive to increased PRC assertiveness, are viewed in Beijing as facilitating Taiwan's permanent separation from China. The PRC responds, in turn, with even more shows of force. The cross-strait sovereignty dispute, in short, is complex, intractable, and potentially volatile.

A COMPLEX MIX OF COMPETING AND REINFORCING TRENDS

In the first part of this book, I described several trends that have complex and at times competing implications for stability in the Taiwan Strait. I began in chapter 1 with a discussion of the cross-strait economic relationship. Even though China-Taiwan economic integration has slowed over the past decade, China remains Taiwan's top trade partner and is the primary destination for Taiwan's outbound foreign direct investment. Extensive cross-strait economic integration is potentially a source of stability in the Taiwan Strait, as it greatly increases the costs of armed conflict. Yet Taiwan's economic linkages to China can also generate vulnerabilities on the island, and Beijing at times tries to leverage economic integration to advance its political goal of unification with Taiwan.

Chapter 2 considered the balance of military power in the Taiwan Strait, which in recent years has been shifting rapidly in China's favor. China, today, can impose extremely high costs on Taiwan as a consequence of improving missile and air capabilities, and Taipei increasingly has difficulty dealing with China's gray zone operations near Taiwan. On the other hand, China's ability to impose an effective blockade is less clear-cut, and analysts generally agree that an attempt to invade and occupy Taiwan remains a very risky gambit for Beijing. Yet as China's military power continues to grow, an increasing number of analysts believe that Beijing could soon be in a position where it could launch a war to seize Taiwan with reasonable probability of success. Whether and when such a day might come ultimately will hinge on factors such as China's ability to sustain robust economic growth, Taiwan's ability to leverage more limited resources into effective asymmetric deterrent capabilities, and the degree to which the United States remains engaged in the region and committed to Taiwan's defense. In chapter 3 I explored this last factor in greater depth, describing the U.S. commitment to Taiwan as being informal, ambiguous, and to some degree conditional on Taiwan's actions. Still, I showed that, even though these basic characteristics persist, the U.S.-Taiwan security relationship has been getting closer in recent years.

Finally, chapter 4 considered domestic political and social trends in China and Taiwan, and how these trends might affect cross-strait relations. I showed that Taiwan-centric identity has been increasing in Taiwan, and interest in unification with China—even under hypothetical favorable future conditions—has been waning. But I also argued that public opinion remains quite pragmatic on sovereignty-related issues, and in particular there is not widespread support for actions—such as a declaration of independence—that would likely trigger conflict with China. Next I highlighted the importance of nationalism in understanding Beijing's interest in Taiwan, and I noted that some recent studies suggest that public opinion in the PRC is quite hawkish in general and on the Taiwan issue in particular. But I also drew attention to several recent studies that suggest that PRC leaders retain considerable room to maneuver despite hawkish public sentiment. Finally, I noted some signs that Xi Jinping views progress on the Taiwan issue as a more urgent priority than his predecessors, but there is also reason to think that other objectives—including maintaining the CCP's grip on power along with continued economic development—remain more important.

In this book's introduction, I suggested that these complex trends are a key reason that analysts have come to divergent conclusions about the likelihood of a cross-strait military conflict. While some trends—such as a shifting balance of military power—appear to raise the risk of conflict, others—such as cross-strait economic integration or continued pragmatism among Taiwan's citizens—appear to help stabilize relations. This book was motivated, in part, by a desire to sift through this complexity, and the second part of the book leveraged a simple model through which to think through, systematically, the prospects for conflict in the Taiwan Strait.

INFORMATION AND CREDIBLE COMMITMENT PROBLEMS MAGNIFY THE RISK OF CONFLICT

The potential horrors of a cross-strait war are difficult to fathom—the loss of life, the physical destruction, the risks to Taiwan's democracy and China's modernization, the possibility of escalating conflict involving two nuclear superpowers. Clearly there should be outcomes that China, Taiwan, and the United States should all prefer to war, meaning the three countries have a shared interest in avoiding a cross-strait conflict. Unfortunately, the same could be said of wars in general, and yet wars are a persistent—if relatively rare—feature of international politics. Understanding why a cross-strait war might occur means grappling with the fact that wars are a costly and inefficient means to resolve disputes, and asking why the relevant states—the United States, China, and Taiwan—couldn't find bargains that would leave all better off than the war outcome. My approach has been to draw from the bargaining theory of conflict to construct a simple model of the cross-strait relationship. Bargaining theory highlights two broad explanations for why wars tend to occur. First, wars can arise because of information problems, where countries tend to have an imperfect understanding of their adversaries' capabilities and resolve and find it difficult to obtain this information. Second, credible commitment problems can lead to war when leaders recognize bargains that are preferable to war in principle but nevertheless doubt the credibility of other leaders to uphold those bargains in practice. I have argued that both types of problems are prevalent in the cross-strait relationship and could lead to conflict through several distinct causal logics.

Two of these logics revolve around the problem of what I have termed, following Ross, *Taiwan revisionism*.[6] The PRC has made clear that it is prepared to use military force if Taiwan crosses certain red lines, such as by formally declaring its independence from China. Taiwan's government, in turn, has strong incentive to avoid crossing these red lines, given the devastating consequences a war would entail for the island. In chapter 6 I showed how information and credible commitment problems could nevertheless help to trigger a conflict rooted in Taiwan revisionism. In the most straightforward manifestation, a conflict could occur simply because it is hard for Taiwan's leaders to discern with confidence the precise location of China's red lines, since the PRC has obvious incentives to overstate its resolve. But I further argued that the risks of major war arising from such a scenario are relatively small, and that Taipei, Beijing, and Washington have been able to manage the risks of this sort of conflict relatively effectively. First, I noted that the risks can be managed via costly signaling, and that the PRC has been relatively successful at credibly conveying its bottom lines. Second, I emphasized that the nature of the good in dispute—Taiwan's sovereign status—means that Taiwan revisionism entails taking concrete risks to obtain primarily symbolic gains. In turn, the United States has discouraged Taiwan from pursuing actions that Washington views as changing the status quo, and Taiwan itself has been relatively cautious in risking conflict to obtain these mostly symbolic gains.

A somewhat more insidious scenario is rooted in potential *future* revisionist Taiwan behavior. Such a scenario could arise if Beijing becomes deeply pessimistic about future trends, believing in essence that Taiwan is slipping away and prospects for unification are becoming more remote (due to, for instance, improving U.S.-Taiwan security ties, or shifts in Taiwan politics and identity). I argued that such pessimism could trigger a war because of a credible commitment problem that resembles the problems that lead to preventive war during power transitions in international politics. But two factors help to mitigate this sort of commitment problem in the Taiwan Strait. First, even though there are reasons for PRC pessimism about certain trends in the Taiwan Strait, Beijing also has reason for optimism if it remains patient; most obviously, the cross-strait balance of military power continues to shift in China's favor. Second, it is not clear that use of military force would alter trends that Beijing views as unfavorable in any event. The limited use of force would likely backfire by further undermining the PRC's image in Taiwan, while an effort to invade and occupy Taiwan remains a highly risky undertaking that could fail. Thus I concluded in chapter 6 that the likelihood of a cross-strait war rooted in actual or potential Taiwan revisionism is quite low.

My conclusions in chapter 7, on the other hand, were somewhat less rosy. There I argued that broad trends in the Taiwan Strait are combining to increase the risk of war rooted in PRC revisionism, where Chinese leaders come to believe that the PRC could win a war to occupy Taiwan at acceptable cost. Should PRC leaders in fact come to this conclusion, then Taiwan would have strong incentives to accommodate Beijing just enough such that Chinese leaders again prefer the status quo over initiating war. I noted, however, that several information and credible commitment problems would make peaceful Taiwanese accommodation difficult. Beijing, for instance, would likely have a hard time credibly communicating a willingness to launch a war absent Taiwanese accommodation on sovereignty issues. Meanwhile, Taiwan would reasonably fear giving ground on sovereignty issues because doing so would likely further erode Taipei's bargaining power in its interactions with Beijing. In turn, finding a peaceful alternative to fighting could become quite difficult if Beijing were ever to conclude that it could obtain a better outcome by fighting a war than it obtains in the status quo.

HOW WAR MIGHT BE AVERTED

My conclusions in this book suggest that, even if it is hyperbole to describe Taiwan as the "most dangerous place on Earth," the risk of armed conflict in the Taiwan Strait is real. Beijing and Taipei are involved in an intractable sovereignty dispute, and several overlapping information and credible commitment problems contribute to an underlying risk of war. How, then, might this outcome be avoided?

To begin, I wish to reiterate a key point that I made at this book's outset: even if the risk of conflict is real, war is *not* an inevitable—or even a highly probable—outcome in the Taiwan Strait. Wars between states are relatively rare occurrences in today's world and have generally declined over time.[7] Wars between great powers are rarer still.[8] Great power war is rare in large part because the costs of such wars have become increasingly catastrophic, and I have emphasized that a war in the Taiwan Strait would likewise risk catastrophic costs for the PRC, for Taiwan, and for the United States. All three countries, in short, have a shared interest in avoiding war, and policy makers in Washington, Taipei, and Beijing should recognize war for what it is: a risk that can be, and has been, successfully managed. Indeed, the Taiwan Strait has been a potential flashpoint for conflict for decades and has seen its share of serious crises, yet none of these have escalated to actual war. For policy makers in Washington, overhyping the risk of war is potentially counterproductive because it helps to legitimize dramatic changes in U.S. policy toward Taiwan. On one extreme, overstating the risk of war can lead to calls for much stronger U.S.-Taiwan security ties, such as formalizing a clear U.S. commitment to Taiwan's defense. Such steps, however, would likely intensify security dilemma dynamics in the Taiwan Strait by stoking nationalism in China and increasing pessimism in Beijing over cross-strait trends; leaders in China would likely respond with even more assertive policies—including even more displays of force—toward Taiwan. On the other extreme, overstating the danger of war can lead to calls for the United States to end all commitments to Taiwan's security so as to help mitigate the risk of a catastrophic U.S.-China war. But if the United States were to abandon Taiwan, the risk of a cross-strait war would likely increase: Beijing's war utility would improve even as the underlying commitment and information problems described in chapter 7 would remain.

Second, military deterrence continues to be important, as it helps to lower China's expected war utility. Washington should thus continue to focus on sustaining a capacity to intervene effectively in a cross-strait conflict should one occur, while continuing to encourage Taiwan to invest more extensively in its own defense capabilities. But deterrence should continue to be paired with clear assurances to Beijing that the United States opposes changes to the status quo initiated on either side of the Taiwan Strait, and in particular that it does not support Taiwan's formal separation from China. Otherwise, the United States risks negating the benefits of deterrence (tempering excessive PRC optimism about the likely outcome of a conflict) by fueling pessimism in Beijing about the likely consequences of peace.[9] More generally, the United States should continue to work within the framework of its long-standing one China policy and avoid symbolic actions that appear to be normalizing the U.S.-Taiwan relationship while doing little in concrete terms to enhance deterrence in the Taiwan Strait.

Finally, there should be a concerted effort in both Washington and Beijing to repair the overall bilateral U.S.-China relationship, which has worsened considerably in recent years. An improved relationship is conducive to stability in the Taiwan Strait in part because it would help to reduce the severity of some of the commitment problems, described in chapter 7, that are partially rooted in U.S.-China rivalry. An improved relationship would also open the door to increased dialogue and perhaps some conversations on how to manage crises in the Taiwan Strait.[10] Perhaps most important, increased cooperation in the broader U.S.-China relationship has the effect of increasing the benefits of peace for both countries; both have more to lose, in turn, if war breaks out. This is especially important in light of the discussion in chapter 7, where I emphasized that if a point is ever reached where PRC leaders believe that war is preferable to the status quo, then finding a way to avoid war will be challenging given underlying commitment and information problems. An improved U.S.-China relationship has the potential to increase Beijing's stake in stability and consequently to make war less attractive. On the other hand, a China that already derives little benefit from cooperating with Washington would simply have less to lose in a cross-strait war.

NOTES

INTRODUCTION

1. "Full Text of President Ma Ying-jeou's Inaugural Address on May 20," *Taiwan News*, May 20, 2012, https://www.taiwannews.com.tw/en/news/1925248.

2. See, for instance, Liu Xuanzun, "PLA Aircraft Again Surround Taiwan with US Intervention on Mind," *Global Times*, March 30, 2021, https://www.globaltimes.cn/page/202103/1219869.shtml.

3. Brad Lendon, "China Building Offensive, Aggressive Military, Top US Pacific Commander Says," *CNN*, March 10, 2021, https://www.cnn.com/2021/03/10/asia/us-pacific-commander-china-threat-intl-hnk-ml/index.html.

4. Brad Lendon, "Chinese Threat to Taiwan 'Closer to Us Than Most Think,' Top US Admiral Says," *CNN*, March 24, 2021, https://www.cnn.com/2021/03/24/asia/indo-pacific-commander-aquilino-hearing-taiwan-intl-hnk-ml/index.html.

5. This quote is from an unnamed senior U.S. official, quoted in Demetri Sevastopulo and Kathrin Hille, "U.S. Fears China Is Flirting with Seizing Taiwan," *Financial Times*, March 26, 2021, https://www.ft.com/content/3ed169b8-3f47-4f66-a914-58b6e2215f7d.

6. See, for instance, Oriana Skylar Mastro, "The Taiwan Temptation: Why Beijing Might Resort to Force," *Foreign Affairs* 100, no. 4 (2021): 58–67.

7. For recent studies along these lines, see, for instance, Ian Easton, *The Chinese Invasion Threat: Taiwan's Defense and America's Strategy in Asia* (Arlington, Va.: Project 2049 Institute, 2017); Oriana Skylar Mastro, "The Precarious State of Cross-Strait Deterrence," testimony before the U.S.-China Economic and Security Review Commission, February 18, 2021, https://www.uscc.gov/sites/default/files/2021-02/Oriana_Skylar_Mastro_Testimony.pdf; Eric Heginbotham et al., *The U.S.-China Military Scorecard: Forces, Geography, and the Evolving Balance of Power, 1996–2017* (Santa

Monica, Calif.: RAND, 2015); Michael A. Hunzeker et al., *A Question of Time: Enhancing Taiwan's Conventional Deterrence Posture* (Arlington, Va.: Schar School of Policy and Government, George Mason University, 2018); and Michael Beckley, *Unrivaled: Why America Will Remain the World's Sole Superpower* (Ithaca, N.Y.: Cornell University Press, 2018).

8. The guidelines did note, however, that unification should occur in the context of a "democratic, free and equitably prosperous China." The full text of the guidelines is available from the Mainland Affairs Council at https://www.mac.gov.tw/en/News _Content.aspx?n=8A319E37A32E01EA&sms=2413CFE1BCE87E0E&s=6913A37D7 83577C2.

9. Mainlanders (*waishengren*) were those Chinese who moved to Taiwan after the island reverted to ROC control in 1945 (mostly in the late 1940s as the KMT retreated to the island).

10. The full text of Lee's speech is available from the East Asia Peace and Security Initiative, https://www.eapasi.com/uploads/5/5/8/6/55860615/appendix_80_—_president _lee_tenghui_cornell_commencement_address.pdf.

11. On Lee's drift from a "one China" principle and a discussion of the events described here, see J. Bruce Jacobs and I-hao Ben Liu, "Lee Teng-Hui and the 'Idea' of Taiwan," *China Quarterly* 190 (2007): 381–83.

12. See Robert S. Ross, "The 1995–96 Taiwan Strait Confrontation: Coercion, Credibility, and the Use of Force," *International Security* 25, no. 2 (2000): 87–123.

13. See Michael D. Swaine, "Chinese Decision-Making Regarding Taiwan, 1979–2000," in *The Making of Chinese Foreign and Security Policy in the Era of Reform, 1978–2000,* ed. David M. Lampton (Stanford Calif.: Stanford University Press, 2001), 289–336.

14. Chen won the election in large part because the KMT split before the election, with former Taiwan governor James Soong running as an independent. After the election, Soong created a new party (the People First Party), which ultimately aligned itself with the KMT in a broader "pan-blue" coalition (the KMT flag is blue). The DPP has remained the main party in an opposing "pan-green" coalition (the DPP flag is green).

15. On Chen's statements after his victory, see "President Chen's Interview with the Washington Post," Office of the President of the Republic of China, March 30, 2004, https://english.president.gov.tw/NEWS/1705.

16. For example, the postal service's name was changed from "China Post" to "Taiwan Post" in 2007. Chen's government also took steps to reconsider the legacy of Chiang Kai-shek in Taiwan, including renaming entities that had been named after Chiang (such as the main international airport in Taiwan), removing the honor guard at and renaming the memorial to Chiang in Taipei, and so forth.

17. See "Full Text of Anti-Secession Law," *People's Daily*, March 14, 2005, http://english .peopledaily.com.cn/200503/14/eng20050314_176746.html.

18. Richard C. Bush, *Uncharted Strait: The Future of China-Taiwan Relations* (Washington, D.C.: Brookings, 2013), 12.

19. For a discussion of Ma's approach to one China and the 1992 consensus, see Bush, 21–22.

20. For an early collection of essays on the possible limits of cross-strait détente, see Wei-xing Hu, ed., *New Dynamics in Cross-Taiwan Straits Relations: How Far Can the Rapprochement Go?* (Hoboken, N.J.: Taylor and Francis, 2013).

21. "China's Xi Says Political Solution for Taiwan Can't Wait Forever," *Reuters*, October 6, 2013, https://www.reuters.com/article/us-asia-apec-china-taiwan/chinas-xi-says-political-solution-for-taiwan-cant-wait-forever-idUSBRE99503Q20131006.

22. Alan D. Romberg, "Squaring the Circle: Adhering to Principle, Embracing Ambiguity," *China Leadership Monitor* 47 (2015): 2.

23. Romberg, 1.

24. The full English translation of the speech is available from Taiwan's Office of the President at https://english.president.gov.tw/News/4893.

25. For an analysis of the PRC's reaction to Tsai's inaugural speech, see Alan D. Romberg, "Tsai Ing-wen Takes Office: A New Era in Cross-Strait Relations," *China Leadership Monitor* 50 (2016).

26. For an overview of Xi's speech and an analysis of some of its key components, see Richard C. Bush, "8 Key Things to Notice from Xi Jinping's New Year Speech on Taiwan," Brookings Institution (2019), https://www.brookings.edu/blog/order-from-chaos/2019/01/07/8-key-things-to-notice-from-xi-jinpings-new-year-speech-on-taiwan/.

27. A translation of Tsai's speech is available from Taiwan's Office of the President at https://english.president.gov.tw/News/5621.

28. It is worth noting here that PRC leaders and scholars have frequently emphasized that the one country, two systems model would be tailored to Taiwan's particular circumstances—meaning it would be very different from the system adopted in Hong Kong. On this point, see Gang Lin, "Beijing's New Strategies Toward a Changing Taiwan," *Journal of Contemporary China* 25, no. 99 (2016): 321–35.

29. For a good overview of the election and detailed discussion of the factors contributing to Tsai's victory, along with its political implications, see Shelley Rigger, "Taiwan's 2020 Election Analysis," *China Leadership Monitor* 63 (2020), https://www.prcleader.org/shelley-rigger-taiwan-election.

30. See Chao Deng, "Biden Brushes Off China's Complaints, Sends First Delegation to Taiwan," *Wall Street Journal*, April 14, 2021, https://www.wsj.com/articles/biden-sends-unofficial-delegation-to-taiwan-as-beijing-ramps-up-pressure-11618384940?mod=hp_listb_pos3.

31. On this point, see Thomas J. Christensen, "The Contemporary Security Dilemma," *Washington Quarterly* 25, no. 4 (2002): 7–21.

32. In other words, the cross-strait relationship is characterized by security dilemma dynamics. For analysis of the security dilemma in the Taiwan Strait, see Christensen, "Contemporary Security Dilemma"; and Scott L. Kastner, "The Taiwan Issue in U.S.-China Relations: Slipping Into a Security Dilemma?" in *After Engagement: Dilemmas in U.S.-China Security Relations*, ed. Jacques deLisle and Avery Goldstein (Washington, D.C.: Brookings, 2021), 244–68.

33. June Teufel Dreyer, "Flashpoint in the Taiwan Strait," *Orbis* 44, no. 4 (2000): 615–29.

34. Alan D. Romberg, *Rein In at the Brink of the Precipice: American Policy Toward Taiwan and U.S.-PRC Relations* (Washington, D.C.: Henry L. Stimson Center, 2003).

35. Matthew Strong, "Taiwan Strait Could be Flashpoint for U.S.-China Conflict: Former U.S. Official," *Taiwan News*, October 31, 2018, https://www.taiwannews.com.tw /en/news/3564943.

36. Robert D. Blackwill and Philip Zelikow, "Can the United States Prevent a War Over Taiwan?," *War on the Rocks*, March 1, 2021, https://warontherocks.com/2021/03/can -the-united-states-prevent-a-war-over-taiwan/.

37. Mastro, "Precarious State," 1.

38. Minxin Pei, "China's Perilous Taiwan Policy," *Project Syndicate*, January 11, 2019, https://www.project-syndicate.org/commentary/china-taiwan-policy-conflict-with -america-by-minxin-pei-2019-01.

39. Peter Gries and Tao Wang, "Taiwan's Perilous Futures: Chinese Nationalism, the 2020 Presidential Elections, and U.S.-China Tensions Spell Trouble for Cross-Strait Relations," *World Affairs* 183, no. 1 (2020): 57.

40. Jacques deLisle, "The Growing Dangers of Potential U.S.-China Conflict," *Taiwan Insight*, June 8, 2021, https://taiwaninsight.org/2021/06/08/the-growing-dangers-of -potential-u-s-china-conflict/.

41. Tyler Cowen, "China's War Against Taiwan Could Come Sooner Rather Than Later," *Bloomberg*, April 6, 2021, https://www.bloomberg.com/opinion/articles/2021-04-07 /china-taiwan-conflict-could-come-sooner-rather-than-later.

42. Mark Cozad, "Factors Shaping China's Use of Force Calculations Against Taiwan," testimony before the U.S.-China Economic and Security Review Commission, February 18, 2021, https://www.uscc.gov/sites/default/files/2021-02/Mark_Cozad_Testi mony.pdf.

43. Dennis J. Blasko, "The Chinese Military Speaks to Itself: Revealing Doubts," *War on the Rocks*, February 18, 2019, https://warontherocks.com/2019/02/the-chinese-military -speaks-to-itself-revealing-doubts/.

44. Richard C. Bush, Bonnie Glaser, and Ryan Hass, "Opinion: Don't Help China by Hyping Risk of War Over Taiwan," *NPR*, April 8, 2021, https://www.npr.org/2021/04/08 /984524521/opinion-dont-help-china-by-hyping-risk-of-war-over-taiwan.

45. On costs, see, e.g., Jon Stokes, "Why a Chinese Invasion of Taiwan Would Be a Catastrophe for China and the World," *Doxa*, April 13, 2021, https://doxa.substack.com/p /why-a-chinese-invasion-of-taiwan; Jordan Schneider, "China's Chip Industry: Running Faster but Still Falling Behind," Rhodium Group note, April 22, 2021, https://rhg .com/research/china-chips/. On the high costs of war as reason for optimism, see Brian Hioe, "No, Taiwan Is Not Going to Be Invaded by China Tomorrow," *New Bloom*, March 29, 2021, https://newbloommag.net/2021/03/29/china-invasion-possibility/.

46. Some of my earlier work has highlighted ambiguity in major trend lines affecting cross-strait relations and has argued for the need for clear theoretical frameworks through which to assess the risks of a cross-strait conflict. See, for instance, Scott L. Kastner, "Is the Taiwan Strait Still a Flashpoint? Assessing the Prospects for Armed Conflict Between China and Taiwan," *International Security* 40, no. 3 (2015/2016):

54–92; Scott L. Kastner, "Rethinking the Prospects for Conflict in the Taiwan Strait," in *Globalization and Security Relations Across the Taiwan Strait: in the Shadow of China*, ed. Ming-chin Monique Chu and Scott L. Kastner (New York: Routledge, 2015), 42–60; and Kastner, "Taiwan Issue." In this book I draw on some of the ideas presented in these earlier works but develop them at greater length and advance a number of new arguments.

47. James D. Fearon, "Rationalist Explanations for War," *International Organization* 49, no. 3 (1995): 379.

48. David A. Lake, "Two Cheers for Bargaining Theory: Assessing Rationalist Explanations for the Iraq War," *International Security* 35, no. 3 (2010/2011): 7–52. My model draws especially on Fearon's ("Rationalist Explanations") seminal study.

1. ECONOMIC INTEGRATION ACROSS THE TAIWAN STRAIT

1. Yun-han Chu, "The Political Economy of Taiwan's Mainland Policy," in *Across the Taiwan Strait: Mainland China, Taiwan, and the 1995–1996 Crisis*, ed. Suisheng Zhao (New York: Routledge, 1999), 163.

2. Nicholas R. Lardy, *Integrating China Into the Global Economy* (Washington, D.C.: Brookings, 2002), 31.

3. I consider the general question of how commerce can flourish despite conflict—focusing on the Taiwan-China case in particular—in Scott L. Kastner, *Political Conflict and Economic Interdependence Across the Taiwan Strait and Beyond* (Stanford, Calif.: Stanford University Press, 2009).

4. Sumner J. La Croix and Yibo Xu, "Political Uncertainty and Taiwan's Investment in Xiamen's Special Economic Zone," in *Emerging Patterns of East Asian Investment in China: From Korea, Taiwan, and Hong Kong*, ed. Sumner J. La Croix, Michael Plummer, and Keun Lee (Armonk, N.Y.: M. E. Sharpe, 1994), 125.

5. On the special economic zones and China's opening to the world economy during the 1980s, see Barry Naughton, "Economic Policy Reform in the PRC and Taiwan," in *The China Circle: Economics and Electronics in the PRC, Taiwan, and Hong Kong*, ed. Barry Naughton (Washington, D.C.: Brookings, 1997), 81–110; Susan L. Shirk, *How China Opened Its Door: The Political Success of the PRC's Foreign Trade and Investment Reforms* (Washington, D.C.: Brookings, 1994).

6. Suisheng Zhao, "Economic Interdependence and Political Divergence: A Background Analysis of the Taiwan Strait Crisis," in *Across the Taiwan Strait: Mainland China, Taiwan, and the 1995–1996 Crisis*, ed. Suisheng Zhao (New York: Routledge, 1999), 22.

7. Thomas B. Gold, *State and Society in the Taiwan Miracle* (Armonk, N.Y.: M. E. Sharpe, 1986), 4–6.

8. Robert Wade, *Governing the Market: Economic Theory and the Role of Government in East Asian Industrialization* (Princeton, N.J.: Princeton University Press, 2004), 35.

9.   Gold, *State and Society*, 5.

10. On the pressures facing Taiwan's low-end manufacturers and incentives to move operations to mainland China, see Naughton, "Economic Policy Reform."

11. See, for instance, Murray Scot Tanner, *Chinese Economic Coercion Against Taiwan: A Tricky Weapon to Use* (Santa Monica, Calif.: RAND Corporation, 2007), 39.

12. See Shelley Rigger, *Why Taiwan Matters: Small Island, Global Powerhouse* (Lanham, Md.: Rowman and Littlefield, 2011), 121.

13. Tanner, *Chinese Economic Coercion*, 40.

14. The ROC government finally legalized mainland investment in 1992, but investment still needed to be done indirectly, via a company that was based in a third location such as Hong Kong. See Syaru Shirly Lin, *Taiwan's China Dilemma: Contested Identities and Multiple Interests in Taiwan's Cross-Strait Economic Policy* (Stanford, Calif.: Stanford University Press, 2016), 62.

15. Chu, "Political Economy," 174.

16. Rigger, "Why Taiwan," 121.

17. Chu, "Political Economy," 174.

18. These statistics are from *Liang'an jingji tongji yuebao* [Cross-strait economic statistics monthly] (Taipei: Mainland Affairs Council of the Executive Yuan, 2002), no. 120.

19. On the post-Tiananmen economic retrenchment, see Barry Naughton, *Growing Out of the Plan: Chinese Economic Reform 1978–1993* (New York: Cambridge University Press), 274–88.

20. Naughton, 302–4.

21. Tse-kang Leng, *The Taiwan-China Connection: Democracy and Development Across the Taiwan Straits* (Boulder, Colo.: Westview, 1996), 90; Chu, "Political Economy," 174.

22. On PRC political motivations, see, for instance, Chu, "Political Economy," 182; Zhao, "Economic Interdependence," 27; Tanner, *Chinese Economic Coercion*.

23. On the "Go South" strategy, see Tanner, *Chinese Economic Coercion*, 45–47; Kastner, *Political Conflict*, 55–58.

24. Chu, "Political Economy," 176.

25. On the "go slow, be patient" (or "no haste") policy, see Tanner, *Chinese Economic Coercion*, 47–48; Kastner, *Political Conflict*, 58–60; Lin, *Taiwan's China Dilemma*, chap. 3.

26. *Liang'an jingji tongji yuebao*, no. 136, 26.

27. On business community pushback, see Tanner, *Chinese Economic Coercion*, 48–49; Lin, *Taiwan's China Dilemma*, 78–81.

28. For instance, the Lee government successfully blocked a planned power plant investment by the Formosa Plastics group, probably the highest-profile success of the policy. On this episode, see Lin, *Taiwan's China Dilemma*, 81–87.

29. Taiwan-approved investments started to increase again after 1999. PRC statistics suggested that contracted investment began to rebound in the late 1990s as well, though realized investment didn't increase until the early 2000s. See *Liang'an jingji tongji yuebao*, no. 136, 26.

30. For a good discussion, see Rigger, *Why Taiwan*, 123–25. See also Tanner, *Chinese Economic Coercion*, 49.

31. On the advisory conference, see Lin, *Taiwan's China Dilemma*, 100–104; Kastner, *Political Conflict*, 63–64; Tanner, *Chinese Economic Coercion*, 52–53.

32. See Kastner, *Political Conflict*, 63–64; Tanner, *Chinese Economic Coercion*, 53. The decision to lift the semiconductor ban was especially contentious in Taiwan and followed an extensive debate; the lifting of the ban was a compromise of sorts, as significant restrictions remained, including a review process and limiting investments to 8-inch wafer production facilities (and not allowing investments in more cutting-edge 12-inch wafer production facilities). For a detailed overview of the debate and policy outcomes, see T. J. Cheng, "China-Taiwan Economic Linkage: Between Insulation and Superconductivity," in *Dangerous Strait: The U.S.-Taiwan-China Crisis*, ed. Nancy Bernkopf Tucker (New York: Columbia University Press, 2005), 93–130. See also Lin, *Taiwan's China Dilemma*, 117–22. On the security implications of semiconductor industry investment in China, see Ming-chin Monique Chu, "Rethinking Globalization-Security Linkages with References to the Semiconductor Industry Across the Taiwan Strait," in *Globalization and Security Relations Across the Taiwan Strait: In the Shadow of China*, ed. Ming-chin Monique Chu and Scott L. Kastner (New York: Routledge, 2015), 183–208.

33. On the mini three links, see Tanner, *Chinese Economic Coercion*, 54; on the holiday charter flights, 66–68.

34. On the political barriers to opening direct links under the Chen administration, see Tanner, 60–62.

35. Calculating actual cross-strait trade was complicated by the large amount of transit trade through Hong Kong. These numbers come from *Liang'an jingji tongji yuebao*, no. 205, 23.

36. *Liang'an jingji tongji yuebao*, no. 205, 26.

37. The MAC estimated trade with the PRC to be US$49 billion in 2003, compared with US$44 billion with the United States. Trade with the United States in 2008 stood at US$58 billion, compared with an estimated US$105 billion with China. *Liang'an jingji tongji yuebao*, no. 205, 23; and Taiwan Ministry of Finance Trade Statistics Database, http://web02.mof.gov.tw/njswww/webproxy.aspx?sys=100&funid=edefjsptgl.

38. *Liang'an jingji tongji yuebao*, no. 205, 28.

39. In 2008 investment in electronic parts and components; computer, electronic and optical products manufacturing; and electrical equipment manufacturing accounted for approximately 46 percent of all approved Taiwan investment in China. See *Liang'an jingji tongji yuebao*, no. 193, 30.

40. See, for instance, "Taiwan to Review China Funding," *International Herald Tribune*, March 30, 2006, 18. At the time, official Taiwan numbers, reported in *Liang'an jingji tongji yuebao*, were lower than US$50 billion.

41. Rigger, *Why Taiwan*, 118. For an example of the one million estimate, see "Direct Flights Between China and Taiwan Start," *New York Times*, July 4, 2008, https://www.nytimes.com/2008/07/04/business/worldbusiness/04iht-04fly.14224270.html.

42. Rigger, 125.

43. For example, Wang Daohan, an advisor to President Jiang Zemin and the head of the Association for Relations Across the Taiwan Straits, told Taiwan investors that

"although political relations across the Taiwan Straits are strained, economic and trade cooperation . . . are not strained and are still developing." See "ARATS Officials Reassure Taiwan Investors," *Xinhua*, October 29, 1995, in *FBIS-China*, October 31, 1995, 71. For other, similar examples of PRC efforts to reassure Taiwan investors during periods of turbulence in the 1990s, see Kastner, *Political Conflict*, 79–82.

44. For a discussion in this regard, see Kastner, *Political Conflict*, 95–99.

45. See Douglas B. Fuller, "The Cross-Strait Economic Relationship's Impact on Development in Taiwan and China: Adversaries and Partners," *Asian Survey* 48, no. 2 (2008): 239–64. See also Rigger, *Why Taiwan*, 128.

46. See Gunter Schubert, Ruihua Lin, and Jean Yu-Chen Tseng, "Are Taiwanese Entrepreneurs a Strategic Group? Reassessing Taishang Political Agency Across the Taiwan Strait," *Asian Survey* 57, no. 5 (2017): 869–74; and Gunter Schubert, Rui-hua Lin and Jean Yu-Chen Tseng, "Taishang Studies: A Rising or Declining Research Field?" *China Perspectives* 2016, no. 1 (2016): 29–36.

47. Richard C. Bush, *Uncharted Strait: The Future of China-Taiwan Relations* (Washington, D.C.: Brookings, 2013), 49. On the agreements, see Yu-Jie Chen and Jerome A. Cohen, "China-Taiwan Relations Reexamined: The '1992 Consensus' and Cross-Strait Agreements," *Asian Law Review* 14, no. 1 (2019): 1–40.

48. "Direct Flights Between China and Taiwan Start," *New York Times*, July 4, 2008.

49. "Direct Flights Between China and Taiwan Begin," *New York Times*, December 15, 2008, https://www.nytimes.com/2008/12/15/news/15iht-15TAIWAN.186758 54.html.

50. See Lin, *Taiwan's China Dilemma*, 175.

51. "Historic Taiwan-China Trade Deal Takes Effect," *BBC News*, September 12, 2010, https://www.bbc.com/news/world-asia-pacific-11275274. An English translation of the agreement is available from the USC US-China Institute, https://china.usc.edu/china -taiwan-economic-cooperation-framework-agreement-ecfa-june-29-2010.

52. *Liang'an jingji tongji yuebao*, no. 320, 2–1.

53. The full text of the agreement is available from Taiwan's Mainland Affairs Council at https://ws.mac.gov.tw/001/Upload/OldFile/public/data/962616363771.pdf. See also Andrew Jacobs, "As Chinese Visit Taiwan, the Cultural Influence Is Subdued," *New York Times*, August 10, 2011, https://www.nytimes.com/2011/08/11/world/asia/11taiwan .html.

54. Numbers come from various issues of *Liang'an jingji tongji yuebao*.

55. See Lin, *Taiwan's China Dilemma*, 179–81; Bush, *Uncharted Strait*, 53; "Protestors Fill Taipei Streets to Oppose ECFA," *Taiwan Today*, June 28, 2010, https://taiwantoday.tw /news.php?unit=2&post=1270.

56. "China and Taiwan Sign Key Investment Protection Pact," *BBC*, August 10, 2012, https://www.bbc.com/news/business-19204608.

57. On the CSSTA and the Sunflower Movement, see Lin, *Taiwan's China Dilemma*, 196–202; JoAnn Fan, "The Economics of the Cross-Strait Services Agreement," Brookings Institution, April 18, 2014, https://www.brookings.edu/opinions/the-economics

-of-the-cross-strait-services-agreement/; J. Michael Cole, *Convergence or Conflict in the Taiwan Strait: The Illusion of Peace?* (New York: Routledge, 2017), chap. 7.

58. According to Taiwan customs statistics, Taiwan's trade with mainland China and Hong Kong combined dropped from approximately US$165 billion in 2012 to approximately US$157 billion in 2016. Trade then increased to approximately US$193 billion in 2018. According to PRC customs statistics, bilateral trade grew until 2014, dropped during 2015–2016, then expanded again in 2017–2018. See *Liang'an jingji tongji yuebao*, various issues.

59. American Chamber of Commerce in Taiwan, "2019 White Paper Overview," https://amcham.com.tw/2019/05/taiwan-white-paper-overview/.

60. For an early analysis of the New Southbound policy, see Bonnie S. Glaser, Scott Kennedy, and Derek Mitchell, "The New Southbound Policy: Deepening Taiwan's Regional Integration," *CSIS* report, January 2018, https://csis-prod.s3.amazonaws.com/s3fs-public/publication/180613_Glaser_NewSouthboundPolicy_Web.pdf?Acoay LFliB9_iAvbmYvP_jM27mEXw5xL.

61. For a detailed discussion of how and why the PRC might undertake economic coercion against Taiwan, as well as a discussion of factors that magnify or mitigate the potential efficacy of economic coercion, see Tanner, *Chinese Economic Coercion*, chap. 2. For a good general discussion of the different reasons states might impose economic sanctions, see Francesco Giumelli, "The Purposes of Targeted Sanctions," in *Targeted Sanctions: The Impacts and Effectiveness of United Nations Action*, ed. Thomas J. Biersteker, Sue E. Eckert, and Marcos Tourinho (Cambridge: Cambridge University Press, 2016), 38–59.

62. On different types of strategic inducement (or "economic engagement") policies, see Miles Kahler and Scott L. Kastner, "Strategic Uses of Economic Interdependence: Engagement Policies on the Korean Peninsula and Across the Taiwan Strait," *Journal of Peace Research* 43, no. 5 (2006): 523–41. For a general discussion on the problems associated with using carrots as a tool of statecraft, see Daniel W. Drezner, "The Trouble with Carrots: Transaction Costs, Conflict Expectations, and Economic Inducements," *Security Studies* 9, no. 1/2 (1999/2000): 188–218.

63. See, e.g., Zhao, "Economic Interdependence," 27.

64. For a good article that explains how this effect can occur, even in the absence of intent, see Rawi Abdelal and Jonathan Kirshner, "Strategy, Economic Relations, and the Definition of National Interests," *Security Studies* 9, no. 1/2 (1999/2000): 119–56.

65. For instance, Jiang Zemin in 1994 argued that "increasing cross-Strait economic exchanges and cooperation . . . will be useful in boosting the development of cross-Strait relations and national unification." See Zhao, "Economic Interdependence," 27.

66. Taiwan businesses operating in China are commonly referred to using their Chinese name, the *Taishang*. For a general overview of Taishang, see Chun-yi Lee, *Taiwanese Business of Chinese Security Asset? A Changing Pattern of Interaction Between Taiwanese Businesses and Chinese Governments* (London: Routledge, 2012).

67. Tanner, *Chinese Economic Coercion*, 114.

68. Local Taiwan Business Associations cooperate with local Taiwan Affairs Offices in China to offer cheap fares. See, for instance, Schubert, Lin, and Tseng, "Taiwanese Entrepreneurs," 867. Entrepreneurs also sometimes arrange for their employees in China to get discounted tickets to return to Taiwan for elections. See Andrew Jacobs, "Taiwan Vote Lures Back Expatriots in China," *New York Times*, January 11, 2012, https://www.nytimes.com/2012/01/12/world/asia/taiwan-vote-lures-back-expatri ates-in-china.html.

69. For extended discussions of the case of PRC coercion against pro-DPP Taishang during the Chen Shui-bian administration, see Tanner, *Chinese Economic Coercion*, esp. chap. 5; Kastner, *Political Conflict*, chap. 5; and William L. Norris, *Chinese Economic Statecraft: Commercial Actors, Grand Strategy, and State Control* (Ithaca, N.Y.: Cornell University Press, 2016), chap. 6.

70. See Norris, *Chinese Economic Statecraft*; Tanner, *Chinese Economic Coercion*.

71. One commonly cited example concerns the *China Times* group (which includes the daily newspaper *China Times*), which was purchased by a conglomerate with extensive economic interests in China in 2008. For a discussion of this case, see Cole, *Convergence or Conflict*, 75. On Taishang media influence, see also Gunter Schubert, "Assessing Political Agency Across the Taiwan Strait: The Case of the Taishang," *China Information* 27, no. 1 (2013): 62–63.

72. On the reluctance of Taiwan business associations to be active on China-related policy discussions, see Schubert, Lin, and Tseng, "Taiwan Entrepreneurs," 869–74. See also Shubert, Lin, and Tseng, "Taishang Studies."

73. See Schubert, Lin, and Tseng, "Taishang Studies," 35; Schubert, "Assessing Political Agency," 60–62; and Shu Keng and Gunter Schubert, "Agents of Taiwan-China Unification? The Political Role of Taiwan Business People in the Process of Cross-Strait Integration," *Asian Survey* 50, no. 2 (2010): 303–4. Taishang do, however, tend to court close relationships with individual politicians in Taiwan; on this point, see Schubert, Lin, and Tseng, "Taishang Studies," 35.

74. For a discussion of recent studies in this regard, see Schubert, Lin, and Tseng, "Taishang Studies," 32–34. See also Shuling Huang, "Re-mediating Identities in the Imagined Homeland: Taiwanese Migrants in China," Ph.D. diss., University of Maryland, College Park, 2010; and Rigger, *Why Taiwan*, chap. 6. On limitations of thinking of the Taishang as a coherent voting bloc in Taiwan elections, see Schubert, "Assessing Political Agency," 58–60.

75. See Tanner, *Chinese Economic Coercion*; Kastner, *Political Conflict*; and Norris, *Chinese Economic Statecraft*. All these studies highlight the difficulties the PRC would face in undertaking a broader coercive campaign against the Taishang. See also Keng and Schubert, "Agents," 298–303.

76. See, e.g., "China Flaunts Buying Power," *Taipei Times*, May, 15, 2010, http://www .taipeitimes.com/News/taiwan/archives/2010/05/15/2003473036.

77. See Annie Huang, "China Uses Trade to Influence Taiwan Election," *Associated Press*, January 9, 2012; Sophia Wu, "Talk of the Day—Beijing's New Strategies toward

Taiwan," *Focus Taiwan (Taiwan Central News Agency)*, February 24, 2012, http://focustaiwan.tw/news/aipl/201202240051.aspx; and Jens Kastner, "Mainland Slips on Fishy Plan to Boost Cross-Strait Business," *Taiwan Reports*, March 23, 2012, http://taiwanreports.wordpress.com/2012/03/23/mainland-slips-on-fishy-plan-to-boost-cross-strait-business/.

78. Stan Hok-wui Wong and Nichole Wu, "Can China Buy Taiwan? An Empirical Assessment of Beijing's Agricultural Trade Concessions to Taiwan," *Journal of Contemporary China* 25, no. 99 (2016): 353–71.

79. Shu Keng, Jean Yu-Chen Tseng, and Qiang Yu, "The Strengths of China's Charm Offensive: Change in the Political Landscape of a Southern Taiwan Town Under Attack from Chinese Economic Power," *China Quarterly*, no. 232 (2017): 956–81. On the limitations of the PRC's agricultural inducement strategy, see also Chi-hung Wei, "China's Economic Offensive and Taiwan's Defensive Measures: Cross-Strait Fruit Trade, 2005–2008," *China Quarterly*, no. 215 (2013): 641–62.

80. PRC tourism in Taiwan statistics can be found in *Liang-an jingji tongji yuebao*, various issues.

81. "China to Stop Issuing Individual Travel Permits to Taiwan," *BBC*, July 31, 2019, https://www.bbc.com/news/world-asia-49178314. The number of PRC tourist visits to Taiwan, in turn, dropped from approximately 200,000 in August 2019 to under 58,000 in October. See *Liang'an jingji tongji yuebao*, no. 320.

82. For a discussion of the tourism case, see Peter Harrell, Elizabeth Rosenberg, and Edoardo Saravalle, "China's Use of Coercive Economic Measures," Center for a New American Security, 2018, https://www.cnas.org/publications/reports/chinas-use-of-coercive-economic-measures. Jason Li argues that the tourism sanctions have been more effective and asserts that PRC actions have harmed Taiwan's tourism industry; Li views PRC actions as contributing to KMT victories in 2018. See Jason Li, "China's Surreptitious Economic Influence on Taiwan's Elections," *Diplomat*, April 12, 2019, https://thediplomat.com/2019/04/chinas-surreptitious-economic-influence-on-taiwans-elections/.

83. It didn't appear as though the incentives had much of an effect on actual behavior by Taiwan businesses or students. See, for instance, Sophia Yang, "China's Pro-Unification 31 Measures for Taiwan Have Failed: Academia Sinica Scholar," *Taiwan News*, January 26, 2019, https://www.taiwannews.com.tw/en/news/3625988.

84. Taipei's mayor, Ko Wen-je, questioned the decision and demanded greater clarity concerning how the project—if developed by a company with Chinese links—would threaten national security. See "Commission Must Explain Twin Towers Decision: Ko," *Taipei Times*, June 28, 2019, http://www.taipeitimes.com/News/taiwan/archives/2019/06/28/2003717741. For a broader discussion concerning the difficulties associated with assessing China's overseas economic influence, see Scott L. Kastner and Margaret M. Pearson, "Exploring the Parameters of China's Economic Influence," *Studies in Comparative International Development* 56, no. 1 (2021): 18–44.

85.   Christina Lai, "More than Carrots and Sticks: Economic Statecraft and Coercion in China-Taiwan Relations from 2000–2019," *Politics* (online first, 2021), https://doi.org /10.1177/0263395720962654.

2. THE SHIFTING BALANCE OF MILITARY POWER IN THE TAIWAN STRAIT

1.   U.S. Secretary of Defense, *Annual Report on the Military Power of the People's Republic of China, 2000,* full text available on the USC US-China Institute webpage, https://china.usc.edu/us-secretary-defense-annual-report-military-power-peoples -republic-china-2000.

2.   David A. Shlapak, David T. Orletsky, and Barry A. Wilson, *Dire Strait? Military Aspects of the China-Taiwan Confrontation and Options for U.S. Policy* (Santa Monica, Calif.: RAND Corporation, 2000), xvi.

3.   All military expenditure data are from Stockholm International Peace Research Institute, SIPRI Military Expenditure Database, https://www.sipri.org/databases/milex.

4.   United States Defense Intelligence Agency, *China Military Power: Modernizing a Force to Fight and Win,* 2019, 33, https://www.dia.mil/Portals/27/Documents/News /Military%20Power%20Publications/China_Military_Power_FINAL_5MB_2019 0103.pdf.

5.   Michael A. Glosny, *Getting Beyond Taiwan? Chinese Foreign Policy and PLA Modernization* (Washington, D.C.: Institute for National Strategic Studies, National Defense University, 2011), 1.

6.   Joel Wuthnow, "System Overload: Can China's Military Be Distracted in a War Over Taiwan?," Center for the Study of Chinese Military Affairs, Institute for National Strategic Studies, *China Strategic Perspectives,* no. 15 (2020): 3.

7.   Eric Heginbotham et al., *The U.S.-China Military Scorecard: Forces, Geography, and the Evolving Balance of Power, 1996–2017* (Santa Monica, Calif.: RAND, 2015).

8.   Robert S. Ross, "Navigating the Taiwan Strait: Deterrence, Escalation Dominance, and U.S.-China Relations," *International Security* 27, no. 2 (2002): 47–85.

9.   Oriana Skylar Mastro and Ian Easton, "Risk and Resiliency: China's Emerging Air Base Strike Threat," Project 2049 Institute (2017), 8.

10. William S. Murray, "Asymmetric Options for Taiwan's Deterrence and Defense," in *Globalization and Security Relations Across the Taiwan Strait: In the Shadow of China,* ed. Monique Ming-chin Chu and Scott L. Kastner (London: Routledge, 2015), 64. See also Piin-Fen Kok and David J. Firestein, *Threading the Needle: Proposals for U.S. and Chinese Actions on Arms Sales to Taiwan* (New York: EastWest Institute, 2013), http:// www.ewi.info/idea/threading-needle-proposals-us-and-chinese-actions-arms-sales -taiwan.

11. U.S.-China Economic and Security Review Commission, *2020 Report to Congress of the U.S.-China Economic and Security Review Commission* (Washington, D.C.: Government Printing Office, 2020), 464.

12. For an overview of Taiwan's active and passive responses to China's missile capabilities, see Mastro and Easton, "Risk and Resiliency."

13. Murray, "Asymmetric Options," 66.

14. David A. Shlapak et al., *A Question of Balance: Political Context and Military Aspects of the China-Taiwan Dispute* (Santa Monica, Calif.: RAND Corporation, 2009), 126.

15. Mark Stokes, testimony before the U.S.-China Economic and Security Review Commission, March 18, 2010, http://origin.www.uscc.gov/sites/default/files/transcripts/3.18.10HearingTranscript.pdf.

16. The PRC numbers include both PLA Air Force and PLA Navy planes. The numbers for 2000 come from U.S.-China Economic and Security Review Commission, *2014 Report to Congress of the U.S.-China Economic and Security Review Commission* (Washington, D.C.: Government Printing Office, 2014), 300–309. The 2020 numbers are from Office of the Secretary of Defense, *Annual Report to Congress: Military and Security Developments Involving the People's Republic of China* (Washington, D.C.: U.S. Department of Defense, 2020), 166.

17. Heginbotham et al., *U.S.-China Military Scorecard*, 75.

18. See Ian Easton, testimony before the U.S.-China Economic and Security Review Commission, June 5, 2014, https://www.uscc.gov/sites/default/files/Easton_USCC_Taiwan_Hearing_Statement_2014.pdf. On PLA Air Force training, see Kevin Lanzit, "Education and Training in the PLAAF," in *The Chinese Air Force: Evolving Concepts, Roles, and Capabilities*, ed. Richard P. Hollion, Roger Cliff, and Phillip C. Saunders (Washington, D.C.: National Defense University Press, 2012), 235–54.

19. Shlapak et al., *Question of Balance*, 131.

20. Heginbotham et al., *U.S.-China Military Scorecard*.

21. Michael A. Hunzeker et al., *A Question of Time: Enhancing Taiwan's Conventional Deterrence Posture* (Arlington, Va.: Schar School of Policy and Government, George Mason University, 2018), 51. To be clear, although the PRC could undoubtedly impose great costs on Taiwan in a strike campaign, this does not mean that Taiwan would be left defenseless. Beckley observes, for instance, that much of Iraq's air force and mobile missile launchers survived a relentless U.S.-led bombing campaign during the Gulf War; it is likely that much of Taiwan's forces would similarly survive a PRC strike campaign. Moreover, Taiwan has the capacity to impose high costs on China as well. Chinese aircraft would face sophisticated surface-to-air missiles and mobile anti-aircraft guns, and Taiwan has its own missiles that could hit military targets in the PRC. For a discussion, see Michael Beckley, *Unrivaled: Why America Will Remain the World's Sole Superpower* (Ithaca, N.Y.: Cornell University Press, 2018), 80.

22. Glosny, writing in 2004, concluded that the risks of a PRC submarine blockade were overstated at the time. See Michael A. Glosny, "Strangulation from the Sea? A PRC Submarine Blockade of Taiwan," *International Security* 28, no. 4 (2004): 125–60.

23. See U.S.-China Economic and Security Review Commission, *2014 Report to Congress*, 300–309, 487.

24. Hunzeker et al., *Question of Time*, 59.

25. Though Cole did suggest that U.S. intervention would shift the naval balance in Tai-
     wan's favor. See Bernard D. Cole, "The Military Instrument of Statecraft at Sea: Naval
     Options in an Escalatory Scenario involving Taiwan, 2007–2016," in *Assessing the
     Threat: the Chinese Military and Taiwan's Security*, ed. Michael D. Swaine, Andrew N.
     D. Yang, and Evan S. Medeiros (Washington D.C.: Carnegie Endowment for Inter-
     national Peace, 2007), 195.
26. For a discussion of China's growing capacity to complicate U.S. intervention in a
     cross-strait conflict, see Thomas H. Shugart III, "Trends, Timelines, and Uncer-
     tainty: An Assessment of the State of Cross-Strait Deterrence," testimony before the
     U.S.-China Economic and Security Review Commission, February 18, 2021, https://
     www.uscc.gov/sites/default/files/2021-02/Thomas_Shugart_Testimony.pdf. Shugart
     highlights in particular China's improving missile capabilities, improving long-range
     bomber capabilities, and rapidly growing blue water navy. For an early statement on the
     PRC's increasing capacity to complicate U.S. intervention in a conflict near China's
     coast, see Thomas J. Christensen, "Posing Problems Without Catching Up: China's Rise
     and Challenges for U.S. Security Policy," *International Security* 25, no. 4 (2001): 5–40.
     See also Thomas J. Christensen, *The China Challenge: Shaping the Choices of a Rising
     Power* (New York: Norton, 2015), chap. 4. On the PRC anti-ship ballistic missile pro-
     gram, see Andrew S. Erickson, *Chinese Anti-Ship Ballistic Missile (ASBM) Develop-
     ment: Drivers, Trajectories, and Strategic Implications* (Washington, D.C.: Jamestown
     Foundation, 2013). For a discussion of the implications of China's A2/AD capabilities,
     see Stephen Biddle and Ivan Oelrich, "Future Warfare in the Western Pacific: Chinese
     Antiaccess/Area Denial, U.S. AirSea Battle, and Command of the Commons in East
     Asia," *International Security* 41, no. 1 (2016): 7–48.
27. Biddle and Oelrich, "Future Warfare," 41–42. See also Lonnie Henley, "PLA Opera-
     tional Concepts and Centers of Gravity in a Taiwan Conflict," testimony before the
     U.S.-China Economic and Security Review Commission, February 18, 2021, https://
     www.uscc.gov/sites/default/files/2021-02/Lonnie_Henley_Testimony.pdf. Henley
     argues that the PRC would likely maintain considerable capacity to impose a block-
     ade on Taiwan even if it were to suffer extensive losses in a war. He emphasizes, in
     particular, the likelihood that the PRC would be able to impose extensive damage on
     Taiwan ports, and that those ports would remain highly vulnerable because they
     mostly lie on the western side of the island.
28. Beckley, *Unrivaled*, 84.
29. Beckley, 85. On the other hand, for reasons to be skeptical that a U.S. cost-imposition
     strategy would be effective in ending a blockade, see Henley, "PRC Operational
     Concepts."
30. See Beckley, *Unrivaled*, 85. For an overview of improving PRC submarine capabili-
     ties, along with continued strong U.S. antisubmarine warfare capabilities, see Hegen-
     botham et al., *U.S.-China Military Scorecard*, 185–89.
31. James Holmes, "Could China Successfully Blockade Taiwan?," *National Inter-
     est*, August 28, 2020, https://nationalinterest.org/feature/could-china-successfully
     -blockade-taiwan-168035.

32. On this point, see also Denny Roy, "Prospects for Taiwan Maintaining Its Autonomy Under Chinese Pressure," *Asian Survey* 57, no. 6 (2017): 1153.

33. On how the PRC might pursue a blockade, based on analysis of PRC strategic writings, see Ian Easton, *The Chinese Invasion Threat: Taiwan's Defense and America's Strategy in Asia* (Arlington, Va.: Project 2049 Institute, 2017), 101–4.

34. Lyle L. Morris et al., *Gaining a Competitive Edge in the Gray Zone: Response Options for Aggression Below the Threshold for Major War* (Santa Monica, Calif.: RAND, 2019), 8.

35. See, for instance, Hunzeker et al., *Question of Time*; U.S.-China Economic and Security Review Commission, *2020 Report to Congress of the U.S.-China Economic and Security Review Commission* (Washington, D.C.: Government Printing Office, 2020); and Center for Strategic and International Studies, "Competing in the Gray Zone," n.d., https://www.csis.org/features/competing-gray-zone.

36. For a description of various actions the PRC has undertaken in recent years to pressure Taiwan using its military forces see U.S.-China Economic and Security Review Commission, *2020 Report to Congress*, 456–64. These actions include, in addition to airspace incursions, sending PRC aircraft carriers into waters near Taiwan and through the Taiwan Strait, and undertaking large-scale military exercises meant to prepare for a Taiwan contingency.

37. J. Michael Cole, "Are the Chinese Gearing Up for War in the Taiwan Strait?" *National Interest*, November 15, 2020: https://nationalinterest.org/blog/reboot/are-chinese-gearing-war-taiwan-strait-172723.

38. "China Launches 'Gray-Zone' Warfare to Subdue Taiwan," *Reuters*, December 10, 2020: https://www.reuters.com/investigates/special-report/hongkong-taiwan-military/.

39. "China Launches 'Gray-Zone' Warfare."

40. Hunzeker et al., *Question of Time*, chap. 4. The authors argue that Taiwan faces a trilemma in its deterrence posture, where it can have only two of the following three things: a reasonably limited defense budget; effective deterrence of a PRC invasion; and effective countering of PRC gray zone incursions. The high costs of advanced air and naval capabilities needed to counter such incursions would either force major increases in defense budgets or detract from investments in things like asymmetrical weapons systems and improved troop readiness that help to deter invasion. The authors conclude that the best option (or, perhaps more accurately, least bad option) for Taiwan is to accept some ceding of the gray zone.

41. Shlapak et al., *Question of Balance*, 118.

42. Office of the Secretary of Defense, *Annual Report to Congress: Military and Security Developments Involving the People's Republic of China* (Washington, D.C.: U.S. Department of Defense, 2014), 55.

43. Ian M. Easton, testimony before the U.S.-China Economic and Security Review Commission, June 5, 2014, https://www.uscc.gov/sites/default/files/Easton_USCC_Taiwan_Hearing_Statement_2014.pdf. On the high costs of a PRC coercive attack on Taiwan, see also Paul H. B. Godwin and Alice L. Miller, *China's Forbearance Has*

      Limits: Chinese Threat and Retaliation Signaling and Its Implications for a Sino-American Military Confrontation (Washington, D.C.: National Defense University Press, 2013), 19–20.

44. Denny Roy, "Prospects for Taiwan Maintaining Its Autonomy Under Chinese Pressure," *Asian Survey* 57, no. 6 (2017): 1154–55.

45. Biddle and Oelrich, "Future Warfare," 13.

46. On a Taiwan invasion scenario, see Beckley, *Unrivaled*, 80–83.

47. Office of the Secretary of Defense, *2020 Annual Report*, 114.

48. Office of the Secretary of Defense, 114.

49. Thomas H. Shugart III, "Trends, Timelines, and Uncertainty: An Assessment of the State of Cross-Strait Deterrence," testimony before the U.S.-China Economic and Security Review Commission, February 18, 2021, https://www.uscc.gov/sites/default /files/2021-02/Thomas_Shugart_Testimony.pdf.

50. Shugart, "Trends."

51. Mastro, "Precarious." On PRC capabilities and writings regarding information warfare, see also Fiona S. Cunningham, Testimony before the U.S.-China Economic and Security Review Commission, February 18, 2021, https://www.uscc.gov/sites/default /files/2021-02/Fiona_Cunningham_Testimony.pdf.

52. Mastro ("Precarious") warns about this possibility and notes that recent Pentagon and RAND Corporation war games have suggested that the United States would likely lose a war with China over Taiwan, and that the PRC would be able to successfully invade the island. See also "The U.S. Has Been 'Getting Its Ass Handed to It' in War Games Simulating Fights Against Russia and China," *Business Insider*, March 8, 2019, https://www.businessinsider.com/the-us-apparently-gets-its-ass-handed-to-it-in -war-games-2019-3.

53. For a discussion, see Mark Cozad, "Factors Shaping China's Use of Force Calculations Against Taiwan," testimony before the U.S.-China Economic and Security Review Commission, February 18, 2021, https://www.uscc.gov/sites/default/files/2021 -02/Mark_Cozad_Testimony.pdf. Mastro ("Precarious") notes, for instance, that PRC military leaders have told her "they will be ready" to compel unification within a year.

54. On China's resilience despite facing numerous financial challenges over the past several decades, see Thomas Orlik, *China: The Bubble That Never Pops* (New York: Oxford University Press, 2020). On some of the economic challenges facing China, see Thomas Fingar and Jean C. Oi, "China's Challenges: Now It Gets Much Harder," *Washington Quarterly* 43, no. 1 (2020): 67–84; Nicholas R. Lardy, *The State Strikes Back: The End of Economic Reform in China?* (Washington, D.C.: Peterson Institute for International Economics, 2019); and George Magnus, *Red Flags: Why Xi's China Is in Jeopardy* (New Haven, Conn.: Yale University Press, 2018).

55. Wuthnow, "System Overload."

56. These findings are from the 2020 Taiwan National Security Survey. The Taiwan National Security Surveys (2002–2020) were conducted by the Election Study Center of the National Chengchi University, Taipei, Taiwan, under the auspices of the Program in Asian Security Studies (PASS) at Duke University. For more detailed

information about each of the surveys, see http:/sites.duke.edu/pass/. Note that participating directly in the war includes those saying they would "resist," "join the military," or "support government decisions." For overviews of the results, see Dennis V. Hickey, "More and More Taiwanese Favor Independence—and Think the US Would Help Fight for It," *Diplomat*, December 3, 2020, https://thediplomat.com/2020/12/more-and-more-taiwanese-favor-independence-and-think-the-us-would-help-fight-for-it/; and "75% of Taiwanese Think Taiwan Independent; 53% Expect US Protection," *Taiwan News*, December 4, 2020, https://www.taiwannews.com.tw/en/news/4069688.

57. See, for instance, Hunzeker et al., *Question of Time*; William S. Murray, "Revisiting Taiwan's Defense Strategy," *Naval War College Review* 61, no. 3 (2008): 12–38; Murray, "Asymmetric Options"; and Colin Carroll and Rebecca Friedman Lissner, "Forget the Subs: What Taipei Can Learn from Tehran About Asymmetric Defense," *War on the Rocks*, April 6, 2017, https://warontherocks.com/2017/04/forget-the-subs-what-taipei-can-learn-from-tehran-about-asymmetric-defense/.

58. See Hsi-min Lee and Eric Lee, "Taiwan's Overall Defense Concept, Explained," *Diplomat*, November 3, 2020, https://thediplomat.com/2020/11/taiwans-overall-defense-concept-explained/. On the Overall Defense Concept, see also Drew Thompson, "Hope on the Horizon: Taiwan's Radical New Defense Concept," *War on the Rocks*, October 2, 2018, https://warontherocks.com/2018/10/hope-on-the-horizon-taiwans-radical-new-defense-concept/; and Kharis A. Templeman, testimony before the U.S.-China Economic and Security Review Commission, February 18, 2021, https://www.uscc.gov/sites/default/files/2021-02/Kharis_Templeman_Testimony.pdf.

59. Some analysts remain skeptical of Taiwan's commitment to the Overall Defense Concept and its urgency in implementing reforms in this regard. See, for instance, Michael A. Hunzeker, testimony before the U.S.-China Economic and Security Review Commission, February 18, 2021, https://www.uscc.gov/sites/default/files/2021-02/Michael_Hunzeker_Testimony.pdf; and Tanner Greer, "Why I Fear for Taiwan," *Scholar's Stage* (blog), September 11, 2020, https://scholars-stage.blogspot.com/2020/09/why-i-fear-for-taiwan.html. Both point to factors such as bureaucratic inertia and domestic politics as undercutting reform. Greer also highlights complex historical legacies (such as deep skepticism of the armed forces by pan-green supporters given Taiwan's martial law past) and reluctance among both political leaders and citizens to make the sacrifices necessary to have a credible deterrent posture.

3. THE U.S. COMMITMENT TO TAIWAN

1. In the U.S.-PRC Joint Communiqué of 1972, the United States "acknowledges that all Chinese on either side of the Taiwan Strait maintain there is but one China and that Taiwan is a part of China." Full text available from the American Institute in Taiwan at https://www.ait.org.tw/our-relationship/policy-history/key-u-s-foreign-policy-documents-region/u-s-prc-joint-communique-1972/.

2. Article 5 of the treaty reads: "Each Party recognizes that an armed attack in the Western Pacific Area directed against the territories of each of the Parties would be dangerous to its own peace and safety and declares that it would act to meet the common danger in accordance with its constitutional processes." See Steven Goldstein and Randall Schriver, "An Uncertain Relationship: The United States, Taiwan and the Taiwan Relations Act," *China Quarterly* 165 (2001): 149.

3. Goldstein and Schriver, 149–50.

4. "U.S. Arms Sales to Taiwan Justified, Declassified Reagan Memo Reveals," *Focus Taiwan*, September 18, 2019, http://focustaiwan.tw/news/aipl/201909180020.aspx. The relevant passage of the joint communiqué of 1982 indicates the United States "does not seek to carry out a long-term policy of arms sales to Taiwan, that its arms sales to Taiwan will not exceed, either in qualitative or in quantitative terms, the level of those supplied in recent years . . . and that it intends gradually to reduce its sale of arms to Taiwan, leading, over a period of time, to a final resolution." The full text is available at https://www.ait.org.tw/our-relationship/policy-history/key-u-s-foreign-policy-documents-region/u-s-prc-joint-communique-1982/.

5. American Institute in Taiwan, "Declassified Cables: Taiwan Arms Sales and Six Assurances (1982)," https://www.ait.org.tw/our-relationship/policy-history/key-u-s-foreign-policy-documents-region/six-assurances-1982/.

6. Phil Stewart and Hyonhee Shin, "Mattis Says U.S. Troop Commitment to South Korea Is 'Ironclad,'" *Reuters*, June 18, 2018, https://www.reuters.com/article/us-southkorea-usa/mattis-says-u-s-troop-commitment-to-south-korea-is-ironclad-idUSKBN1JO0IR.

7. Lawrence Chung, "U.S. National Security Advisor John Bolton Rebukes Beijing for Incursions Into Taiwanese Airspace," *South China Morning Post*, April 2, 2019: https://www.scmp.com/news/china/diplomacy/article/3004261/us-national-security-adviser-john-bolton-rebukes-beijing. Some recent statements during the Biden administration have been stronger, as I elaborate on later in this chapter.

8. Richard C. Bush, "The United States Security Partnership with Taiwan," Brookings Institution, 2016, 3, https://www.brookings.edu/wp-content/uploads/2016/07/Paper-7v3.pdf.

9. Full text of the testimony available from the State Department at https://2001-2009.state.gov/p/eap/rls/rm/2004/31649.htm.

10. See especially the speech given by Thomas J. Christensen, then deputy assistant secretary of state for East Asian and Pacific affairs, to the U.S.-Taiwan Business Council, September 11, 2007, https://2001-2009.state.gov/p/eap/rls/rm/2007/91979.htm.

11. My discussion in this section draws from and builds on some of my earlier work, including Scott L. Kastner, "The Taiwan Issue in U.S.-China Relations: Slipping Into a Security Dilemma?," in *After Engagement: Dilemmas in U.S.-China Security Relations*, ed. Jacques deLisle and Avery Goldstein (Washington, D.C.: Brookings, 2021), 244–68; and Scott L. Kastner, "Ambiguity, Interdependence, and the U.S. Strategic Dilemma in the Taiwan Strait," *Journal of Contemporary China* 15, no. 49 (2006): 651–69.

12. It is worth noting here that "steps toward independence" or "moving toward independence" are obviously subjective evaluations on some level. Moreover, such steps could include both formal policy changes (changing the formal name of the country; writing a completely new constitution, etc.), but also changes that occur on a societal level (such as a shift in Taiwan centric identity, which will be discussed in the next chapter), which might themselves be partially endogenous to policy choices such as school curriculum. Different observers might come to different conclusions on whether a particular policy, speech, etc., is "changing the status quo" in this regard. Ultimately, the PRC's reaction to any particular policy decision in Taiwan that touches on sovereignty issues will be informed by Chinese leaders' interpretation of the policy and what it means for PRC long-term goals of preventing formal Taiwan independence and accomplishing formal unification.

13. See Christensen, U.S.-Taiwan Business Council speech.

14. On entrapment, see Glenn Snyder, "The Security Dilemma in Alliance Politics," *World Politics* 36, no. 4 (1984): 461–95.

15. For classic discussions of extended deterrence problems, see Thomas C. Schelling, *Arms and Influence* (New Haven, Conn.: Yale University Press, 1966); and Paul Huth, *Extended Deterrence and the Prevention of War* (New Haven, Conn.: Yale University Press, 1988).

16. This section draws in part from Scott L. Kastner, "Stronger Than Ever? US-Taiwan Relations During the First Tsai Administration," in *Navigating in Stormy Waters: Taiwan During the First Administration of Tsai Ing-wen*, ed. Gunter Schubert and Chun-Yi Lee (London: Routledge, 2021), 303–27. There I outline some of the trends discussed here in greater detail, with a particular focus on trends during the first Tsai Ing-wen administration.

17. See, for instance, Charles L. Glaser, "A U.S.-China Grand Bargain? The Hard Choice Between Military Competition and Accommodation," *International Security* 39, no. 4 (2015): 49–90; Bruce Gilley, "Not So Dire Straits: How the Finlandization of Taiwan Benefits US Security," *Foreign Affairs* 89, no. 1 (2010): 44–60; and Bill Owens, "America Must Start Treating China as a Friend," *Financial Times*, November 17, 2009, http://www.ft.com/cms/s/0/69241506-d3b2-11de-8caf-00144feabdco.html#axzz3d9SM9kwf.

18. See especially John J. Mearsheimer, "Say Goodbye to Taiwan," *National Interest*, March–April 2014, http://nationalinterest.org/article/say-goodbye-taiwan-9931; and Robert Sutter, *Taiwan's Future: Narrowing Straits* (Seattle: National Bureau of Asian Research, 2011).

19. Nancy Bernkopf Tucker and Bonnie Glaser, "Should the United States Abandon Taiwan?" *Washington Quarterly* 34, no. 4 (2011): 23–37; Shelley Rigger, "Why Giving Up Taiwan Will Not Help Us with China," American Enterprise Institute report, 2011, https://www.aei.org/research-products/report/why-giving-up-taiwan-will-not-help-us-with-china/.

20. See, for instance, Joseph Bosco, "Strategic Ambiguity on Taiwan No Longer Works—It's Time for Strategic Clarity," *Hill*, September 1, 2020, https://thehill.com/opinion

/international/514503-strategic-ambiguity-on-taiwan-no-longer-works-its-time-for -strategic; Richard Haass and David Sacks, "American Support for Taiwan Must Be Unambiguous," *Foreign Affairs*, September 2, 2020, https://www.foreignaffairs.com /articles/united-states/american-support-taiwan-must-be-unambiguous.   For counterarguments, see, e.g., Bonnie Glaser, "A Guarantee Isn't Worth the Risk," *Foreign Affairs*, September 24, 2020, https://www.foreignaffairs.com/articles/united -states/2020-09-24/dire-straits; and Nien-chung Chang-Liao and Chi Fang, "The Case for Maintaining Strategic Ambiguity in the Taiwan Strait," *Washington Quarterly* 44, no. 2 (2021): 45–60. For earlier debates on strategic ambiguity, see, e.g., Thomas J. Christensen, "The Contemporary Security Dilemma," *Washington Quarterly* 25, no. 4 (2002): 7–21.

21. For instance, President Tsai Ing-wen has called recent U.S.-Taiwan relations "better than ever," and Foreign Minister Joseph Wu has echoed this view. See "The Taiwan Relations Act at Forty and U.S.-Taiwan Relations," *CSIS*, April 9, 2019, https://www .csis.org/analysis/taiwan-relations-act-forty-and-us-taiwan-relations; Ralph Jennings, "Foreign Minister: Taiwan-US Relations Probably at Their Best Ever," *VOA*, August 30, 2019, https://www.voanews.com/usa/foreign-minister-taiwan-us-relations -probably-their-best-ever.

22. See, for instance, Raymond Zhong, "China Vows Sanctions on U.S. Firms Selling Arms to Taiwan," *New York Times*, July 12, 2019, https://www.nytimes.com/2019/07 /12/world/asia/taiwan-arms-china-sanctions.html.

23. For an elaboration of this line of argument, see Scott L. Kastner, William L. Reed, and Ping-Kuei Chen, "Mostly Bark, Little Bite? Modeling US Arms Sales to Taiwan and the Chinese Response," *Issues & Studies* 49, no. 3 (2013): 111–50.

24. Taiwan's legislature passed a bill funding the purchase of the F-16s in October, 2019. See "Bill Paving Way for NT$250 Billion Purchase Passes," *Focus Taiwan*, October 29, 2019, http://focustaiwan.tw/news/aipl/201910290006.aspx.

25. See U.S.-China Economic and Security Review Commission, *2019 Report to Congress of the U.S.-China Economic and Security Review Commission* (Washington, D.C.: Government Printing Office, 2019), 457.

26. For a discussion, see Shirly Kan, "Congressional Support for Taiwan's Defense Through the National Defense Authorization Act," National Bureau of Asian Research, 2018, https://www.nbr.org/wp-content/uploads/pdfs/us-taiwan_defense_ relations_roundtable_may2018.pdf.

27. On these cases, see Richard C. Bush, *At Cross-Purposes: US-Taiwan Relations Since 1942* (Armonk, N.Y.: M. E. Sharpe, 2004), 223–26; and Susan V. Lawrence and Wayne M. Morrison, "Taiwan: Issues for Congress," CRS Report, 2017, 21, https://fas .org/sgp/crs/row/R44996.pdf.

28. For a summary of U.S. cabinet-level visits to Taiwan since 1979, see Lawrence and Morrison, "Taiwan," 21.

29. See Chris Horton, "U.S. Unveils an Office in Taiwan, but Sends No Top Officials," *New York Times*, June 12, 2018, https://www.nytimes.com/2018/06/12/world/asia /trump-taiwan-ait.html.

30. On the meeting, see "China Bridles at Rare Meeting Between Taiwan and U.S. Security Officials," *Reuters*, May 26, 2019, https://www.reuters.com/article/us-usa-taiwan /china-bridles-at-rare-meeting-between-taiwan-and-u-s-security-officials -idUSKCN1SX077.

31. Yasmeen Abutaleb, "Azar Criticizes China's Response to Coronavirus During Taiwan Visit," *Washington Post*, August 12, 2020, https://www.washingtonpost.com /health/2020/08/12/azar-criticizes-chinas-response-coronavirus-during-taiwan -visit/.

32. See "Under Secretary Keith Krach's Travel to Taiwan," State Department Press Statement, September 16, 2020, https://www.state.gov/under-secretary-keith-krachs -travel-to-taiwan/. Robert Sutter notes, moreover, that meetings at the deputy assistant level have been more frequent and publicized in recent years than was the case in the past, and that recent years have seen an increase in military-to-military consultations and planning that often occurs "out of public view." See Robert Sutter, "The US and Taiwan Embrace Despite China's Objections, but Will It Last?" *Pacific Forum PacNet*, no. 58, November 12, 2019, https://www.pacforum.org/analysis/pacnet-58-us -and-taiwan-embrace-despite-china%E2%80%99s-objections-will-it-last.

33. Lawrence and Morrison, "Taiwan," 21–22. The one exception to the stopover rule occurred with Lee Teng-hui's trip to Cornell University in 1995, discussed in the introduction. This was a special case where the Clinton administration had little choice but to allow Lee's visit given strong congressional support for such action.

34. For a discussion of these episodes and a nice general overview of stopover visits, see Kristian McGuire, "Tsai Ing-wen's U.S. Transit Stops in Historical Context," *Diplomat*, July 5, 2016, https://thediplomat.com/2016/07/tsai-ing-wens-u-s-transit-stops-in -historical-context/.

35. These numbers are based on extensive internet searches using Google.

36. Kensaku Ihara, "Taiwan's Tsai Makes Historic Trip to NASA Space Center," *Nikkei Asian Review*, August 20, 2018, https://asia.nikkei.com/Politics/International -relations/Taiwan-s-Tsai-makes-historic-trip-to-NASA-space-center.

37. Prior to 2003, the Defense Department relied on contractors. See Lawrence and Morrison, "Taiwan," 16.

38. Bonnie Glaser, Richard C. Bush, and Michael J. Green, "Toward a Stronger U.S.-Taiwan Relationship," Center for Strategic and International Studies, report of the CSIS Task Force on U.S. Policy Toward Taiwan, 2020, https://csis-website-prod.s3 .amazonaws.com/s3fs-public/publication/201021_Glaser_TaskForce_Toward_A_ Stronger_USTaiwan_Relationship_0.pdf, 23.

39. See, e.g., "US Warship Transits Taiwan Strait for Second Time in Two Weeks," *Reuters*, August 31, 2020, https://www.reuters.com/article/us-taiwan-usa-defence/u-s-warship -transits-taiwan-strait-for-second-time-in-two-weeks-idUSKBN25R0LC. The US-China Economic and Security Review Commission Annual Report to Congress for 2019, 457–58, lists recent U.S. Naval transits through the Taiwan Strait as one of several indicators that the report takes as evidence of "expanded U.S. efforts to support Taiwan's security." Others have argued, however, that the transits are a relatively muted signal.

See, for instance, David Lague and Benjamin Kang Lim, "The China Challenge: China's Vast Fleet Is Tipping the Balance in the Pacific," *Reuters* Special Report, April 30, 2019, https://www.reuters.com/investigates/special-report/china-army-navy/.

40.   See John Power, "US Warships Made 92 Trips Through the Taiwan Strait Since 2007," *South China Morning Post*, May 3, 2019, https://www.scmp.com/week-asia/geopolitics /article/3008621/us-warships-made-92-trips-through-taiwan-strait-2007. This report draws on data made available by the U.S. Pacific Fleet, including with regard to previously unannounced transits. On the uptick in 2019, see U.S.-China Economic and Security Review Commission, *2019 Annual Report*, 457.

41.   Sam LaGrone, "Two U.S. Warships Pass Through Taiwan Strait in 7th Transit Since 2018," *USNI News*, April 29, 2019, https://news.usni.org/2019/04/29/two-u-s-warships -pass-through-taiwan-strait-in-7th-transit-since-2018.

42.   The (arguably) key passage in the Taiwan Travel Act reads that "it should be the policy of the United States to . . . allow officials at all levels of the United States Government, including Cabinet-level national security officials, general officers, and other executive branch officials, to travel to Taiwan to meet their Taiwanese counterparts." The act does not present specifics concerning how frequently such meetings should occur nor does it outline consequences should the president ignore it. Text available at Congress.gov.

43.   Information about relevant Taiwan-related bills comes from Congress.gov.

44.   See Kan, "Congressional Support." The language directing the secretary of defense to undertake a review was included in the conference committee explanatory statement for the FY2010 bill but not in the final version of the bill that became law. For the text of the conference committee explanatory statement relating to Taiwan, *Congressional Record*, October 7, 2009, 290, https://www.congress.gov/111/crec/2009/10 /07/CREC-2009-10-07-pt1-PgH10565.pdf.

45.   Michael Mazza, "The National Defense Authorization Act and U.S. Policy Toward Taiwan," National Bureau of Asian Research, 2018, https://www.nbr.org/wp-content /uploads/pdfs/us-taiwan_defense_relations_roundtable_may2018.pdf. Note that the NDAA of 2018 contained other Taiwan-related provisions as well, including a requirement that the secretaries of defense and state should provide regular briefings on Taiwan's security to Congress.

46.   Text of NDAAs is available at Congress.gov.

47.   Mark Landler, "Trump Suggests Using Bedrock China Policy as Bargaining Chip," *New York Times*, December 11, 2016, https://www.nytimes.com/2016/12/11/us/politics /trump-taiwan-one-china.html.

48.   Mark Landler and Michael Forsythe, "Trump Tells Xi Jinping US Will Honor 'One China' Policy," *New York Times*, February 9, 2017, https://www.nytimes.com/2017/02 /09/world/asia/donald-trump-china-xi-jinping-letter.html.

49.   Pence's remarks are available from the Hudson Institute at https://www.hudson.org /events/1610-vice-president-mike-pence-s-remarks-on-the-administration-s-policy -towards-china102018.

50.   The full text of the report is available from the U.S. Department of Defense at https:// media.defense.gov/2019/Jul/01/2002152311/-1/-1/1/department-of-defense-indo

-pacific-strategy-report-2019.pdf. The indirect reference to Taiwan as a country occurs on page 30, where, after referencing Singapore, Taiwan, Mongolia, and New Zealand as reliable partners of the United States, the report notes that "all four countries contribute to U.S. missions around the world."

51. This quote is from page 31 of the report. The relevant section of the National Security Strategy on page 47 reads: "We will maintain our strong ties with Taiwan in accordance with our 'One China' policy, including our commitments under the Taiwan Relations Act to provide for Taiwan's legitimate defense needs and deter coercion." See https://www.whitehouse.gov/wp-content/uploads/2017/12/NSS-Final-12-18-2017-0905.pdf. The 2015 report does not mention Taiwan, and the 2010 report briefly notes that the United States would "encourage the continued reduction of tension between the People's Republic of China and Taiwan." The 2010 report is available at https://obamawhitehouse.archives.gov/sites/default/files/rss_viewer/national_security_strategy.pdf.

52. See https://www.state.gov/prc-military-pressure-against-taiwan-threatens-regional-peace-and-stability/; and "US Says Commitment to Taiwan 'Rock Solid,'" *Taipei Times*, April 9, 2021, https://www.taipeitimes.com/News/taiwan/archives/2021/04/09/2003755372.

53. The full text of the Biden-Suga joint statement is at https://www.whitehouse.gov/briefing-room/statements-releases/2021/04/16/u-s-japan-joint-leaders-statement-u-s-japan-global-partnership-for-a-new-era/. The full text of the Biden-Moon joint statement is at https://www.whitehouse.gov/briefing-room/statements-releases/2021/05/21/u-s-rok-leaders-joint-statement/.

54. David E. Sanger, "Biden Said the US Would Protect Taiwan. But It's Not That Clear Cut," *New York Times*, October 22, 2021, https://www.nytimes.com/2021/10/22/us/politics/biden-taiwan-defense-china.html.

55. Bush, "Cross-Purposes."

56. See, for instance, comments from PRC officials at a 2019 dialogue, summarized in Ambassador Stephen M. Young (Ret.), "A Conference with the Taiwan Affairs Office of the PRC State Council," National Committee on American Foreign Policy, June 2019, https://www.ncafp.org/2016/wp-content/uploads/2019/07/NCAFP-2019-TAO-Conference-Report_FINAL.pdf. In his virtual summit with President Biden in November 2021, Xi Jinping warned U.S. politicians not to "play with fire" by using Taiwan as a point of leverage with China. See "Biden and Xi Pledge More Cooperation, but Offer No Breakthroughs," *New York Times*, November 15, 2021, https://www.nytimes.com/live/2021/11/15/world/biden-xi-summit.

4. DOMESTIC DYNAMICS IN CHINA AND TAIWAN

1. Data are available from Freedom House at https://freedomhouse.org/report/freedom-world. On Taiwan's democratization, see Shelley Rigger, *Politics in Taiwan: Voting for Democracy* (London: Routledge, 1999); Alan M. Wachman, *Taiwan: National Identity and Democratization* (Armonk, N.Y.: M. E. Sharpe, 1994); and Dafydd Fell, *Government and Politics in Taiwan: Second Edition* (London: Routledge, 2018).

2.   The full text of the speech is at https://www.president.gov.tw/NEWS/25319.

3.   Nathan Batto, "The NPP's Internal Divisions, Ko's New Party, and the China Cleavage," *Frozen Garlic: A Blog on Elections in Taiwan*, August 7, 2019, https://frozengarlic.wordpress.com/2019/08/07/the-npps-internal-divisions-kos-new-party-and-the-china-cleavage/.

4.   Batto, "NPP's Internal Divisions."

5.   Fell, *Government and Politics*, 24.

6.   Shelley Rigger, *Why Taiwan Matters: Small Island, Global Powerhouse* (Lanham, Md.: Rowman and Littlefield, 2011), 35.

7.   Rigger, 35; Teng-hui Lee, "Understanding Taiwan: Bridging the Perception Gap," *Foreign Affairs* 78, no. 6 (1999): 9.

8.   On nation-building during the Chen administration, see also Daniel C. Lynch, "Taiwan's Self-Conscious Nation-Building Project," *Asian Survey* 44, no. 4 (2004): 513–33.

9.   Rigger, "Why Taiwan," 36.

10. T. Y. Wang, "Changing Boundaries: The Development of the Taiwan Voters' Identity," in *The Taiwan Voter*, ed. Christopher Henry Achen and T. Y. Wang (Ann Arbor: University of Michigan Press, 2017), 53. It is also worth emphasizing that the distinction between "mainlanders" and "native Taiwanese" is much less important as a social cleavage than it was in the years after 1945, for a variety of reasons (including the simple fact that more than seventy years have passed since the end of the Chinese Civil War). See Wang, "Changing Boundaries," 50–51; and Rigger, *Why Taiwan*, 38.

11. Wang, "Changing Boundaries," 57, 54.

12. Rigger, *Why Taiwan*.

13. Yang Zhong, "Explaining National Identity Shift in Taiwan," *Journal of Contemporary China* 25, no. 99 (2016): 336–52.

14. Rou-lan Chen, "Beyond National Identity in Taiwan: A Multidimensional and Evolutionary Conceptualization," *Asian Survey* 52, no. 5 (2012): 845–71.

15. Wang, "Changing Boundaries," 61.

16. Yun-han Chu, "Taiwan's National Identity Politics and the Prospect of Cross-Strait Relations," *Asian Survey* 44, no. 4 (2004): 484–512.

17. Emerson M. S. Niou, "Understanding Taiwan Independence and Its Policy Implication," *Asian Survey* 44, no. 4 (2004): 555–67.

18. Taiwan's Election and Democratization Study, Survey of the Presidential and Legislative Elections, 2012, http://teds.nccu.edu.tw/teds_plan/list.php?g_isn=61.

19. Taiwan's Election and Democratization Study, Survey of the Presidential and Legislative Elections, 2020, http://teds.nccu.edu.tw/teds_plan/item.php?cat_choose=64.

20. The Taiwan National Security Surveys (2002–2020) were conducted by the Election Study Center of the National Chengchi University, Taipei, under the auspice of the Program in Asian Security Studies (PASS) at Duke University. For more detailed information about each of the surveys (and for the results described here), see http://sites.duke.edu/pass/.

21. While surveys generally find limited support for the one country, two systems model in Taiwan, just how low that support is appears to depend heavily on how survey

questions are framed. The TNSS of 2020, for instance, frames one country, two systems in a fairly positive light in asking: "Mainland China hopes Taiwan will accept one country, two systems, which it says will guarantee that the lives of the Taiwan people will not change and war will be avoided. Do you agree or disagree that this would be an acceptable outcome?" Some 32.6 percent of survey respondents agreed or strongly agreed. On the other hand, Taiwan's Mainland Affairs Council fielded a survey in 2020 (implemented by the NCCU Election Study Center) that asked: "The CCP has put forward '1 country, two systems,' which will make Taiwan a local government and a special administrative region, and will mean accepting CCP governance and that the ROC will cease to exist. Do you approve or disapprove of this proposition?" Perhaps not surprisingly, support was much lower, at less than 5 percent. The survey results are available at https://ws.mac.gov.tw/001/Upload/295/relfile/7837/76094/f02a6ff0-7720-425e-8f37-cc4c4002ef22.pdf.

22. See Fang-yu Chen et al., "What Do Taiwan's People Think About Their Relationship to China?," *Diplomat*, May 29, 2020, https://thediplomat.com/2020/05/what-do-taiwans-people-think-about-their-relationship-to-china/. The authors conducted a survey that asked some respondents whether they viewed Taiwan as a sovereign state and other respondents whether they viewed the ROC as a sovereign state. In both cases, over 90 percent agreed. The authors interpret this to mean the Taiwan "public considers Taiwan, as a synonym to the ROC, to be a sovereign state."

23. Batto, "NPP's Internal Divisions."

24. John Fuh-sheng Hsieh, "Ethnicity, National Identity, and Domestic Politics in Taiwan," *Journal of Asian and African Studies* 40, no. 1/2 (2005): 13–28; Shing-yuan Sheng and Hsiao-chuan (Mandy) Liao, "Issues, Political Cleavages, and Party Competition in Taiwan," in *The Taiwan Voter*, ed. Christopher Henry Achen and T. Y. Wang (Ann Arbor: University of Michigan Press, 2017), 98–138.

25. Christopher H. Achen and T. Y. Wang, "Conclusion: The Power of Identity in Taiwan," in *The Taiwan Voter*, ed. Christopher Henry Achen and T. Y. Wang (Ann Arbor: University of Michigan Press, 2017), 273–92.

26. Alexander C. Tan and Karl Ho, "Cross-Strait Relations and the Taiwan Voter," in *The Taiwan Voter*, ed. Christopher Henry Achen and T. Y. Wang (Ann Arbor: University of Michigan Press, 2017), 158–69.

27. Sheng and Liao, "Issues."

28. For a succinct summary of shifts in each party's approach to the China issue over time, see Sheng and Liao, "Issues."

29. Sheng and Liao, "Issues."

30. Data on party support come from "Changes in Party Identification of Taiwanese as Tracked in Surveys by the Election Study Center, NCCU (1992 2020.12)," https://esc.nccu.edu.tw/upload/44/doc/6964/Party202012.jpg.

31. On the cross-strait policy dilemmas facing the KMT, see Derek Grossman and Brandon Alexander Millan, "Taiwan's KMT May Have a Serious '1992 Consensus' Problem," RAND Corporation, September 25, 2020, https://www.rand.org/blog/2020/09/taiwans-kmt-may-have-a-serious-1992-consensus-problem.html.

32. Alan Wachman, *Why Taiwan? Geostrategic Rationales for China's Territorial Integrity* (Stanford, Calif.: Stanford University Press, 2007), 39.

33. See especially Wachman, *Why Taiwan?*, for an elaboration of the strategic logic of Chinese interest in Taiwan, with references to Chinese strategic writings on the subject earlier this century. It is worth noting here that there are other strategic logics to Beijing's interest in Taiwan. Beijing's handling of the Taiwan issue, for instance, can have implications for separatist movements elsewhere in China, where a failure to take a strong stand against separatism in Taiwan could lead separatist groups on China's periphery—such as in Xinjiang and Tibet—to conclude that Beijing lacks resolve in opposing separatism more generally. Indeed, Christensen writes that Chinese leaders "subscribe to a domestic domino theory in which the loss of one piece of sovereign territory will encourage separatists elsewhere and hurt morale among the Chinese forces who must defend national unity." See Thomas J. Christensen, "Chinese Realpolitik," *Foreign Affairs* 75, no. 5 (1996): 46. For a summary of some of the reasons China cares about Taiwan, including its strategic motivations, see Rigger, *Why Taiwan*, 172–73.

34. On the South Korean television show, see Keoni Everington, "Chinese Netizens Cry Foul Over Taiwan Flag on South Korea's 'Running Man,'" *Taiwan News*, December 8, 2020, https://www.taiwannews.com.tw/en/news/4072355. For examples of corporations changing their depictions of Taiwan in response to PRC pressure, see Chris Horton and Shuhei Yamada, "How Beijing Enlists Global Companies to Pressure Taiwan," *Nikkei Asia*, July 25, 2018, https://asia.nikkei.com/Spotlight/The-Big-Story/How-Beijing-enlists-global-companies-to-pressure-Taiwan; on Hollywood, see Aynne Kokas, "Mulan Is a Movie About How Much Hollywood Needs China," *Washington Post*, September 9, 2020, https://www.washingtonpost.com/outlook/2020/09/09/mulan-is-movie-about-how-much-hollywood-needs-china/. Kokas describes a recent case where the Taiwan flag was removed from the jacket of the Tom Cruise character in the Top Gun sequel.

35. Thomas J. Christensen, "China," in *Strategic Asia: Power and Purpose*, ed. Richard J. Ellings and Aaron L. Friedberg (Seattle: National Bureau of Asian Research, 2001–2002), 41.

36. Susan L. Shirk, *China, Fragile Superpower: How China's Internal Politics Could Derail its Peaceful Rise* (New York: Oxford University Press, 2007), 186.

37. See, for instance, Allen Carlson, *Unifying China, Integrating with the World: Securing Chinese Sovereignty in the Reform Era* (Stanford, Calif.: Stanford University Press, 2005), 134; Gregory J. Moore, "The Power of 'Sacred Commitments'—Chinese Interests in Taiwan," *Foreign Policy Analysis* 12, no. 2 (2016): 214–35.

38. Christensen, "China," 41. See also Christensen, "Chinese Realpolitik"; and Yinan He, "History, Chinese Nationalism, and the Emerging Sino-Japanese Conflict," *Journal of Contemporary China* 16, no. 50 (2007): 1–24.

39. Shirk, *Fragile Superpower*, 186–87.

40. Christensen, "China"; Yu-Shan Wun and Kuan-Wu Chen, "Domestic Politics and Cross-Strait Relations: A Synthetic Perspective," *Journal of Asian and African Studies* 55, no. 2 (2020): 168–86.

41. See, e.g., Shirk, *Fragile Superpower*; He, "History"; and Jessica Chen Weiss, *Powerful Patriots: Nationalist Protest in China's Foreign Relations* (New York: Oxford University Press, 2014).

42. Weiss, *Powerful Patriots*, 7.

43. Alastair Iain Johnston, "Is Chinese Nationalism Rising? Evidence from Beijing," *International Security* 41, no. 3 (2017): 7–43.

44. Jessica Chen Weiss, "How Hawkish Is the Chinese Public? Another Look at 'Rising Nationalism' and Chinese Foreign Policy," *Journal of Contemporary China* 28, no. 119 (2019): 679–95.

45. Hsin-Hsin Pan, Wen-Chin Wu, and Yu-Tzung Chang, "How Chinese Citizens Perceive Cross-Strait Relations: Survey Results from Ten Major Cities in China," *Journal of Contemporary China* 26, no. 106 (2017): 616–31.

46. The survey was conducted on university students in Beijing. Elina Sinkkonen, "Nationalism, Patriotism, and Foreign Policy Attitudes Among Chinese University Students," *China Quarterly* 216 (2013): 1045–63.

47. Peter Gries and Tao Wang, "Taiwan's Perilous Futures: Chinese Nationalism, the 2020 Presidential Elections, and U.S.-China Tensions Spell Trouble for Cross-Strait Relations," *World Affairs* 183, no. 1 (2020): 40–61.

48. Weiss, *Powerful Patriots*.

49. Michael Tomz, "Domestic Audience Costs in International Relations: An Experimental Approach," *International Organization* 61, no. 4 (2007): 821–40; Xiaojun Li and Dingding Chen, "Public Opinion, International Reputation, and Audience Costs in an Authoritarian Regime," *Conflict Management and Peace Science* 38, no. 5 (2021): 543–60.

50. Kai Quek and Alastair Iain Johnston, "Can China Back Down? Crisis De-escalation in the Shadow of Popular Opposition," *International Security* 42, no. 3 (2018): 7–36; Jessica Chen Weiss and Alan Dafoe, "Authoritarian Audiences, Rhetoric, and Propaganda in International Crises: Evidence from China," *International Studies Quarterly* 63, no. 4 (2019): 963–73.

51. On the PRC government's ability to change course in its foreign policy and subsequently build support for that new course, see also James Reilly, *Strong Society, Smart State: The Rise of Public Opinion in China's Japan Policy* (New York: Columbia University Press, 2012).

52. Shirk, *Fragile Superpower*, 191, cites Taiwan policy advisors in China on this point.

53. The White Paper listed three conditions under which force would be justified against Taiwan: a Taiwan declaration of independence, a foreign invasion of Taiwan, or indefinite delay by Taiwan officials on negotiating reunification. For a discussion, see Alan D. Romberg, *Rein in at the Brink of the Precipice: American Policy Toward Taiwan and U.S.-PRC Relations* (Washington, D.C.; Henry L. Stimson Center, 2003), 190–91.

54. Chien-kai Chen, "Comparing Jiang Zemin's Impatience with Hu Jintao's Patience Regarding the Taiwan Issue, 1989–2012," *Journal of Contemporary China* 21, no. 78 (2012): 955–72. Still, it is worth noting that no explicit timetables were ever released during the Jiang years, and PRC officials denied that a timetable had been set. See

Chen-yuan Tung, "An Assessment of China's Taiwan Policy under the Third Generation Leadership," *Asian Survey* 45, no. 3 (2005): 352.

55.   Hu's six-point proposal was delivered to commemorate the thirtieth anniversary of the "Message to Taiwan Compatriots," which signaled the shift in the PRC's Taiwan policy toward "peaceful reunification." The speech was generally seen as conciliatory and pragmatic; the six points emphasized increased interactions and flexibility in terms of Taiwan's international space. For a discussion, see Russell Hsiao, "Hu Jintao's 'Six-Points' Proposition to Taiwan," Jamestown Foundation, January 12, 2009, https://jamestown.org/program/hu-jintaos-six-points-proposition-to-taiwan/.

56.   Richard C. Bush, "8 Key Things to Notice from Xi Jinping's New Year Speech on Taiwan," Brookings Institution, 2019, https://www.brookings.edu/blog/order-from-chaos/2019/01/07/8-key-things-to-notice-from-xi-jinpings-new-year-speech-on-taiwan/.

57.   Bush, "8 Key Things"; Qiang Xin, "Having Much in Common? Changes and Continuity in China's Taiwan Policy," *Pacific Review* 34, no. 6 (2021): 926–45.

58.   See, e.g., Xi's speech to the CCP National Congress in 2017, available at http://www.xinhuanet.com/english/download/Xi_Jinping's_report_at_19th_CPC_National_Congress.pdf. Note that Xi, even in his 2019 speech noted earlier, has not publicized any explicit unification deadlines.

59.   Xin, "Having Much."

60.   Chen, "Comparing Jiang," makes this argument explicitly; Shirk, *Fragile Superpower*, highlights similar factors.

61.   Shirk, *Fragile Superpower*.

62.   Xin, "Having Much."

5. MODELING CROSS-STRAIT RELATIONS

1.   For a discussion of different types of models, and their purposes, see Kevin A. Clarke and David M. Primo, *A Model Discipline: Political Science and the Logic of Representations* (New York: Oxford University Press, 2012).

2.   For a critique of the use of formal theory in security studies, see Stephen M. Walt, "Rigor or Rigor Mortis? Rational Choice and Security Studies," *International Security* 23, no. 4 (1999): 5–48. I do not construct a formal mathematical model here.

3.   Clarke and Primo, *Model Discipline*.

4.   On organizational models, see Clarke and Primo, 87–90.

5.   For a book that considers different types of PRC invasion scenarios, see Ian Easton, *The Chinese Invasion Threat: Taiwan's Defense and America's Strategy in Asia* (Arlington, Va.: Project 2049 Institute, 2017).

6.   James D. Fearon, "Rationalist Explanations for War," *International Organization* 49, no. 3 (1995): 379–414.

7.   David A. Lake, "Two Cheers for Bargaining Theory: Assessing Rationalist Explanations for the Iraq War," *International Security* 35, no. 3 (2010/2011): 7–52. Key works in this literature include Thomas C. Schelling, *Arms and Influence* (New Haven,

Conn.: Yale University Press, 1966); Thomas C. Schelling, *The Strategy of Conflict* (Cambridge, Mass.: Harvard University Press, 1960); Fearon, "Rationalist Explanations"; Stephen Van Evera, *Causes of War: Power and the Roots of Conflict* (Ithaca, N.Y.: Cornell University Press, 1999); Robert Powell, "Bargaining Theory and International Conflict," *Annual Review of Political Science* 5, no. 1 (2002): 1–30; Robert Powell, "War as a Commitment Problem," *International Organization* 60, no. 1 (2006): 169–203; Erik Gartzke, "War Is in the Error Term," *International Organization* 53, no. 3 (1999): 567–87; William Reed, "Information, Power, and War," *American Political Science Review* 97, no. 4 (2003): 633–41; Dan Reiter, "Exploring the Bargaining Model of War," *Perspectives of Politics* 1, no. 1 (2002): 27–43. Branislav L. Slanchev, "The Power to Hurt: Costly Conflict with Completely Informed States," *American Political Science Review* 97, no. 1 (2003): 123–33; R. Harrison Wagner, *War and the State: The Theory of International Politics* (Ann Arbor: University of Michigan Press, 2007); Alex Weisiger, *Logics of War: Explanations for Limited and Unlimited Conflicts* (Ithaca, N.Y.: Cornell University Press, 2013); and Oriana Skylar Mastro, *The Costs of Conversation: Obstacles to Peace in Wartime* (Ithaca, N.Y.: Cornell University Press, 2019), among others.

8. See especially Fearon, "Rationalist Explanations," on this point.

9. For a discussion of the war's costs, see Lake, "Two Cheers." Those costs continued to accrue after Lake wrote the article.

10. See, e.g., Fearon, "Rationalist Explanations"; Reiter, "Exploring."

11. Lake, "Two Cheers."

12. David A. Lake and Robert Powell, eds., *Strategic Choice and International Relations* (Princeton, N.J.: Princeton University Press, 1999).

13. Fearon, "Rationalist Explanations."

14. See, e.g., Jacques deLisle, "The China-Taiwan Relationship: Law's Spectral Answers to the Cross-Strait Sovereignty Question," *Orbis* 46, no. 4 (2002): 733–52.

15. Fearon, "Rationalist Explanations."

16. For studies that conceptualize Taiwan's status as a continuum of potential outcomes, see, for instance, David M. Lampton, "Preparing for a Better Time in Cross-Strait Relations: Short-Term Stalemate, Possible Medium-Term Opportunities," in *Breaking the China-Taiwan Impasse*, ed. Donald S. Zagoria (Westport, Conn.: Praeger, 2003), 105 14; Roger Cliff and David A. Shlapak, *U.S.-China Relations after Resolution of Taiwan's Status* (Santa Monica, Calif.: RAND, 2007); Richard C. Bush, *Untying the Knot: Making Peace in the Taiwan Strait* (Washington, D.C.: Brookings, 2005). For a more general study that presents a similar approach, see, for instance, Chad Rector, *Federations: The Dynamics of International Cooperation* (Ithaca, N.Y.: Cornell University Press, 2009). For a counterargument relating to the cross-strait case, see deLisle, "China-Taiwan Relationship," who argues that the core issue in cross-strait relations is actually less divisible than meets the eye: while a range of possible divisions of sovereignty are possible in theory, the core issue of contention is more one of principle. DeLisle (749) notes in particular "Beijing's insistence on the unitary sovereignty of a China that includes Taiwan while Taiwanese leaders asymptotically approach declaring separate sovereign statehood for Taiwan."

17. On core national interests, see Michael D. Swaine, "China's Assertive Behavior—Part One: On "Core Interests," *China Leadership Monitor* 34 (2011), https://www.hoover.org/research/chinas-assertive-behavior-part-one-core-interests.

18. For a brief overview, see Susan V. Lawrence and Wayne M. Morrison, "Taiwan: Issues for Congress," CRS Report, 2017, https://fas.org/sgp/crs/row/R44996.pdf, 45.

19. In the Resolution on Taiwan's Future (1999), the DPP outlined a policy which emphasized that Taiwan is a "sovereign and independent country"; that any effort to change this status quo would require approval from the Taiwan electorate in a referendum; that the PRC's one China principle and one country, two systems model "fundamentally don't apply to Taiwan"; and that Taiwan is named the "Republic of China" according to the current constitution (among other policy stances). The resolution effectively superseded the DPP's revisions to the party charter in 1991 calling for the establishment of a Republic of Taiwan. The text of the charter is available from the DPP's website at https://www.dpp.org.tw/upload/download/%E9%BB%A8%E7%B6%B1.pdf, with the 1999 resolution on pp. 31–33. Tsai Ing-wen has emphasized that Taiwan has no need to declare independence because "we are an independent country already and we call ourselves the Republic of China (Taiwan)." See John Sudworth, "China Needs to Show Taiwan Respect, Says President," *BBC*, January 14, 2020, https://www.bbc.com/news/world-asia-51104246.

20. For a discussion of Tsai's views on the 1992 consensus, and in particular how she formulated her position during her inaugural address in 2016, see Lawrence and Morrison, "Taiwan," 42–44; and Alan D. Romberg, "Tsai Ing-wen Takes Office: A New Era in Cross-Strait Relations," *China Leadership Monitor* 50 (2016): 4–6, https://www.hoover.org/sites/default/files/research/docs/clm50ar.pdf#overlay-context=research/chinese-views-presumptive-us-presidential-candidates-hillary-r-clinton-and-donald-j-trump.

21. Fearon, "Rationalist Explanations."

22. Christensen, "Contemporary Security Dilemma."

23. See especially Fearon, "Rationalist Explanations." On feigning weakness, see Branislav L. Slanchev, "Feigning Weakness," *International Organization* 64, no. 3 (2010): 357–88. Slanchev shows that leaders sometimes have contradictory incentives during bargaining to signal strength (to get a better bargain) and to signal weakness (to obtain tactical advantages should bargaining fail and war break out). Mao, for instance, appeared to feign weakness to lure U.S. troops deep into North Korea in 1950.

24. Fearon, "Rationalist Explanations"; Powell, "Commitment Problem."

6. THE PROBLEM OF TAIWAN REVISIONISM

1. I do not mean for the term *Taiwan revisionism* to carry any positive or negative connotations. I simply use it here as shorthand to describe dissatisfaction with the status quo in cross-strait relations, and efforts by leaders and citizens in Taiwan to

redefine Taiwan's sovereign status in a way that more closely resembles formal independence. For an analysis of the factors that give rise to Taiwan revisionism, see Robert S. Ross, "Explaining Taiwan's Revisionist Diplomacy," *Journal of Contemporary China* 15, no. 48 (2006): 443–58.

2. The transcripts from these interviews, including the quotes in this paragraph, are available from PBS at https://www.pbs.org/wgbh/pages/frontline/shows/china/experts/taiwan.html.

3. For studies published during the Chen administration that point toward Taiwan revisionism as a likely trigger for PRC use of military force, see, for instance, Richard C. Bush and Michael E. O'Hanlon, *A War Like No Other: The Truth About China's Challenge to America* (Hoboken, N.J.: Wiley, 2007); Ted Galen Carpenter, *America's Coming War with China: A Collision Course Over Taiwan* (New York: Palgrave Macmillan, 2005); Gabe T. Wang, *China and the Taiwan Issue: Impending War at the Taiwan Strait* (Lanham, Md.: University Press of America, 2006); and Michael A. Glosny, "Strangulation from the Sea? A PRC Submarine Blockade of Taiwan," *International Security* 28, no. 4 (2004): 125–60.

4. For instance, CATO Institute's Ted Galen Carpenter warns in a recent paper that warming U.S.-Taiwan relations and "the growing strength of staunchly pro-independence figures in Taiwan" could provoke conflict in the Taiwan Strait. Ted Galen Carpenter, "Is American Prodding Taiwan Toward Conflict with China?" *American Conservative*, May 30, 2019, https://www.cato.org/publications/commentary/america-prodding-taiwan-towards-conflict-china.

5. These quotes come from Xi's January 2, 2019, speech on Taiwan. See "Highlights of Xi's Speech at Taiwan Message Anniversary Event," *China Daily*, January 2, 2019, https://www.chinadaily.com.cn/a/201901/02/WS5c2c1ad2a310d91214052069_2.html.

6. To be clear, just because a potential gain is mostly symbolic does not mean it lacks important meaning or value to people seeking such a gain.

7. Steve Tsang, ed., *If China Attacks Taiwan: Military Strategy, Politics, and Economics* (London: Routledge, 2006), 1.

8. Scott L. Kastner, "Is the Taiwan Strait Still a Flashpoint? Assessing the Prospects for Armed Conflict Between China and Taiwan." *International Security* 40, no. 3 (2015/2016): 54–92.

9. The arguments that I advance in the next two sections draw from—but also extend—the analysis developed in Kastner, "Is the Taiwan Strait," and Scott L. Kastner, "Rethinking the Prospects for Conflict in the Taiwan Strait," in *Globalization and Security Relations Across the Taiwan Strait: In the Shadow of China*, ed. Ming-chin Monique Chu and Scott L. Kastner, 42–60 (New York: Routledge, 2015).

10. The full text of the speech can be found on the website *Taiwan Today* (Ministry of Foreign Affairs, ROC), https://taiwantoday.tw/news.php?post=3961&unit=4,29,31,45.

11. Robert S. Ross, "The 1995–96 Taiwan Strait Confrontation: Coercion, Credibility, and the Use of Force," *International Security* 25, no. 2 (2000): 87–123.

12. On ambiguity in PRC red lines, see Tsang, *If China Attacks Taiwan*.

13. Geoffrey Blainey, *The Causes of War* (New York: Free Press, 1988); Dominic D. P. Johnson, *Overconfidence and War: The Havoc and Glory of Positive Illusions* (Cambridge, Mass.: Harvard University Press, 2004); Stephen Van Evera, *Causes of War: Power and the Roots of Conflict* (Ithaca, N.Y.: Cornell University Press, 1999); Alex Weisiger, *Logics of War: Explanations for Limited and Unlimited Conflicts* (Ithaca, N.Y.: Cornell University Press, 2013).

14. Van Evera, *Causes of War*, 16; Weisiger, *Logics of War*, 34.

15. On incentives to misrepresent private information as a source of conflict, see James D. Fearon, "Rationalist Explanations for War," *International Organization* 49, no. 3 (1995): 379–414.

16. Seth Faison, "Taiwan President Implies His Island Is a Sovereign State," *New York Times*, July 13, 1999, https://www.nytimes.com/1999/07/13/world/taiwan-president -implies-his-island-is-sovereign-state.html.

17. Catherine Sung, "China's New Demands 'Unfounded,'" *Taipei Times*, September 10, 1999, https://www.taipeitimes.com/News/front/archives/1999/09/10/0000001547.

18. "Invasion Fears Are Unrealistic: Tang," *Taipei Times*, August 31, 1999, https://www .taipeitimes.com/News/local/archives/1999/08/31/0000000144.

19. See Margaret MacMillan, *The War That Ended Peace: How Europe Abandoned Peace for the First World War* (London: Profile Books, 2013), 593. On Saddam's misplaced confidence, see Johnson, *Overconfidence*, chap. 8.

20. For a discussion of signaling in international relations and how it can help to overcome information problems, see James D. Morrow, "The Strategic Setting of Choices: Signaling, Commitment and Negotiations in International Politics," in *Strategic Choice and International Relations*, ed. David A. Lake and Robert Powell (Princeton, N.J.: Princeton University Press, 1999), 77–114. See also James D. Morrow, "How Could Trade Affect Conflict," *Journal of Peace Research* 36, no. 4 (1999): 481–89; Erik Gartzke, Quan Li, and Charles Boehmer, "Investing in the Peace: Economic Interdependence and International Conflict," *International Organization* 55, no. 2 (2001): 391–438.

21. Ross, "1995–1996 Taiwan Strait Confrontation"; Robert S. Ross, "Navigating the Taiwan Strait: Deterrence, Escalation Dominance, and U.S.-China Relations," *International Security* 27, no. 2 (2002): 47–85; and Robert S. Ross, "Comparative Deterrence: The Taiwan Strait and the Korean Peninsula," in *New Directions in the Study of China's Foreign Policy*, ed. Alastair Iain Johnston and Robert S. Ross (Stanford, Calif.: Stanford University Press, 2006), 13–49.

22. It is also worth noting that overtly revisionist behavior by Taiwan can backfire internationally by undercutting international support for Taiwan. The decision to pursue a UN referendum to occur during the 2008 election, for instance, led to considerable international criticism, including from the United States.

23. See Thomas J. Christensen, speech to the U.S.-Taiwan Business Council, September 11, 2007, https://2001-2009.state.gov/p/eap/rls/rm/2007/91979.htm.

24. See Ron E. Hassner, *War on Sacred Grounds* (Ithaca, N.Y.: Cornell University Press, 2009).

25.   See Stacie E. Goddard, *Indivisible Territory and the Politics of Legitimacy: Jerusalem and Northern Ireland* (New York: Cambridge University Press, 2010).

26.   The DPP primary uses public opinion polls where candidates are matched up against likely challengers from other parties in the general election. The system thus prizes electability over "playing to the base." On the lack of political differences between Tsai and Lai, see Brian Hioe, "Lai Fails to Differentiate Political Program from Tsai During Presidential Primary Debate," *New Bloom Magazine*, June 2019, https://newbloommag.net/2019/06/08/dpp-presidential-debate-2020/. On the primary results, see also Nick Aspinwall, "Taiwan's President Clears Her Primary Challenge: Will Her Party Get on Board?," *Diplomat*, June 21, 2019, https://thediplomat.com/2019/06/taiwans-president-clears-her-primary-challenge-will-her-party-get-on-board/.

27.   This sort of opportunity cost logic is central to much of the literature linking economic interdependence to a reduced likelihood of war. See, for instance, Bruce Russett and John R. Oneal, *Triangulating Peace: Democracy, Interdependence, and International Organizations* (New York: Norton, 2001). For reviews of this literature, see Edward D. Mansfield and Brian M. Pollins, "The Study of Interdependence and Conflict: Recent Advances, Open Questions, and Directions for Future Research," *Journal of Conflict Resolution* 45, no. 6 (2001): 834–59; Erik Gartzke and Jiakun Jack Zhang, "Trade and War," in *The Oxford Handbook of the Political Economy of International Trade*, ed. Lisa Martin (Oxford: Oxford University Press, 2015), 419–38; and Hyo-Joon Chang and Scott L. Kastner, "Economic Interdependence and Conflict," in *Oxford Research Encyclopedia of Politics*, 2017, https://oxfordre.com/politics/view/10.1093/acrefore/9780190228637.001.0001/acrefore-9780190228637-e-563.

28.   This assessment is based on my discussions with numerous PRC Taiwan experts over the past several years.

29.   I elaborate on this point in Scott L. Kastner, *Political Conflict and Economic Interdependence Across the Taiwan Strait and Beyond* (Stanford, Calif.: Stanford University Press, 2009).

30.   Accidents are most likely to lead to war when there are strong advantages to striking first (and fear of being the target of a first strike), which Van Evera (*Causes of War*, 43) notes could lead to a "shoot first, ask questions later" mentality. In the Taiwan Strait, it is unlikely that the PRC would interpret an accident as the beginning of a Taiwan attack on the mainland—something that hasn't been a realistic concern since the 1960s. And even if Taiwan's leaders were to worry that an accident were the beginning of a PRC attack, the risks of preemption would be massive (virtually guaranteeing a massive PRC response). For further elaboration of this line of argument, see Kastner, "Is the Taiwan Strait."

31.   See, for instance, Ryan L. Hass, "Cross-Taiwan Strait Relations: Managing Triangular Dynamics," National Committee on American Foreign Policy, April 2019, https://www.ncafp.org/2016/wp-content/uploads/2019/04/NCAFP-Report_Cross-Strait-Dialogue_April-2019.pdf.

32.   See the following works by Thomas J. Christensen, "Posing Problems Without Catching Up: China's Rise and Challenges for U.S. Security Policy," *International Security*

25, no. 4 (2001): 5–40; "The Contemporary Security Dilemma," *Washington Quarterly* 25, no. 4 (2002): 7–21; "Tracking China's Security Relations: Reasons for Optimism and Pessimism," *China Leadership Monitor* 1 (2002), https://www.hoover.org/research /tracking-chinas-security-relations-causes-optimism-and-pessimism; "Beijing's Views of Taiwan and the United States in Early 2002: The Renaissance of Pessimism," *China Leadership Monitor* 3 (2002), http://media.hoover.org/sites/default/files /documents/clm3_TC.pdf; "Taiwan's Legislative Yuan Elections and Cross-Strait Security Relations: Reduced Tensions and Remaining Challenges," *China Leadership Monitor* 13 (2005): https://www.hoover.org/research/taiwans-legislative-yuan -elections-and-cross-strait-security-relations-reduced-tensions-and; and "Windows and War: Trend Analysis and Beijing's Use of Force," in *New Directions in the Study of China's Foreign Policy*, ed. Alastair Iain Johnston and Robert S. Ross (Stanford, Calif.: Stanford University Press, 2006), 50–85.

33. On the windows metaphor, see especially Christensen, "Windows and War."

34. Christensen, "Taiwan's Legislative Yuan Elections." I likewise found considerable pes-simism in my own interviews with analysts in China during the summer of 2004.

35. Indeed, some argue that China has already lost Taiwan. See, for instance, Nick Frisch, "How China Lost Taiwan," *New York Times*, January 27, 2016, https://www.nytimes .com/2016/01/28/opinion/how-china-lost-taiwan.html.

36. See Fearon, "Rationalist Explanations"; Powell, "War as a Commitment Problem"; and Weisiger, *Logics of War*. On preventive wars, see also Van Evera, *Causes of War*; and Jack S. Levy, "Declining Power and the Preventive Motivation for War," *World Poli-tics* 40, no. 1 (1987): 82–107.

37. See, e.g., Weisiger, *Logics of War*, 19. For a discussion of the windows logic, see Van Evera, *Causes of War*, chap. 4.

38. Both conditions are highlighted in Christensen, "Tracking China's Security Relations."

39. On the debate inside the KMT, see for instance, "KMT Criticized for Sidestepping Consensus That Enabled Good Relations," *Focus Taiwan*, June 19, 2020, https:// focustaiwan.tw/politics/202006190020.

40. Qiang Xin, "Having Much in Common? Changes and Continuity in China's Taiwan Policy," *Pacific Review* 34, no. 6 (2021): 926–45; see also Qiang Xin, "Selective Engage-ment: Mainland China's Dual Track Taiwan Policy," *Journal of Contemporary China* 29, no. 124 (2020): 535–52.

41. PRC analysts have expressed considerable concern about trends in the U.S.-Taiwan security relationship, with one analyst noting in a recent dialogue that the United States is "testing China's bottom line" on the issue. See Ambassador Stephen M. Young, "A Conference with the Taiwan Affairs Office of the PRC State Council," National Committee on American Foreign Policy, June, 2019, https://www.ncafp.org /2016/wp-content/uploads/2019/07/NCAFP-2019-TAO-Conference-Report_FINAL .pdf. Similar sentiments have been shared at other dialogues bringing together U.S. and PRC Taiwan experts. See, for instance, Hass, "Cross-Taiwan Strait Relations." On trends in U.S.-Taiwan security relations, see also Xiying Zuo, "Unbalanced

Deterrence: Coercive Threat, Reassurance and the US-China Rivalry in the Taiwan Strait," *Pacific Review* 34, no. 4 (2021): 547–76. Other worrisome trends highlighted by PRC analysts in the dialogue summarized by Young, "Conference with the Taiwan Affairs Office," include efforts by the DPP to marginalize the KMT within Taiwan, such as via "transitional justice" initiatives, which could lead to DPP political dominance and the ability to pursue independence.

42. See, for instance, Peng Li, "The Nature of the Economic Cooperation Framework Agreement and Its Implications for Peaceful Development of Cross-Strait Relations," in *New Dynamics in Cross–Taiwan Straits Relations: How Far Can the Rapprochement Go?*, ed. Weixing Hu (Hoboken, N.J.: Taylor and Francis, 2013), 47–59; Gang Lin, "Beijing's Evolving Policy and Strategic Thinking on Taiwan," in Hu, *New Dynamics in Cross–Taiwan Straits Relations*, 63–77; Zhang Hua, "2012 Taiwan 'daxuan' xuanmin toupiao xingwei xin tedian ji qi dui liang'an guanxi de yingxiang yanjiu" [A study of the new characteristics of Taiwan voting behavior during the 2012 Taiwan "election" and their impact on cross-strait relations], *Taiwan yanjiu jikan* [Taiwan research journal] 123, no. 5 (2012): 24–32; Chen Xing, "Lun heping fazhan zhanlue dui Taiwan zhengdang zhengzhi de yingxiang" [On the influence of the peaceful development strategy on Taiwan's political parties and politics], *Beijing Lianhe Daxue xuebao* [Journal of Beijing Union University] 10, no. 3 (2012): 87–92.

43. Xin, "Having Much."

44. Christensen, "Windows and War."

45. M. Taylor Fravel, *Strong Borders, Secure Nation: Cooperation and Conflict in China's Territorial Disputes* (Princeton, N.J.: Princeton University Press, 2008); M. Taylor Fravel, "Power Shifts and Escalation: Explaining China's Use of Force in Territorial Disputes," *International Security* 32, no. 3 (2008): 44–83.

46. Ketian Zhang, "Cautious Bully: Reputation, Resolve, and Beijing's Use of Coercion in the South China Sea," *International Security* 44, no. 1 (2019): 117–59.

47. Xin, "Having Much." Some PRC analysts have long held the view that time is on Beijing's side in cross-strait relations. See, for instance, Lin ("Beijing's Evolving Policy," 74), who writes that the "expanding gap" between China and Taiwan's relative economic power "has made more people on the mainland believe that time is on their side." This sentiment is consistent with my own discussions with several PRC-based analysts in the past few years. Recently, during the coronavirus crisis, there were some increased calls among Chinese nationalists on social media to launch a war of unification while the United States appeared distracted and bogged down (several aircraft carriers, for instance, had large outbreaks). However, some prominent analysts, such as retired air force major general Qiao Liang, generally considered a foreign policy hawk, pointedly rebutted these calls, emphasizing the need for continued patience and the downside risks of launching a war. See, for instance, Minnie Chan, " 'Too Costly': Chinese Military Strategist Warns Now Is Not the Time to Take Back Taiwan by Force," *South China Morning Post*, May 4, 2020, https://www.scmp.com/news/china/military/article/3082825/too-costly-chinese-military-strategist-warns-now-not-time-take; Minnie Chan, "China Tries to Calm 'Nationalist Fever' as Calls for

Invasion of Taiwan Grow," *South China Morning Post*, May 10, 2020, https://www
.scmp.com/print/news/china/politics/article/3083696/china-tries-calm-nationalist
-fever-calls-invasion-taiwan-grow.

7. THE PROBLEM OF PRC REVISIONISM

1. The quote is from Lai I-chung, a prominent DPP official, in Nathan Vanderklippe,
"A More Confident China Threatens to Use Military Force in Taiwan, Holds Up Hong
Kong as a Model," *Globe and Mail*, January 2, 2019, https://www.theglobeandmail
.com/world/article-a-more-confident-china-threatens-military-force-in-taiwan
-holds-up/. Similar language is used in the U.S.-China Economic and Security Review
Commission Annual Report to Congress in 2019 (p. 445), which describes Xi as
possessing a "sense of urgency regarding unification."

2. John Pomfret, "China's Xi Jinping Is Growing Impatient with Taiwan, Adding to Tensions with U.S.," *Washington Post*, February 18, 2019, https://www.washingtonpost
.com/opinions/2019/02/18/chinas-xi-jinping-is-growing-impatient-with-taiwan
-adding-tensions-with-united-states/. Not everyone viewed the speech as a major
departure from past policy. See especially Richard C. Bush, "8 Key Things to Notice
from Xi Jinping's New Year Speech on Taiwan," Brookings Institution, 2019, https://
www.brookings.edu/blog/order-from-chaos/2019/01/07/8-key-things-to-notice
-from-xi-jinpings-new-year-speech-on-taiwan/. Some PRC-based analysts have
expressed frustration at what they see as a twisting of Xi's speech to make it seem
more threatening than it was intended to be (based on my own interaction with several PRC Taiwan experts).

3. Ian Easton warns, for instance, that "with every passing year, the risk goes up that
Beijing might decide to pull the trigger." See Ian Easton, "America Should Put Military Forces in Taiwan," *Taipei Times*, March 9, 2020, https://www.taipeitimes.com
/News/editorials/archives/2020/03/09/2003732335. See also U.S.-China Economic and
Security Review Commission, *2019 Report to Congress*, 451, which warns that the PRC
is "not yet capable of carrying out a full invasion of Taiwan. Nevertheless, the PLA is
improving its capabilities to conduct such an operation."

4. See especially Minnie Chan, "'Too Costly': Chinese Military Strategist Warns Now
Is Not the Time to Take Back Taiwan by Force," *South China Morning Post*, May 4,
2020, https://www.scmp.com/news/china/military/article/3082825/too-costly-chinese
-military-strategist-warns-now-not-time-take.

5. John J. Mearsheimer, "Say Goodbye to Taiwan," *National Interest*, March–April 2014,
http://nationalinterest.org/article/say-goodbye-taiwan-9931."

6. Robert Sutter, *Taiwan's Future: Narrowing Straits* (Seattle: National Bureau of Asian
Research, 2011).

7. Bruce Gilley, "Not So Dire Straits: How the Finlandization of Taiwan Benefits US
Security," *Foreign Affairs* 89, no. 1 (2010): 44–60.

8. Eli Binder, "Chas Freeman on Picking Fights the U.S. Can Win," *Wire China*, June 28, 2020, https://www.thewirechina.com/2020/06/28/chas-freeman-on-picking-fights-the-us-can-win/.

9. Charles L. Glaser, "A U.S.-China Grand Bargain? The Hard Choice Between Military Competition and Accommodation," *International Security* 39, no. 4 (2015): 49–90.

10. Lauly Li, "Taiwan Presidential Favorite Says Peace Talks with China 'Inevitable,'" *Nikkei Review*, February 22, 2019, https://asia.nikkei.com/Politics/International-relations/Taiwan-presidential-favorite-says-peace-talks-with-China-inevitable.

11. Lawrence Chung, "Taiwan Presidential Hopeful Han Kuo-yu Says 'No Peace Deal with Beijing Until Threats End,'" *South China Morning Post*, November 15, 2019, https://www.scmp.com/news/china/politics/article/3037798/taiwan-presidential-hopeful-han-kuo-yu-says-no-peace-deal.

12. Indeed, some hard-liners in Beijing have suggested that Beijing's National Security Law, which limits dissent in Hong Kong, could be a model for dealing with dissent in postunification Taiwan. See John Pomfret, "The Hong Kong Security Law Could Be Beijing's Blueprint to Deal with the 'Taiwan Problem,'" *Washington Post*, July 6, 2020, https://www.washingtonpost.com/opinions/2020/07/06/hong-kong-security-law-could-be-chinas-blueprint-deal-with-taiwan-problem/?fbclid=IwAR3A146WVGayS8-QRsfpQj106F3dCNr3335_wqKaWmZiZaG-CQIvPmkowYo.

13. Thomas C. Schelling, *Arms and Influence* (New Haven, Conn.: Yale University Press, 1966).

14. Daniel Kahneman and Amos Tversky, "Prospect Theory: An Analysis of Decision under Risk," *Econometrica* 47, no. 2 (1979): 263–92. On the use of prospect theory in international relations, see Jack S. Levy, "Prospect Theory, Rational Choice, and International Relations," *International Studies Quarterly* 41, no. 1 (1997): 87–112. For applications to cross-Taiwan Strait relations, see Kai He and Huiyun Feng, "Leadership, Regime Security, and China's Policy Toward Taiwan: Prospect Theory and Taiwan Crises," *Pacific Review* 22, no. 4 (2009): 501–21; and Yves-Heng Lim, "The Future Instability of Cross-Strait Relations: Prospect Theory and Ma Ying-jeou's Paradoxical Legacy," *Asian Security* 14, no. 3 (2018): 318–38.

15. Alan D. Romberg, "Taiwan Elections Head to the Finish: Concerns, Cautions, and Challenges," *China Leadership Monitor* 36 (2012), http://www.hoover.org/research/taiwan-elections-head-finish-concerns-cautions-and-challenges.

16. James D. Fearon, "Rationalist Explanations for War," *International Organization* 49, no. 3 (1995): 408–9.

17. Bush, "8 Key Things."

18. For example, arms sales to Taiwan would almost certainly cease were Taiwan to move toward a formal unification agreement, as the United States would naturally worry that these weapons would end up in PLA hands.

19. For an elaboration of this line of argument, see Scott L. Kastner and Chad Rector, "National Unification and Mistrust: Bargaining Power and the Prospects for a PRC/Taiwan Agreement," *Security Studies* 17, no. 1 (2008): 39–71.

20. See Nadia Tsao, "Rohrabacher to Leave Taiwan Caucus Position," *Taipei Times*, March 15, 2009, http://www.taipeitimes.com/News/taiwan/archives/2009/03/15 /2003438534.

21. For additional examples, and a critique of this line of thinking, see J. Michael Cole, "Washington Celebrates, but Others Are Fretful," *Taipei Times*, March 26, 2008, http://www.taipeitimes.com/News/editorials/archives/2008/03/26/2003407160.

22. On the problem of asymmetric economic dependence in the context of political integration, see Chad Rector, *Federations: The Dynamics of International Cooperation* (Ithaca, N.Y.: Cornell University Press, 2009).

23. Fearon, "Rationalist Explanations," 408–9.

24. Full text available from China.org at http://www.china.org.cn/english/7945.htm.

25. "Jan 30, 1995: President Jiang Zemin Puts Forward Eight Propositions on Development of Relations Between Two Sides of Taiwan Straits," *China Daily* archives, https:// www.chinadaily.com.cn/china/19thcpcnationalcongress/2011-01/30/content_2971 5090.htm.

26. On Xi's speech, see Bush, "8 Key Things." As noted earlier, Bush emphasizes that Xi's promises concerning one country, two systems appear less generous than in the past: Xi makes no mention, for instance, of Taiwan retaining its armed forces, nor does he provide explicit assurances about the island's political system.

27. For a good overview of CCP institutions, and a conceptualization of authority relations, see Susan Shirk, *China: Fragile Superpower: How China's Internal Politics Could Derail its Peaceful Rise* (New York: Oxford University Press, 2007).

28. For a brief overview of PRC repression in Xinjiang, and particularly the targeting of Uyghurs, see Lindsay Maizland, "China's Repression of Uyghurs in Xinjiang," Council on Foreign Relations *Backgrounder*, updated March 1, 2021, https://www.cfr .org/backgrounder/chinas-repression-uyghurs-xinjiang. On the camps, see James Millward, " 'Reeducating' Xinjiang's Muslims," *New York Review of Books*, February 7, 2019, https://www.nybooks.com/articles/2019/02/07/reeducating-xinjiangs -muslims/.

29. Allen Carlson, "What's in Store for Hong Kong? Look at Tibet," *Washington Post Monkey Cage*, June 2, 2020, https://www.washingtonpost.com/politics/2020/06/02/whats -store-hong-kong-look-tibet/.

30. For a short discussion of the law's effects, see Javier C. Hernández, "Harsh Penalties, Vaguely Described Crimes: China's New National Security Law Explained," *New York Times*, June 30, 2020, https://www.nytimes.com/2020/06/30/world/asia/hong-kong -security-law-explain.html.

31. Several PRC-based analysts have emphasized this point to me in discussions.

32. To be clear, Taiwan's government viewed one country, two systems as lacking credibility from the moment the formula was developed in the 1980s. And the proposal had very little support in Taiwan even before the recent crackdown in Hong Kong.

33. Amy Qin and Tiffany May, "To 'Protect Young Minds,' Hong Kong Moves to Overhaul Schools," *New York Times*, July 11, 2020, https://www.nytimes.com/2020/07/11 /world/asia/china-hong-kong-security-schools.html.

34. One PLA general suggested in 2019 that the PRC would treat Taiwan independence supporters as war criminals in the event of a cross-strait military conflict. See "Chinese General Issues 'War Criminal' Warning to Taiwan," *Straits Times*, January 10, 2019, https://www.straitstimes.com/asia/east-asia/chinese-general-issues-war-criminal-warning-to-taiwan.

35. See, for instance, Chris Horton, "Specter of Meddling by Beijing Looms Over Taiwan Elections," *New York Times*, November 22, 2018, https://www.nytimes.com/2018/11/22/world/asia/taiwan-elections-meddling.html; Joshua Kurlantzick, "How China is Interfering in Taiwan's Election," Council on Foreign Relations, November 7, 2020, https://www.cfr.org/in-brief/how-china-interfering-taiwans-election; Russell Hsiao, "CCP Influence Operations and Taiwan's 2020 Elections," *Diplomat*, December 1, 2019, https://thediplomat.com/2019/11/ccp-influence-operations-and-taiwans-2020-elections/.

36. See, for instance, Graham Allison, *Destined for War: Can America and China Escape Thucydides's Trap?* (Boston: Houghton Mifflin Harcourt, 2017), who applies the concept of a "Thucydides trap" to China-U.S. relations. For pessimistic takes, see Gregory J. Moore, "Avoiding a Thucydides Trap in Sino-American Relations (. . . and 7 Reasons Why That Might Be Difficult)," *Asian Security* 13, no. 2 (2017): 98–115; and John J. Mearsheimer, *The Tragedy of Great Power Politics*, updated ed. (New York: Norton, 2014). For more measured conclusions, see Oriana Skylar Mastro, "In the Shadow of the Thucydides Trap: International Relations Theory and the Prospects for Peace in U.S.-China Relations," *Journal of Chinese Political Science* 24 (2019): 25–45. A massive literature explores the idea that war becomes more likely during power transitions in world politics. For key studies in this literature, see A. F. K. Organski and Jacek Kugler, *The War Ledger* (Chicago: University of Chicago Press, 1980); and Robert Gilpin, *War and Change in World Politics* (Cambridge: Cambridge University Press, 1981). For a detailed discussion and critique of this literature, see Jonathan M. DiCicco and Jack S. Levy, "Power Shifts and Problem Shifts: The Evolution of the Power Transition Research Program," *Journal of Conflict Resolution* 43, no. 6 (1999): 675–704. For good critiques of the application of power transition theory, or the "Thucydides trap," to China's rise and U.S.-China relations, see David A. Welch, "China, the United States, and the Thucydides's Trap," in *China's Challenges and International Order Transition: Beyond the Thucydides's Trap*, ed. Huiyun Feng and Kai He (Ann Arbor: University of Michigan Press, 2020), 47–69; Jack S. Levy, "Power Transition Theory and the Rise of China," in *China's Ascent: Power, Security, and the Future of International Politics*, ed. Robert S. Ross and Zhu Feng (Ithaca, N.Y.: Cornell University Press, 2008), 11–33; Steve Chan, *China, the U.S., and the Power Transition Theory: A Critique* (London: Routledge, 2008); and Steve Chan, "China and Thucydides's Trap," in *China's Challenges and International Order Transition: Beyond the Thucydides's Trap*, ed. Huiyun Feng and Kai He (Ann Arbor: University of Michigan Press, 2020), 27–46.

37. For arguments along these lines, see John F. Copper, "Why We Need Taiwan," *National Interest*, August 29, 2011, https://nationalinterest.org/commentary/why-we

-need-taiwan-5815; Joseph Bosco, "Taiwan and Strategic Security," *Diplomat*, May 15, 2015, https://thediplomat.com/2015/05/taiwan-and-strategic-security/. For counterarguments, see, for instance, Glaser, "U.S.-China Grand Bargain?," 75–76.

38.   See, e.g., James E. Auer and Tetsuo Kotani, "Reaffirming the 'Taiwan Clause': Japan's National Interest in Taiwan Strait and the U.S.-Japan Alliance, *NBR Analysis* 16, no. 1 (2005), https://www.nbr.org/publication/reaffirming-the-taiwan-clause-japans-national-interest-in-the-taiwan-strait-and-the-u-s-japan-alliance/; Grant Newsham, "Japan Must Help Defend Taiwan," *Taipei Times*, April 15, 2020, https://www.taipeitimes.com/News/editorials/archives/2020/04/15/2003734631.

39.   See Glaser, "U.S.-China Grand Bargain?," 75, for a skeptical take on this argument. Glaser notes that trade can easily be diverted via bypass routes.

40.   "China, Taiwan, and the United States" (U.S. Senate, March 7, 1996). From the Congressional Record, 104th Congress, S1634, https://www.congress.gov/congressional-record. For counterarguments, see David C. Kang, *China Rising: Peace, Power, and Order in East Asia* (New York: Columbia University Press, 2007), 93. Kang writes that Taiwan is not a bellwether because "Taiwan-China relations are categorically different in Chinese eyes than are relations between China and the other East Asian states."

41.   Shelley Rigger, Why Giving Up Taiwan Will Not Help Us with China," American Enterprise Institute Report, 2011, https://www.aei.org/research-products/report/why-giving-up-taiwan-will-not-help-us-with-china/.

42.   Nancy Bernkopf Tucker and Bonnie Glaser, "Should the United States States Abandon Taiwan?," *Washington Quarterly* 34, no. 4 (2011): 23–37. See also Richard C. Bush, *Uncharted Strait: The Future of China-Taiwan Relations* (Washington, D.C.: Brookings, 2013), for similar arguments. For counterarguments, see Charles L. Glaser, "A U.S.-China Grand Bargain? The Hard Choice Between Military Competition and Accommodation," *International Security* 39, no. 4 (2015): 49–90.

43.   Daniel W. Drezner, "Bad Debts: Assessing China's Financial Influence in Great Power Politics," *International Security* 34, no. 2 (2009): 20. See also Daniel W. Drezner, *The Sanctions Paradox: Economic Statecraft and International Relations* (Cambridge: Cambridge University Press, 1999).

44.   Glaser, "U.S.-China Grand Bargain."

CONCLUSION

1.   "The Most Dangerous Place on Earth," *Economist*, May 1, 2021, https://www.economist.com/leaders/2021/05/01/the-most-dangerous-place-on-earth.

2.   See, e.g., "Taiwan deng shangfengmian Jingji Xueren: Diqiushang zui weixian de difang" [Taiwan on the cover of the *Economist*: The most dangerous place on Earth], *Ziyou shibao*, April 30, 2021, https://news.ltn.com.tw/news/world/breakingnews/3516217.

3.   "Taiwan Responds to Magazine Cover Depicting It as a Target," *Radio Free Asia*, May 3, 2021, https://www.rfa.org/english/news/china/target-05032021110008.html.

4. Sun Guoxiang, "Zhongguo shi Diqiushang zui weixian guojia" [China is the most dangerous country on Earth], *Newtalk*, May 7, 2021, https://newtalk.tw/citizen/view /57032; Brian Hioe, "Idealization and Fearmongering Opposite Sides of the Same Coin for International Media Reporting on Taiwan," *Taiwan Insight*, May 27, 2021, https:// taiwaninsight.org/2021/05/27/idealization-and-fearmongering-opposite-sides-of -the-same-coin-for-international-media-reporting-on-taiwan/.

5. Rhoda Kwan, "'The Most Dangerous Place on Earth': Taiwan Twitter Derides the Economist's Latest Cover Story," *Hong Kong Free Press*, April 30, 2021, https:// hongkongfp.com/2021/04/30/most-dangerous-place-on-earth-taiwan-twitter -derides-the-economists-latest-cover-story/.

6. Robert S. Ross, "Explaining Taiwan's Revisionist Diplomacy," *Journal of Contemporary China* 15, no. 48 (2006): 443–58.

7. Kristian Skrede Gleditsch and Steve Pickering, "Wars Are Becoming Less Frequent: A Response to Harrison and Wolf," *Economic History Review* 67, no. 1 (2014): 214–30.

8. John Mueller, *The Stupidity of War: American Foreign Policy and the Case for Complacency* (Cambridge: Cambridge University Press, 2021).

9. Thomas J. Christensen, "The Contemporary Security Dilemma," *Washington Quarterly* 25, no. 4 (2002): 7–21; T. Y. Wang, "Strategic Ambiguity or Strategic Clarity? US Policy Toward the Taiwan Issue," *Taiwan Insight*, June 7, 2021, https://taiwaninsight .org/2021/06/07/strategic-ambiguity-or-strategic-clarity-us-policy-towards-the -taiwan-issue/.

10. On this point, see Douglas Paal, "Too Much Taiwan Tension, Not Enough Management," *Taiwan Insight*, June 4, 2021, https://taiwaninsight.org/2021/06/04/too-much -taiwan-tension-not-enough-management/.

REFERENCES

Abdelal, Rawi, and Jonathan Kirschner. "Strategy, Economic Relations, and the Definition of National Interests." *Security Studies* 9, no. 1/2 (1999/2000): 119–56.

Achen, Christopher H., and T. Y. Wang. "Conclusion: The Power of Identity in Taiwan." In *The Taiwan Voter*, ed. Christopher Henry Achen and T. Y. Wang, 273–92. Ann Arbor: University of Michigan Press, 2017.

Allison, Graham. *Destined for War: Can America and China Escape Thucydides's Trap?* Boston: Houghton Mifflin Harcourt, 2017.

Auer, James E., and Tetsuo Kotani. "Reaffirming the 'Taiwan Clause': Japan's National Interest in Taiwan Strait and the U.S.-Japan Alliance." *NBR Analysis* 16, no. 1 (2005). https://www.nbr.org/publication/reaffirming-the-taiwan-clause-japans-national-interest-in-the-taiwan-strait-and-the-u-s-japan-alliance/.

Batto, Nathan. "The NPP's Internal Divisions, Ko's New Party, and the China Cleavage." *Frozen Garlic: A Blog on Elections in Taiwan*, August 7, 2019. https://frozengarlic.wordpress.com/2019/08/07/the-npps-internal-divisions-kos-new-party-and-the-china-cleavage/.

Beckley, Michael. *Unrivaled: Why America Will Remain the World's Sole Superpower.* Ithaca, N.Y.: Cornell University Press, 2018.

Biddle, Stephen, and Ivan Oelrich. "Future Warfare in the Western Pacific: Chinese Antiaccess/Area Denial, U.S. AirSea Battle, and Command of the Commons in East Asia." *International Security* 41, no. 1 (2016): 7–48.

Blackwill, Robert D., and Philip Zelikow. "Can the United States Prevent a War Over Taiwan?" *War on the Rocks*, March 1, 2021. https://warontherocks.com/2021/03/can-the-united-states-prevent-a-war-over-taiwan/.

Blainey, Geoffrey. *The Causes of War.* New York: Free Press, 1988.

Blasko, Dennis J. "The Chinese Military Speaks to Itself: Revealing Doubts." *War on the Rocks*, February 18, 2019. https://warontherocks.com/2019/02/the-chinese-military-speaks-to-itself-revealing-doubts/.

Bosco, Joseph. "Taiwan and Strategic Security." *Diplomat*, May 15, 2015. https://thediplomat
.com/2015/05/taiwan-and-strategic-security/.

——. "Strategic Ambiguity on Taiwan No Longer Works—It's Time for Strategic Clarity."
Hill, September 1, 2020. https://thehill.com/opinion/international/514503-strategic
-ambiguity-on-taiwan-no-longer-works-its-time-for-strategic.

Bush, Richard C. *At Cross-Purposes: US-Taiwan Relations Since 1942*. Armonk, N.Y.: M. E.
Sharpe, 2004.

——. "8 Key Things to Notice from Xi Jinping's New Year Speech on Taiwan." Brookings
Institution, 2019. https://www.brookings.edu/blog/order-from-chaos/2019/01/07/8-key
-things-to-notice-from-xi-jinpings-new-year-speech-on-taiwan/.

——. *Uncharted Strait: The Future of China-Taiwan Relations*. Washington, D.C.: Brookings,
2013.

——. *Untying the Knot: Making Peace in the Taiwan Strait*. Washington, D.C.: Brookings,
2005.

——. "The United States Security Partnership with Taiwan." Brookings Institution, 2016.
https://www.brookings.edu/wp-content/uploads/2016/07/Paper-7v3.pdf.

Bush, Richard C., and Ryan Hass. "Taiwan's Democracy and the China Challenge." Brookings Institution Policy Brief, 2018. https://www.brookings.edu/wp-content/uploads/2018
/12/FP_20190226_taiwan_bush_hass.pdf.

Bush, Richard C., and Michael E. O'Hanlon. *A War Like No Other: The Truth About China's
Challenge to America*. Hoboken, N.J.: Wiley, 2007.

Bush, Richard C., Bonnie Glaser, and Ryan Hass. "Opinion: Don't Help China by Hyping
Risk of War Over Taiwan." *NPR*, April 8, 2021. https://www.npr.org/2021/04/08/984524521
/opinion-dont-help-china-by-hyping-risk-of-war-over-taiwan.

Carlson, Allen. *Unifying China, Integrating with the World: Securing Chinese Sovereignty in
the Reform Era*. Stanford, Calif.: Stanford University Press, 2005.

——. "What's in Store for Hong Kong? Look at Tibet." *Washington Post Monkey Cage*, June 2,
2020. https://www.washingtonpost.com/politics/2020/06/02/whats-store-hong-kong
-look-tibet/.

Carpenter, Ted Galen. *America's Coming War with China: A Collision Course Over Taiwan*.
New York: Palgrave Macmillan, 2005.

——. "Is American Prodding Taiwan Toward Conflict with China?" *American Conservative*,
May 30, 2019. https://www.cato.org/publications/commentary/america-prodding-taiwan
-towards-conflict-china.

Carroll, Colin, and Rebecca Friedman Lissner. "Forget the Subs: What Taipei Can Learn from
Tehran About Asymmetric Defense." *War on the Rocks*, April 6, 2017. https://
warontherocks.com/2017/04/forget-the-subs-what-taipei-can-learn-from-tehran-about
-asymmetric-defense/.

Chan, Steve. "China and Thucydides's Trap." In *China's Challenges and International Order
Transition: Beyond the Thucydides's Trap*, ed. Huiyun Feng and Kai He, 27–46. Ann Arbor:
University of Michigan Press, 2020.

——. *China, the U.S., and the Power Transition Theory: A Critique*. London: Routledge, 2008.

Chang, Hyo-Joon, and Scott L. Kastner. "Economic Interdependence and Conflict." In *Oxford Research Encyclopedia of Politics*, 2017, https://oxfordre.com/politics/view/10.1093/acrefore /9780190228637.001.0001/acrefore-9780190228637-e-563.

Chang-Liao, Nien-chung, and Chi Fang. "The Case for Maintaining Strategic Ambiguity in the Taiwan Strait." *Washington Quarterly* 44, no. 2 (2021): 45–60.

Chen, Chien-kai. "Comparing Jiang Zemin's Impatience with Hu Jintao's Patience Regarding the Taiwan Issue, 1989–2012." *Journal of Contemporary China* 21, no. 78 (2012): 955–72.

Chen, Fang-yu, Austin Wang, Charles K. S. Wu, and Yao-yuan Yeh. "What Do Taiwan's People Think About Their Relationship to China?" *Diplomat*, May 29, 2020. https://thediplomat .com/2020/05/what-do-taiwans-people-think-about-their-relationship-to-china/.

Chen, Rou-lan. "Beyond National Identity in Taiwan: A Multidimensional and Evolutionary Conceptualization." *Asian Survey* 52, no. 5 (2012): 845–71.

Chen, Xing. "Lun Heping Fazhan Zhanlue Dui Taiwan Zhengdang Zhengzhi de Yingxiang" [On the influence of the peaceful development strategy on Taiwan's political parties and politics]. *Beijing Lianhe Daxue xuebao* [Journal of Beijing Union University] 10, no. 3 (2012): 87–92.

Chen, Yu-Jie, and Jerome A. Cohen. "China-Taiwan Relations Reexamined: The '1992 Consensus' and Cross-Strait Agreements." *Asian Law Review* 14, no. 1 (2019): 1–40.

Cheng, T. J. "China-Taiwan Economic Linkage: Between Insulation and Superconductivity." In *Dangerous Strait: The U.S.-Taiwan-China Crisis*, ed. Nancy Bernkopf Tucker, 93–130. New York: Columbia University Press, 2005.

Christensen, Thomas J. "Beijing's Views of Taiwan and the United States in Early 2002: The Renaissance of Pessimism." *China Leadership Monitor*, no. 3 (2002). http://media.hoover .org/sites/default/files/documents/clm3_TC.pdf.

——. "China." In *Strategic Asia: Power and Purpose*, ed. Richard J. Ellings and Aaron L. Friedberg. Seattle: National Bureau of Asian Research, 2001/2002. https://www.nbr.org /publication/strategic-asia-2001-02-power-and-purpose/.

——. *The China Challenge: Shaping the Choices of a Rising Power*. New York: Norton, 2015.

——. "Chinese Realpolitik." *Foreign Affairs* 75, no. 5 (1996): 37–52.

——. "The Contemporary Security Dilemma." *Washington Quarterly* 25, no. 4 (2002): 7–21.

——. "Posing Problems Without Catching Up: China's Rise and Challenges for U.S. Security Policy." *International Security* 25, no. 4 (2001): 5–40.

——. "Taiwan's Legislative Yuan Elections and Cross-Strait Security Relations: Reduced Tensions and Remaining Challenges." *China Leadership Monitor*, no. 13 (2005). https://www .hoover.org/research/taiwans-legislative-yuan-elections-and-cross-strait-security -relations-reduced-tensions-and.

——. "Tracking China's Security Relations: Reasons for Optimism and Pessimism." *China Leadership Monitor*, no. 1 (2002). https://www.hoover.org/research/tracking-chinas -security-relations-causes-optimism-and-pessimism.

——. "Windows and War: Trend Analysis and Beijing's Use of Force." In *New Directions in the Study of China's Foreign Policy*, ed. Alastair Iain Johnston and Robert S. Ross, 50–85. Stanford, Calif.: Stanford University Press, 2006.

Chu, Ming-chin Monique. "Rethinking Globalization-Security Linkages with References to the Semiconductor Industry Across the Taiwan Strait." In *Globalization and Security Relations Across the Taiwan Strait: In the Shadow of China*, ed. Ming-chin Monique Chu and Scott L. Kastner, 183–2008. New York: Routledge, 2015.

Chu, Yun-han. "The Political Economy of Taiwan's Mainland Policy." In *Across the Taiwan Strait: Mainland China, Taiwan, and the 1995–1996 Crisis*, ed. Suisheng Zhao, 163–96. New York: Routledge, 1999.

——. "Taiwan's National Identity Politics and the Prospect of Cross-Strait Relations." *Asian Survey* 44, no. 4 (2004): 484–512.

Clarke, Kevin A., and David M. Primo. *A Model Discipline: Political Science and the Logic of Representations.* New York: Oxford University Press, 2012.

Cliff, Roger, and David A. Shlapak. *U.S.-China Relations After Resolution of Taiwan's Status.* Santa Monica, Calif.: RAND Corporation, 2007.

Cole, Bernard D. "The Military Instrument of Statecraft at Sea: Naval Options in an Escalatory Scenario Involving Taiwan, 2007–2016." In *Assessing the Threat: The Chinese Military and Taiwan's Security*, ed. Michael D. Swaine, Andrew N. D. Yang, and Evan S. Medeiros, 185–209. Washington, D.C.: Carnegie Endowment for International Peace, 2007.

Cole, J. Michael. "Are the Chinese Gearing Up for War in the Taiwan Strait?" *National Interest*, November 15, 2020. https://nationalinterest.org/blog/reboot/are-chinese-gearing-war-taiwan-strait-172723.

——. *Convergence or Conflict in the Taiwan Strait: the Illusion of Peace?* New York: Routledge, 2017.

Copper, John F. "Why We Need Taiwan." *National Interest*, August 29, 2011. https://nationalinterest.org/commentary/why-we-need-taiwan-5815.

Cowen, Tyler. "China's War Against Taiwan Could Come Sooner Rather Than Later." *Bloomberg*, April 6, 2021. https://www.bloomberg.com/opinion/articles/2021-04-07/china-taiwan-conflict-could-come-sooner-rather-than-later.

Cozad, Mark. "Factors Shaping China's Use of Force Calculations Against Taiwan." Testimony before the U.S.-China Economic and Security Review Commission, February 18, 2021. https://www.uscc.gov/sites/default/files/2021-02/Mark_Cozad_Testimony.pdf.

Cunningham, Fiona S. Testimony before the U.S.-China Economic and Security Review Commission, February 18, 2021. https://www.uscc.gov/sites/default/files/2021-02/Fiona_Cunningham_Testimony.pdf.

deLisle, Jacques. "The China-Taiwan Relationship: Law's Spectral Answers to the Cross-Strait Sovereignty Question." *Orbis* 46, no. 4 (2002): 733–52.

——. "The Growing Dangers of Potential U.S.-China Conflict." *Taiwan Insight*, June 8, 2021. https://taiwaninsight.org/2021/06/08/the-growing-dangers-of-potential-u-s-china-conflict/.

——. "United States-Taiwan Relations: Tsai's Presidency and Washington's Policy." *China Review* 18, no. 3 (2018): 13–60.

DiCicco, Jonathan M., and Jack S. Levy. "Power Shifts and Problem Shifts: The Evolution of the Power Transition Research Program." *Journal of Conflict Resolution* 43, no. 6 (1999): 675–704.

Dreyer, June Teufel. "Flashpoint in the Taiwan Strait." *Orbis* 44, no. 4 (2000): 615–29.

Drezner, Daniel W. "Bad Debts: Assessing China's Financial Influence in Great Power Politics." *International Security* 34, no. 2 (2009): 7–45.

——. *The Sanctions Paradox: Economic Statecraft and International Relations*. Cambridge: Cambridge University Press, 1999.

——. "The Trouble with Carrots: Transaction Costs, Conflict Expectations, and Economic Inducements." *Security Studies* 9, no. 1/2 (1999/2000): 188–218.

Easton, Ian. *The Chinese Invasion Threat: Taiwan's Defense and America's Strategy in Asia*. Arlington, Va.: Project 2049 Institute, 2017.

——. Testimony before the U.S.-China Economic and Security Review Commission, June 5, 2014. https://www.uscc.gov/sites/default/files/Easton_USCC_Taiwan_Hearing_Statement_2014.pdf.

Erickson, Andrew S. *Chinese Anti-Ship Ballistic Missile (ASBM) Development: Drivers, Trajectories, and Strategic Implications*. Washington, D.C.: Jamestown Foundation, 2013.

Fearon, James D. "Rationalist Explanations for War." *International Organization* 49, no. 3 (1995): 379–414.

Fell, Dafydd. *Government and Politics in Taiwan: Second Edition*. London: Routledge, 2018.

Fingar, Thomas, and Jean C. Oi. "China's Challenges: Now It Gets Much Harder." *Washington Quarterly* 43, no. 1 (2020): 67–84.

Fravel, M. Taylor. "Power Shifts and Escalation: Explaining China's Use of Force in Territorial Disputes." *International Security* 32, no. 3 (2008): 44–83.

——. *Strong Borders, Secure Nation: Cooperation and Conflict in China's Territorial Disputes*. Princeton, N.J.: Princeton University Press, 2008.

Fuller, Douglas B. "The Cross-Strait Economic Relationship's Impact on Development in Taiwan and China: Adversaries and Partners." *Asian Survey* 48, no. 2 (2008): 239–64.

Gartzke, Erik. "War Is in the Error Term." *International Organization* 53, no. 3 (1999): 567–587.

Gartzke, Erik, Quan Li, and Charles Boehmer. "Investing in the Peace: Economic Interdepedence and International Conflict." *International Organization* 55, no. 2 (2001): 391–438.

Gartzke, Erik, and Jiakun Jack Zhang. "Trade and War." In *The Oxford Handbook of the Political Economy of International Trade*, ed. Lisa Martin, 419–38. Oxford: Oxford University Press, 2015.

Gilley, Bruce. "Not So Dire Straits. How the Finlandization of Taiwan Benefits US Security." *Foreign Affairs* 89, no. 1 (2010): 44–60.

Gilpin, Robert. *War and Change in World Politics*. Cambridge: Cambridge University Press, 1981.

Giumelli, Francesco. "The Purposes of Targeted Sanctions." In *Targeted Sanctions: The Impacts and Effectiveness of United Nations Action*, ed. Thomas J. Biersteker, Sue E. Eckert, and Marcos Tourinho, 38–59. Cambridge: Cambridge University Press, 2016.

Glaser, Bonnie. "A Guarantee Isn't Worth the Risk." *Foreign Affairs*, September 24, 2020. https://www.foreignaffairs.com/articles/united-states/2020-09-24/dire-straits.

Glaser, Bonnie, Richard C. Bush, and Michael J. Green. "Toward a Stronger U.S.-Taiwan Relationship." Center for Strategic and International Studies, Report of the CSIS Task Force

on U.S. Policy Toward Taiwan, 2020. https://csis-website-prod.s3.amazonaws.com/s3fs
-public/publication/201021_Glaser_TaskForce_Toward_A_Stronger_USTaiwan_Rela-
tionship_0.pdf.

Glaser, Charles L. "A U.S.-China Grand Bargain? The Hard Choice Between Military Competition and Accommodation." *International Security* 39, no. 4 (2015): 49–90.

Gleditsch, Kristian Skrede, and Steve Pickering. "Wars Are Becoming Less Frequent: A
Response to Harrison and Wolf." *Economic History Review* 67, no. 1 (2014): 214–30.

Glosny, Michael A. *Getting Beyond Taiwan? Chinese Foreign Policy and PLA Modernization.*
Washington, D.C.: Institute for National Strategic Studies, National Defense University,
2011.

——. "Strangulation from the Sea? A PRC Submarine Blockade of Taiwan." *International
Security* 28, no. 4 (2004): 125–60.

Goddard, Stacie E. *Indivisible Territory and the Politics of Legitimacy: Jerusalem and Northern Ireland.* New York: Cambridge University Press, 2010.

Godwin, Paul H. B., and Alice L. Miller. *China's Forbearance Has Limits: Chinese Threat and
Retaliation Signaling and Its Implications for a Sino-American Military Confrontation.*
Washington, D.C.: National Defense University Press, 2013.

Gold, Thomas B. *State and Society in the Taiwan Miracle.* Armonk, N.Y.: M. E. Sharpe, 1986.

Goldstein, Steven M. and Randall Schriver. "An Uncertain Relationship: The United States,
Taiwan and the Taiwan Relations Act." *China Quarterly* no. 165 (2001): 147–72.

Greer, Tanner. "Why I Fear for Taiwan." *Scholar's Stage* (blog), September 11, 2020. https://
scholars-stage.blogspot.com/2020/09/why-i-fear-for-taiwan.html.

Gries, Peter, and Tao Wang. "Taiwan's Perilous Futures: Chinese Nationalism, the 2020 Presidential Elections, and U.S.-China Tensions Spell Trouble for Cross-Strait Relations."
World Affairs 183, no. 1 (2020): 40–61.

Grossman, Derek, and Brandon Alexander Millan. "Taiwan's KMT May Have a Serious '1992
Consensus' Problem." RAND Corporation, September 2020. https://www.rand.org/blog
/2020/09/taiwans-kmt-may-have-a-serious-1992-consensus-problem.html.

Haass, Richard, and David Sacks. "American Support for Taiwan Must Be Unambiguous."
Foreign Affairs, September 2, 2020. https://www.foreignaffairs.com/articles/united-states
/american-support-taiwan-must-be-unambiguous.

Hall, Todd H. "We Will Not Swallow This Bitter Fruit: Theorizing a Diplomacy of Anger."
Security Studies 20, no. 4 (2011): 521–55.

Harrell, Peter, Elizabeth Rosenberg, and Edoardo Saravalle. "China's Use of Coercive Economic Measures." Center for a New American Security, 2018. https://www.cnas.org
/publications/reports/chinas-use-of-coercive-economic-measures.

Hass, Ryan L. "Cross-Taiwan Strait Relations: Managing Triangular Dynamics,"
National Committee on American Foreign Policy, April 2019. https://www.ncafp
.org/2016/wp-content/uploads/2019/04/NCAFP-Report_Cross-Strait-Dialogue_April
-2019.pdf.

Hassner, Ron E. *War on Sacred Grounds.* Ithaca, N.Y.: Cornell University Press, 2009.

He, Kai, and Huiyun Feng. "Leadership, Regime Security, and China's Policy Toward Taiwan: Prospect Theory and Taiwan Crises." *Pacific Review* 22, no. 4 (2009): 501–21.

He, Yinan. "History, Chinese Nationalism, and the Emerging Sino-Japanese Conflict." *Journal of Contemporary China* 16, no. 50 (2007): 1–24.

Heginbotham, Eric, Michael Nixon, Forrest E. Morgan, Jacob L. Heim, Jeff Hagen, Sheng Li, Jeffrey Engstrom, Martin C. Libicki, Paul DeLuca, David A. Shlapak, David R. Frelinger, Burgess Laird, Kyle Brady, and Lyle J. Morris. *The U.S.-China Military Scorecard: Forces, Geography, and the Evolving Balance of Power, 1996–2017.* Santa Monica, Calif.: RAND Corporation, 2015.

Henley, Lonnie. Testimony before the U.S.-China Economic and Security Review Commission, February 18, 2021. https://www.uscc.gov/sites/default/files/2021-02/Lonnie_Henley _Testimony.pdf.

Hickey, Dennis V. "More and More Taiwanese Favor Independence—and Think the US Would Help Fight for It." *Diplomat*, December 3, 2020. https://thediplomat.com/2020/12 /more-and-more-taiwanese-favor-independence-and-think-the-us-would-help-fight -for-it/.

Hioe, Brian. "Idealization and Fearmongering: Opposite Sides of the Same Coin for International Media Reporting on Taiwan." *Taiwan Insight*, May 27, 2021. https://taiwaninsight .org/2021/05/27/idealization-and-fearmongering-opposite-sides-of-the-same-coin-for -international-media-reporting-on-taiwan/.

——. "No, Taiwan Is Not Going to Be Invaded by China Tomorrow." *New Bloom*, March 29, 2021. https://newbloommag.net/2021/03/29/china-invasion-possibility/.

Holmes, James. "Could China Successfully Blockade Taiwan?" *National Interest*, August 28, 2020. https://nationalinterest.org/feature/could-china-successfully-blockade-taiwan -168035.

Hsiao, Russell. "CCP Influence Operations and Taiwan's 2020 Elections." *Diplomat*, December 1, 2019. https://thediplomat.com/2019/11/ccp-influence-operations-and-taiwans -2020-elections/.

——. "Hu Jintao's 'Six-Points' Proposition to Taiwan." Jamestown Foundation, January 12, 2009. https://jamestown.org/program/hu-jintaos-six-points-proposition-to-taiwan/.

Hsieh, John Fuh-sheng. "Ethnicity, National Identity, and Domestic Politics in Taiwan." *Journal of Asian and African Studies* 40, no. 1/2 (2005): 13–28.

Hu, Weixing, ed. *New Dynamics in Cross-Taiwan Straits Relations: How Far Can the Rapprochement Go?* Hoboken, N.J.: Taylor and Francis, 2013.

Huang, Shuling. "Re-mediating Identities in the Imagined Homeland: Taiwanese Migrants in China." Ph.D. diss., University of Maryland, College Park, 2010.

Hunzeker, Michael A. Testimony before the U.S.-China Economic and Security Review Commission, February 18, 2021. https://www.uscc.gov/sites/default/files/2021-02/Michael_ Hunzeker_Testimony.pdf.

Hunzeker, Michael A., Alexander Lanoszka, with Brian Davis, Matthew Fay, Erik Goepner, Joseph Petrucelli, and Erica Seng-White. *A Question of Time: Enhancing Taiwan's Conventional Deterrence Posture.* Arlington, Va: Schar School of Policy and Government, George Mason University, 2018.

Huth, Paul. *Extended Deterrence and the Prevention of War.* New Haven, Conn.: Yale University Press, 1988.

Jacobs, J. Bruce,and I-hao Ben Liu. "Lee Teng-Hui and the 'Idea' of Taiwan." *China Quarterly*, no. 190 (2007): 375–93.

Johnson, Dominic D. P. *Overconfidence and War: The Havoc and Glory of Positive Illusions.* Cambridge, Mass.: Harvard University Press, 2004.

Johnston, Alastair Iain. "Is Chinese Nationalism Rising? Evidence from Beijing." *International Security* 41, no. 3 (2017): 7–43.

Kahler, Miles, and Scott L. Kastner. "Strategic Uses of Economic Interdependence: Engagement Policies on the Korean Peninsula and Across the Taiwan Strait." *Journal of Peace Research* 43, no. 5 (2006): 523–41.

Kahneman, Daniel, and Amos Tversky. "Prospect Theory: An Analysis of Decision Under Risk." *Econometrica* 47, no. 2 (1979): 263–92.

Kan, Shirly A. "Congressional Support for Taiwan's Defense Through the National Defense Authorization Act." National Bureau of Asian Research, May 2018. https://www.nbr.org/wp-content/uploads/pdfs/us-taiwan_defense_relations_roundtable_may2018.pdf.

——. "Taiwan: Major U.S. Arms Sales Since 1990." CRS Report, August 29, 2014. https://fas.org/sgp/crs/weapons/RL30957.pdf.

Kang, David C. *China Rising: Peace, Power, and Order in East Asia.* New York: Columbia University Press, 2007.

Kastner, Scott L. "Ambiguity, Interdependence, and the U.S. Strategic Dilemma in the Taiwan Strait." *Journal of Contemporary China* 15, no. 49 (2006): 651–69.

——. "International Relations Theory and the Relationship Across the Taiwan Strait." *International Journal of Taiwan Studies* 1, no. 1 (2018): 161–83.

——. "Is the Taiwan Strait Still a Flashpoint? Assessing the Prospects for Armed Conflict between China and Taiwan." *International Security* 40, no. 3 (2015/2016): 54–92.

——. *Political Conflict and Economic Interdependence Across the Taiwan Strait and Beyond.* Stanford, Calif.: Stanford University Press, 2009.

——. "Rethinking the Prospects for Conflict in the Taiwan Strait." In *Globalization and Security Relations Across the Taiwan Strait: In the Shadow of China*, ed. Ming-chin Monique Chu and Scott L. Kastner, 42–60. New York: Routledge, 2015.

——. "Stronger Than Ever? US-Taiwan Relations During the First Tsai Administration." In *Navigating in Stormy Waters: Taiwan During the First Administration of Tsai Ing-wen*, ed. Gunter Schubert and Chun-Yi Lee, 303–27. London: Routledge, 2021.

——. "The Taiwan Issue in U.S.-China Relations: Slipping Into a Security Dilemma?" In *After Engagement: Dilemmas in U.S.-China Security Relations*, ed. Jacques deLisle and Avery Goldstein, 244–68. Washington, D.C.: Brookings, 2021.

Kastner, Scott L., and Margaret M. Pearson. "Exploring the Parameters of China's Economic Influence." *Studies in Comparative International Development* 56, no. 1 (2021): 18–44.

Kastner, Scott L., and Chad Rector. "National Unification and Mistrust: Bargaining Power and the Prospects for a PRC/Taiwan Agreement." *Security Studies* 17, no. 1 (2008): 39–71.

Kastner, Scott L., William L. Reed, and Ping-Kuei Chen. "Mostly Bark, Little Bite? Modeling US Arms Sales to Taiwan and the Chinese Response." *Issues & Studies* 49, no. 3 (2013): 111–50.

Keng, Shu and Gunter Schubert. "Agents of Taiwan-China Unification? The Political Role of Taiwan Business People in the Process of Cross-Strait Integration." *Asian Survey* 50, no. 2 (2010): 287–310.

Keng, Shu, Jean Yu-Chen Tseng, and Qiang Yu. "The Strengths of China's Charm Offensive: Change in the Political Landscape of a Southern Taiwan Town Under Attack from Chinese Economic Power." *China Quarterly* no. 232 (2017): 956–81.

Kok, Piin-Fen, and David J. Firestein. *Threading the Needle: Proposals for U.S. and Chinese Actions on Arms Sales to Taiwan.* New York: EastWest Institute, 2013. http://www.ewi.info/idea/threading-needle-proposals-us-and-chinese-actions-arms-sales-taiwan.

Kokas, Aynne. "Mulan Is a Movie About How Much Hollywood Needs China." *Washington Post*, September 9, 2020. https://www.washingtonpost.com/outlook/2020/09/09/mulan-is-movie-about-how-much-hollywood-needs-china/.

Kurlantzick, Joshua. "How China Is Interfering in Taiwan's Election." Council on Foreign Relations, November 7, 2019. https://www.cfr.org/in-brief/how-china-interfering-taiwans-election.

La Croix, Sumner J., and Yibo Xu. "Political Uncertainty and Taiwan's Investment in Xiamen's Special Economic Zone." In *Emerging Patterns of East Asian Investment in China: From Korea, Taiwan, and Hong Kong*, ed. Sumner J. La Croix, Michael Plummer, and Keun Lee, 123–41. Armonk, N.Y.: M. E. Sharpe, 1994.

Lai, Christina. "More than Carrots and Sticks: Economic Statecraft and Coercion in China-Taiwan Relations from 2000–2019." *Politics* (online first, 2021). https://doi.org/10.1177/0263395720962654.

Lake, David A. "Two Cheers for Bargaining Theory: Assessing Rationalist Explanations for the Iraq War." *International Security* 35, no. 3 (2010/2011): 7–52.

Lake, David A., and Robert Powell, eds. *Strategic Choice and International Relations*. Princeton, N.J.: Princeton University Press, 1999.

Lampton, David M. "Preparing for a Better Time in Cross-Strait Relations: Short-Term Stalemate, Possible Medium-Term Opportunities." In *Breaking the China-Taiwan Impasse*, ed. Donald S. Zagoria, 105–14. Westport, Conn.: Praeger, 2003.

Lanzit, Kevin. "Education and Training in the PLAAF." In *The Chinese Air Force: Evolving Concepts, Roles, and Capabilities*, ed. Richard P. Hollion, Roger Cliff, and Phillip C. Saunders, 235–54. Washington, D.C.: National Defense University Press, 2012.

Lardy, Nicholas R. *Integrating China Into the Global Economy*. Washington, D.C.: Brookings, 2002.

Lardy, Nicholas R. *The State Strikes Back: The End of Economic Reform in China?* Washington, D.C.: Peterson Institute for International Economics, 2019.

Lawrence, Susan V., and Wayne M. Morrison. "Taiwan: Issues for Congress." CRS Report, 2017. https://fas.org/sgp/crs/row/R44996.pdf.

Lee, Chun-yi. *Taiwanese Business of Chinese Security Asset? A Changing Pattern of Interaction Between Taiwanese Businesses and Chinese Governments*. London: Routledge, 2012.

Lee, Hsi-min, and Eric Lee. "Taiwan's Overall Defense Concept, Explained." *Diplomat*, November 3, 2020. https://thediplomat.com/2020/11/taiwans-overall-defense-concept-explained/.

Lee, Teng-hui. "Understanding Taiwan: Bridging the Perception Gap." *Foreign Affairs* 78, no. 6 (1999): 9–14.

Leng, Tse-kang. *The Taiwan-China Connection: Democracy and Development Across the Taiwan Straits*. Boulder, Colo.: Westview, 1996.

Levy, Jack S. "Declining Power and the Preventive Motivation for War." *World Politics* 40, no. 1 (1987): 82–107.

——. "Power Transition Theory and the Rise of China." In *China's Ascent: Power, Security, and the Future of International Politics*, ed. Robert S. Ross and Zhu Feng, 11–33. Ithaca, N.Y.: Cornell University Press, 2008.

——. "Prospect Theory, Rational Choice, and International Relations." *International Studies Quarterly* 41, no. 1 (1997): 87–112.

Li, Jason. "China's Surreptitious Economic Influence on Taiwan's Elections." *Diplomat*, April 12, 2019. https://thediplomat.com/2019/04/chinas-surreptitious-economic-influence -on-taiwans-elections/.

Li, Peng. "The Nature of the Economic Cooperation Framework Agreement and Its Implications for Peaceful Development of Cross-Strait Relations." In *New Dynamics in Cross–Taiwan Straits Relations: How Far Can the Rapprochement Go?*, ed. Weixing Hu, 47–59. Hoboken, N.J.: Taylor and Francis, 2013.

Li, Xiaojun, and Dingding Chen. "Public Opinion, International Reputation, and Audience Costs in an Authoritarian Regime." *Conflict Management and Peace Science* 38, no. 5 (2021): 543–60.

Liang'an jingji tongji yuebao [Cross-strait economic statistics monthly]. Taipei: Mainland Affairs Council of the Executive Yuan.

Lim, Yves-Heng. "The Future Instability of Cross-Strait Relations: Prospect Theory and Ma Ying-jeou's Paradoxical Legacy." *Asian Security* 14, no. 3 (2018): 318–38.

Lin, Gang. "Beijing's Evolving Policy and Strategic Thinking on Taiwan." In *New Dynamics in Cross–Taiwan Straits Relations: How Far Can the Rapprochement Go?*, ed. Weixing Hu, 63–77. Hoboken, N.J.: Taylor and Francis, 2013.

——. "Beijing's New Strategies Toward a Changing Taiwan." *Journal of Contemporary China* 25, no. 99 (2016): 321–35.

Lin, Syaru Shirly. *Taiwan's China Dilemma: Contested Identities and Multiple Interests in Taiwan's Cross-Strait Economic Policy*. Stanford, Calif.: Stanford University Press, 2016.

Lynch, Daniel C. "Taiwan's Self-Conscious Nation-Building Project." *Asian Survey* 44, no. 4 (2004): 513–33.

MacMillan, Margaret. *The War That Ended Peace: How Europe Abandoned Peace for the First World War*. London: Profile Books, 2013.

Magnus, George. *Red Flags: Why Xi's China Is in Jeopardy*. New Haven, Conn.: Yale University Press, 2018.

Maizland, Lindsay. "China's Repression of Uighurs in Xinjiang." Council on Foreign Relations *Backgrounder*, 2018. https://www.cfr.org/backgrounder/chinas-repression-uighurs -xinjiang.

Mann, James. *About Face: A History of America's Curious Relationship with China, from Nixon to Clinton*. New York: Vintage, 1998.

Mansfield, Edward D., and Brian M. Pollins. "The Study of Interdependence and Conflict: Recent Advances, Open Questions, and Directions for Future Research." *Journal of Conflict Resolution* 45, no. 6 (2001): 834–59.

Mastro, Oriana Skylar. *The Costs of Conversation: Obstacles to Peace in Wartime*. Ithaca, N.Y.: Cornell University Press, 2019.

——. "In the Shadow of the Thucydides Trap: International Relations Theory and the Prospects for Peace in U.S.-China Relations." *Journal of Chinese Political Science* 24, no. 1 (2019): 25–45.

——. "The Taiwan Temptation: Why Beijing Might Resort to Force." *Foreign Affairs* 100, no. 4 (2021): 58–67.

——. Testimony before the U.S.-China Economic and Security Review Commission, February 18, 2021. https://www.uscc.gov/sites/default/files/2021-02/Oriana_Skylar_Mastro _Testimony.pdf.

Mastro, Oriana Skylar, and Ian Easton. "Risk and Resiliency: China's Emerging Air Base Strike Threat." Project 2049 Institute, 2017. https://project2049.net/2017/11/08/risk-and -resiliency-chinas-emerging-air-base-strike-threat/.

Mazza, Michael. "The National Defense Authorization Act and U.S. Policy Toward Taiwan." National Bureau of Asian Research, May 2018. https://www.nbr.org/wp-content/uploads /pdfs/us-taiwan_defense_relations_roundtable_may2018.pdf.

McGuire, Kristian. "Tsai Ing-wen's U.S. Transit Stops in Historical Context." *Diplomat*, July 5, 2016. https://thediplomat.com/2016/07/tsai-ing-wens-u-s-transit-stops-in -historical-context/.

Mearsheimer, John J. "Say Goodbye to Taiwan." *National Interest*, March–April 2014. http:// nationalinterest.org/article/say-goodbye-taiwan-9931.

——. *The Tragedy of Great Power Politics*. Updated ed. New York: Norton, 2014.

Millward, James. "'Reeducating' Xinjiang's Muslims." *New York Review of Books*, February 2019. https://www.nybooks.com/articles/2019/02/07/reeducating-xinjiangs -muslims/.

Moore, Gregory J. "The Power of 'Sacred Commitments'—Chinese Interests in Taiwan." *Foreign Policy Analysis* 12, no. 2 (2016): 214–35.

Moore, Gregory J. "Avoiding a Thucydides Trap in Sino-American Relations (. . . and 7 Reasons Why That Might Be Difficult)." *Asian Security* 13, no. 2 (2017): 98–115.

Morris, Lyle L., Michael J. Mazarr, Jeffrey W. Hornung, Stephanie Pezard, Anika Binnendijk, and Marta Kepe. *Gaining a Competitive Edge in the Gray Zone: Response Options for Aggression Below the Threshold for Major War*. Santa Monica, Calif.: RAND Corporation, 2019.

Morrow, James D. "How Could Trade Affect Conflict." *Journal of Peace Research* 36, no. 4 (1999): 481–89.

Morrow, James D. "The Strategic Setting of Choices: Signaling, Commitment and Negotiations in International Politics." In *Strategic Choice and International Relations*, ed. David A. Lake and Robert Powell, 77–114. Princeton, N.J.: Princeton University Press, 1999.

Mueller, John. *The Stupidity of War: American Foreign Policy and the Case for Complacency*. Cambridge: Cambridge University Press, 2021.

Murray, William S. "Asymmetric Options for Taiwan's Deterrence and Defense." In *Globalization and Security Relations Across the Taiwan Strait: In the Shadow of China*, ed. Monique Ming-chin Chu and Scott L. Kastner, 61–79. London: Routledge, 2015.

——. "Revisiting Taiwan's Defense Strategy." *Naval War College Review* 61, no. 3 (2008): 12–38.

Naughton, Barry. "Economic Policy Reform in the PRC and Taiwan." In *The China Circle: Economics and Electronics in the PRC, Taiwan, and Hong Kong*, ed. Barry Naughton, 81–110. Washington, D.C.: Brookings, 1997.

——. *Growing Out of the Plan: Chinese Economic Reform 1978–1993*. New York: Cambridge University Press, 1996.

Niou, Emerson M. S. "Understanding Taiwan Independence and Its Policy Implication." *Asian Survey* 44, no. 4 (2004): 555–67.

Norris, William L. *Chinese Economic Statecraft: Commercial Actors, Grand Strategy, and State Control*. Ithaca, N.Y.: Cornell University Press, 2016.

Office of the Secretary of Defense. *Annual Report on the Military Power of the People's Republic of China*. Washington, D.C.: U.S. Department of Defense, 2000. http://archive.defense.gov/news/Jun2000/china06222000.htm.

——. *Annual Report to Congress: Military and Security Developments Involving the People's Republic of China*. Washington, D.C.: U.S. Department of Defense, 2014. http://www.defense.gov/Portals/1/Documents/pubs/2014_DoD_China_Report.pdf.

——. *Annual Report to Congress: Military and Security Developments Involving the People's Republic of China*. Washington, D.C.: U.S. Department of Defense, 2020. https://media.defense.gov/2020/Sep/01/2002488689/-1/-1/1/2020-dod-china-military-power-report-final.pdf.

Organski, A. F. K., and Jacek Kugler. *The War Ledger*. Chicago: University of Chicago Press, 1980.

Orlik, Thomas. *China: The Bubble That Never Pops*. New York: Oxford University Press, 2020.

Owens, Bill. "America Must Start Treating China as a Friend." *Financial Times*, November 17, 2009. http://www.ft.com/cms/s/0/69241506-d3b2-11de-8caf-00144feabdc0.html#axz z3d9SM9kwf.

Paal, Douglas. "Too Much Taiwan Tension, Not Enough Management." *Taiwan Insight*, June 4, 2021. https://taiwaninsight.org/2021/06/04/too-much-taiwan-tension-not-enough-management/.

Pan, Hsin-Hsin, Wen-Chin Wu, and Yu-Tzung Chang. "How Chinese Citizens Perceive Cross-Strait Relations: Survey Results from Ten Major Cities in China." *Journal of Contemporary China* 26, no. 106 (2017): 616–31.

Pei, Minxin. "China's Perilous Taiwan Policy." *Project Syndicate*, January 11, 2019. https://www.project-syndicate.org/commentary/china-taiwan-policy-conflict-with-america-by-minxin-pei-2019-01.

Powell, Robert. "Bargaining Theory and International Conflict." *Annual Review of Political Science* 5, no. 1 (2002): 1–30.

——. "War as a Commitment Problem." *International Organization* 60, no. 1 (2006): 169–203.

Quek, Kai, and Alastair Iain Johnston. "Can China Back Down? Crisis De-escalation in the Shadow of Popular Opposition." *International Security* 42, no. 3 (2018): 7–36.

Rector, Chad. *Federations: The Dynamics of International Cooperation*. Ithaca, N.Y.: Cornell University Press, 2009.

Reed, William. "Information, Power, and War." *American Political Science Review* 97, no. 4 (2003): 633–41.

Reilly, James. *Strong Society, Smart State: The Rise of Public Opinion in China's Japan Policy*. New York: Columbia University Press, 2012.

Reiter, Dan. "Exploring the Bargaining Model of War." *Perspectives of Politics* 1, no. 1 (2003): 27–43.

Rigger, Shelley. *Politics in Taiwan: Voting for Democracy*. London: Routledge, 1999.

——. "Taiwan's 2020 Election Analysis." *China Leadership Monitor* no. 63 (2020). https://www.prcleader.org/shelley-rigger-taiwan-election.

——. "Why Giving up Taiwan Will Not Help Us with China." American Enterprise Institute, 2011. https://www.aei.org/research-products/report/why-giving-up-taiwan-will-not-help-us-with-china/.

——. *Why Taiwan Matters: Small Island, Global Powerhouse*. Lanham, Md.: Rowman and Littlefield, 2011.

Romberg, Alan D. *Rein in at the Brink of the Precipice: American Policy toward Taiwan and U.S.-PRC Relations*. Washington, D.C.: Henry L. Stimson Center, 2003.

——. "Squaring the Circle: Adhering to Principle, Embracing Ambiguity." *China Leadership Monitor*, no. 47 (2015). https://www.hoover.org/sites/default/files/research/docs/clm47ar.pdf.

——. "Taiwan Elections Head to the Finish: Concerns, Cautions, and Challenges." *China Leadership Monitor*, no. 36 (2012). http://www.hoover.org/research/taiwan-elections-head-finish-concerns-cautions-and-challenges.

——. "Tsai Ing-wen Takes Office: A New Era in Cross-Strait Relations." *China Leadership Monitor*, no. 50 (2016). https://www.hoover.org/sites/default/files/research/docs/clm50ar.pdf#overlay-context=research/chinese-views-presumptive-us-presidential-candidates-hillary-r-clinton-and-donald-j-trump.

Ross, Robert S. "Comparative Deterrence: The Taiwan Strait and the Korean Peninsula." In *New Directions in the Study of China's Foreign Policy*, ed. Alastair Iain Johnston and Robert S. Ross, 13–49. Stanford, Calif.: Stanford University Press, 2006.

——. "Explaining Taiwan's Revisionist Diplomacy." *Journal of Contemporary China* 15, no. 48 (2006): 443–58.

——. "Navigating the Taiwan Strait: Deterrence, Escalation Dominance, and U.S.-China Relations." *International Security* 27, no. 2 (2002): 47–85.

——. "The 1995–96 Taiwan Strait Confrontation: Coercion, Credibility, and the Use of Force." *International Security* 25, no. 2 (2000): 87–123.

Roy, Denny. "Prospects for Taiwan Maintaining its Autonomy Under Chinese Pressure." *Asian Survey* 57, no. 6 (2017): 1135–58.

Russett, Bruce, and John R. Oneal. *Triangulating Peace: Democracy, Interdependence, and International Organizations*. New York: Norton, 2001.

Saunders, Phillip C., and Scott L. Kastner. "Bridge Over Troubled Water? Envisioning a China-Taiwan Peace Agreement." *International Security* 33, no. 1 (2009): 87–114.

Schelling, Thomas C. *Arms and Influence*. New Haven, Conn.: Yale University Press, 1966.

——. *The Strategy of Conflict*. Cambridge, Mass.: Harvard University Press, 1960.

Schneider, Jordan. "China's Chip Industry: Running Faster but Still Falling Behind." Rhodium Group, April 22, 2021. https://rhg.com/research/china-chips/.

Schubert, Gunter. "Assessing Political Agency Across the Taiwan Strait: The Case of the Taishang." *China Information* 27, no. 1 (2013): 51–79.

Schubert, Gunter, Ruihua Lin, and Jean Yu-Chen Tseng. "Are Taiwanese Entrepreneurs a Strategic Group? Reassessing Taishang Political Agency Across the Taiwan Strait." *Asian Survey* 57, no. 5 (2017): 856–84.

——. "Taishang Studies: A Rising or Declining Research Field?" *China Perspectives* 2016, no. 1 (2016): 29–36.

Sheng, Shing-yuan, and Hsiao-chuan (Mandy) Liao. "Issues, Political Cleavages, and Party Competition in Taiwan." In *The Taiwan Voter*, ed. Christopher Henry Achen and T. Y. Wang, 98–138. Ann Arbor: University of Michigan Press, 2017.

Shirk, Susan L. *China, Fragile Superpower: How China's Internal Politics Could Derail Its Peaceful Rise*. New York: Oxford University Press, 2007.

——. *How China Opened Its Door: The Political Success of the PRC's Foreign Trade and Investment Reforms*. Washington, D.C.: Brookings, 1994.

Shlapak, David A., David T. Orletsky, Toy I. Reid, Murray Scot Tanner, and Barry A. Wilson. *A Question of Balance: Political Context and Military Aspects of the China-Taiwan Dispute*. Santa Monica, Calif.: RAND Corporation, 2009.

Shlapak, David A., David T. Orletsky, and Barry A. Wilson. *Dire Strait? Military Aspects of the China-Taiwan Confrontation and Options for U.S. Policy*. Santa Monica, Calif.: RAND Corporation, 2000.

Shugart III, Thomas H. Testimony before the U.S.-China Economic and Security Review Commission,February 18, 2021. https://www.uscc.gov/sites/default/files/2021-02/Thomas_Shugart_Testimony.pdf.

Sinkkonen, Elina. "Nationalism, Patriotism, and Foreign Policy Attitudes Among Chinese University Students." *China Quarterly*, no. 216 (2013): 1045–63.

Slanchev, Branislav L. "Feigning Weakness." *International Organization* 64, no. 3 (2010): 357–88.

——. "The Power to Hurt: Costly Conflict with Completely Informed States." *American Political Science Review* 97, no. 1 (2003): 123–33.

Snyder, Glenn. "The Security Dilemma in Alliance Politics." *World Politics* 36, no. 4 (1984): 461–95.

Stokes, Jon. "Why a Chinese Invasion of Taiwan Would Be a Catastrophe for China and the World." *Doxa*, April 13, 2021. https://doxa.substack.com/p/why-a-chinese-invasion-of-taiwan.

Stokes, Mark. Testimony before the U.S.-China Economic and Security Review Commission, March 18, 2010. http://origin.www.uscc.gov/sites/default/files/transcripts/3.18.10HearingTranscript.pdf.

Sun, Guoxiang. "Zhongguo shi Diqiushang Zui Weixian Guojia" [China is the most dangerous country on Earth]. *Newtalk*, May 7, 2021. https://newtalk.tw/citizen/view/57032.

Sutter, Robert. *Taiwan's Future: Narrowing Straits*. Seattle: National Bureau of Asian Research, 2011.

——. "The US and Taiwan Embrace Despite China's Objections, but Will It Last?" *Pacific Forum PacNet*, no. 58, November 12, 2019. https://www.pacforum.org/analysis/pacnet-58-us-and-taiwan-embrace-despite-china%E2%80%99s-objections-will-it-last.

Swaine, Michael D. "China's Assertive Behavior—Part One: On 'Core Interests.'" *China Leadership Monitor*, no. 34 (2011). https://www.hoover.org/research/chinas-assertive-behavior-part-one-core-interests.

——. "Chinese Decision-Making Regarding Taiwan, 1979–2000." In *The Making of Chinese Foreign and Security Policy in the Era of Reform, 1978–2000*, ed. David M. Lampton, 289–336. Stanford, Calif.: Stanford University Press, 2001.

Tan, Alexander C., and Karl Ho. "Cross-Strait Relations and the Taiwan Voter." In *The Taiwan Voter*, ed. Christopher Henry Achen and T. Y. Wang, 158–69. Ann Arbor: University of Michigan Press, 2017.

Tanner, Murray Scot. *Chinese Economic Coercion Against Taiwan: A Tricky Weapon to Use*. Santa Monica, Calif.: RAND Corporation, 2007.

Templeman, Kharis A. Testimony before the U.S.-China Economic and Security Review Commission, February 18, 2021. https://www.uscc.gov/sites/default/files/2021-02/Kharis_Templeman_Testimony.pdf.

Thompson, Drew. "Hope on the Horizon: Taiwan's Radical New Defense Concept." *War on the Rocks*, October 2, 2018. https://warontherocks.com/2018/10/hope-on-the-horizon-taiwans-radical-new-defense-concept/.

Tomz, Michael. "Domestic Audience Costs in International Relations: An Experimental Approach." *International Organization* 61, no. 4 (2007): 821–40.

Tsang, Steve, ed. *If China Attacks Taiwan: Military Strategy, Politics, and Economics*. London: Routledge, 2006.

Tucker, Nancy Bernkopf, and Bonnie Glaser. "Should the United States Abandon Taiwan?" *Washington Quarterly* 34, no. 4 (2011): 23–37.

Tung, Chen-yuan. "An Assessment of China's Taiwan Policy Under the Third Generation Leadership." *Asian Survey* 45, no. 3 (2005): 343–61.

United States Defense Intelligence Agency. *China Military Power: Modernizing a Force to Fight and Win*. 2019. https://www.dia.mil/Portals/27/Documents/News/Military%20Power%20Publications/China_Military_Power_FINAL_5MB_20190103.pdf.

U.S.-China Economic and Security Review Commission. *2014 Report to Congress of the U.S.-China Economic and Security Review Commission*. Washington, D.C.: Government Printing Office, 2014.

——. *2019 Report to Congress of the U.S.-China Economic and Security Review Commission*. Washington, D.C.: Government Printing Office, 2019.

——. *2020 Report to Congress of the U.S.-China Economic and Security Review Commission*. Washington, D.C.: Government Printing Office, 2020.

Van Evera, Stephen. *Causes of War: Power and the Roots of Conflict.* Ithaca, N.Y.: Cornell University Press, 1999.

Wachman, Alan M. *Taiwan: National Identity and Democratization.* Armonk, N.Y.: M. E. Sharpe, 1994.

——. *Why Taiwan? Geostrategic Rationales for China's Territorial Integrity.* Stanford, Calif.: Stanford University Press, 2007.

Wade, Robert. *Governing the Market: Economic Theory and the Role of Government in East Asian Industrialization.* Princeton, N.J.: Princeton University Press, 2004.

Wagner, R. Harrison. *War and the State: The Theory of International Politics.* Ann Arbor: University of Michigan Press, 2007.

Walt, Stephen M. "Rigor or Rigor Mortis? Rational Choice and Security Studies." *International Security* 23, no. 4 (1999): 5–48.

Wang, Gabe T. *China and the Taiwan Issue: Impending War at the Taiwan Strait.* Lanham, Md.: University Press of America, 2006.

Wang, T. Y. "Changing Boundaries: The Development of the Taiwan Voters' Identity." In *The Taiwan Voter,* ed. Christopher Henry Achen and T. Y. Wang, 45–70. Ann Arbor: University of Michigan Press, 2017.

——. "Strategic Ambiguity or Strategic Clarity? US Policy Toward the Taiwan Issue." *Taiwan Insight,* June 7, 2021. https://taiwaninsight.org/2021/06/07/strategic-ambiguity-or-strategic-clarity-us-policy-towards-the-taiwan-issue/.

Wei, Chi-hung. "China's Economic Offensive and Taiwan's Defensive Measures: Cross-Strait Fruit Trade, 2005–2008." *China Quarterly,* no. 215 (2013): 641–62.

Weisiger, Alex. *Logics of War: Explanations for Limited and Unlimited Conflicts.* Ithaca, N.Y.: Cornell University Press, 2013.

Weiss, Jessica Chen. "How Hawkish Is the Chinese Public? Another Look at 'Rising Nationalism' and Chinese Foreign Policy." *Journal of Contemporary China* 28, no. 119 (2019): 679–95.

——. *Powerful Patriots: Nationalist Protest in China's Foreign Relations.* New York: Oxford University Press, 2014.

Weiss, Jessica Chen, and Alan Dafoe. "Authoritarian Audiences, Rhetoric, and Propaganda in International Crises: Evidence from China." *International Studies Quarterly* 63, no. 4 (2019): 963–73.

Welch, David A. "China, the United States, and the Thucydides's Trap." In *China's Challenges and International Order Transition: Beyond the Thucydides's Trap,* ed. Huiyun Feng and Kai He, 47–69. Ann Arbor: University of Michigan Press, 2020.

Whiting, Allen S. "China's Use of Force, 1950–96, and Taiwan." *International Security* 26, no. 2 (2001): 103–31.

Wong, Stan Hok-wui, and Nichole Wu. "Can China Buy Taiwan? An Empirical Assessment of Beijing's Agricultural Trade Concessions to Taiwan." *Journal of Contemporary China* 25, no. 99 (2016): 353–71.

Wu, Yu-Shan. "Theorizing on Relations Across the Taiwan Strait: Nine Contending Approaches." *Journal of Contemporary China* 9, no. 25 (2000): 407–28.

Wu, Yu-Shan, and Kuan-Wu Chen. "Domestic Politics and Cross-Strait Relations: A Synthetic Perspective." *Journal of Asian and African Studies* 55, no. 2 (2020): 168–86.

Wuthnow, Joel. "System Overload: Can China's Military Be Distracted in a War Over Taiwan?" Center for the Study of Chinese Military Affairs, Institute for National Strategic Studies, China Strategic Perspectives, no. 15 (2020). https://inss.ndu.edu/Media/News/Article/2232448/system-overload-can-chinas-military-be-distracted-in-a-war-over-taiwan/.

Xin, Qiang. "Having Much in Common? Changes and Continuity in China's Taiwan Policy." *Pacific Review* 34, no. 6 (2021): 926–45.

——. "Selective Engagement: Mainland China's Dual Track Taiwan Policy." *Journal of Contemporary China* 29, no. 124 (2020): 535–52.

Young, Stephen M. "A Conference with the Taiwan Affairs Office of the PRC State Council." National Committee on American Foreign Policy, June 2019. https://www.ncafp.org/2016/wp-content/uploads/2019/07/NCAFP-2019-TAO-Conference-Report_FINAL.pdf.

Zhang, Hua. "2012 Taiwan 'daxuan' xuanmin toupiao xingwei xin tedian ji qi dui liang'an guanxi de yingxiang yanjiu" [A study of the new characteristics of Taiwan voting behavior during the 2012 Taiwan "election" and their impact on cross-strait relations]. *Taiwan yanjiu jikan* [Taiwan research journal] 123, no. 5 (2012): 24–32.

Zhang, Ketian. "Cautious Bully: Reputation, Resolve, and Beijing's Use of Coercion in the South China Sea." *International Security* 44, no. 1 (2019): 117–59.

Zhao, Suisheng. "Economic Interdependence and Political Divergence: A Background Analysis of the Taiwan Strait Crisis." In *Across the Taiwan Strait: Mainland China, Taiwan, and the 1995–1996 Crisis*, ed. Suisheng Zhao, 21–40. New York: Routledge, 1999.

Zhong, Yang. "Explaining National Identity Shift in Taiwan." *Journal of Contemporary China* 25, no. 99 (2016): 336–52.

Zuo, Xiying. "Unbalanced Deterrence: Coercive Threat, Reassurance and the US-China Rivalry in the Taiwan Strait." *Pacific Review* 34, no. 4 (2021): 547–76.

INDEX

CONTEMPORARY ASIA IN THE WORLD

David C. Kang and Victor D. Cha, Editors

GPSR Authorized Representative: Easy Access System Europe, Mustamäe tee
50, 10621 Tallinn, Estonia, gpsr.requests@easproject.com

www.ingramcontent.com/pod-product-compliance
Lightning Source LLC
Chambersburg PA
CBHW032123020426
42334CB00016B/1051